1968

University of St. Francis

S0-AHZ-662

3 0301 00041827 3

954
D897
1

45465

A HISTORY *of* INDIA
*from the Earliest Times
to Nineteen Thirty-nine*

—

VOLUME I

By the same Author

FRONTIERS
OTHER MEN'S LIVES

HEAD OF THE LARGEST STONE STATUE IN THE WORLD,
THE 60-FT. JAIN STATUE OF GOMATA, IN MYSORE
Single granite Monolith, late tenth century
From a photograph by Frances M. Flaherty

A HISTORY OF
INDIA

FROM THE EARLIEST TIMES

TO

NINETEEN THIRTY-NINE

Sir George Dunbar, Bt.

VOLUME I

1949

NICHOLSON & WATSON
LIMITED . . LONDON

LIBRARY
College of St. Francis
JOLIET, ILL.

[ALL RIGHTS RESERVED]

First Edition	. .	*January*, 1936
Second Edition	. .	*February*, 1939
Third Edition	. .	*November*, 1943
Fourth Revised Edition		*February*, 1949

Printed in Great Britain
by T. and A. Constable Ltd., Hopetoun Street,
Printers to the University of Edinburgh

954
D897
1

PREFACE

A HISTORY of India is equivalent in range to the history of Europe excluding Russia and starting in the fourth century B.C. From the early dawn of definite Indian history, which came with the Macedonian phalanx of Alexander, the intricate and often shadowy story begins of invasion, of the rise and fall of kingdoms and the conflicts of warring Hindu States.

When the armies of Islam began, in the eleventh century, to pour through the grim gateways of the north-western passes, the religious question was added to the general political confusion. In the eighteenth century a further complication was introduced when the two leading European trading companies, the French and the English, in their manœuvres against each other, plunged into Indian politics.

Up to this time only two governments had given the sub-continent anything approaching unity and frontiers secure from invasion. These were the Empires of the Mauryas and of the Moguls at the height of their power. The Guptas and Harsha, who gave Hindu India her golden age between the fourth and seventh centuries A.D., did not extend their sway over all India. The short-lived almost universal paramountcy of the Afghan Sultanate of Delhi, about the beginning of the fourteenth century, was threatened by Mongol invasions, while the authority of the central government was challenged in the more distant parts of the Empire.

But when the Sikh kingdom of the Punjab, the last of the independent Indian sovereignties, was overthrown in the middle of the nineteenth century, British dominion was supreme throughout the whole country. This power was exercised first by the East India Company and then by the Crown and Parliament, through the direct government of British India and by the acknowledged

a 1   v

45465

paramountcy of the Crown over the States. Indian India and British India became united by the common interests of peace and security.

Under the shelter of the Stability of Order the politically minded educated classes of British India, influenced by Western democratic ideas, began, in the second half of the nineteenth century, to develop Nationalist ambitions. With the twentieth century came India's progress towards responsible government.

It is clearly impossible to compress the history of India into a single volume and deal adequately with every period. All that is hoped for in this attempt is to give, without too great a loss of perspective, some idea of the story of India and to indicate the stages which have led to the political situation of 1935.

Religion which, when all is said, dominates the country; the causes of the decline of empires into chaos; the form of these governments and how they affected the mass of the people; literature and art; commerce and industry; the influence of sea-power upon India's destinies; the building up of British paramountcy; the effect of western ideas upon the politically minded classes—these are the features upon which emphasis has been laid. The details of almost innumerable wars from Alexander's expedition up to the latest frontier campaign can be read in military publications. The geology and geography of the country are left to their own text-books.

In the spelling of Indian names, a matter of infinite variety, the course has been taken of using the forms in most general use, and following the authority of the *Imperial Gazetteer of India*. The bibliographies at the end of the chapters are not exhaustive, nor do they include all the sources consulted. But, taken with the references given in footnotes to the text, they suggest authorities for the study of special periods and subjects which cannot be detailed in a general History. Wherever possible the most accessible books of reference have been given.

This attempt to compile a History of India from the standpoint of the governed, rather than the many rulers of the country, owes much to the illustrations which make so admirable a running commentary. I take this opportunity to express my most grateful thanks to

Mrs. Holmes for the wide and illuminating selection of subjects she has made.

Sincere thanks are also due to Sir John Cumming, K.C.I.E., C.S.I., Dr. H. N. Randle, Head of the India Office Library, Mr. W. T. Ottewill, M.B.E., Keeper of the India Office Records, Mr. M. Young, I.C.S. (retired), and Mr. H. G. Rawlinson. Their most kindly and valuable help so generously given it is my privilege here to acknowledge.

G. D.

LONDON,
3rd August 1935.

PREFACE TO SECOND EDITION

THIS book was first published between the passing of the Government of India Act in 1935 and the introduction of the reforms in British India. It was thought better at that stage to state the main facts of this development, and exclude, as far as possible, matters of a controversial nature. Chapter XX, as now presented, is an attempt to give a more complete account of recent events.

From 1904 to the first session of the Round Table Conference the writer was in a position, with certain broken periods, to draw upon his own observation, while he was fortunate in his contacts and what he was enabled to gain from them. He wishes here to tender his thanks and express his indebtedness to Sir Akbar Hydari for invaluable advice upon the early relationship between the English in India and the people of the country.

He takes this opportunity to thank the reviewers of the first edition for their helpful criticism, and Sir Algernon Law for the material on which tardy justice has now been rendered to Lord Ellenborough.

The writer was handicapped by illness when the first edition was going to press, but it is hoped that the revised work may be free from those slips he then overlooked. He has also compiled the index now provided.

G. D.

LONDON,
24th January 1939.

PREFACE TO THIRD EDITION

THIS edition includes a Postscript covering the period from the outbreak of war in 1939 to the end of 1942.

In a world-war for existence, for the survival of human decencies and justice, history is being made, it cannot be written stop-press. But this addition to the book is an attempt to present a factual statement of the contrasting reactions in an India where freedom of government in any form could not exist after an Axis victory.

The passages dealing with the Bactrian Greeks have been rewritten in the light of Dr. Tarn's researches, and statistics of population have been revised in accordance with the 1941 Census.

These are the only material alterations in the text. Chapter XX has been left as a picture of pre-war India in her clouded progress towards responsible government. Only when Indian statesmanship points to a solution of the present political deadlock can the chapter which should follow be written.

G. D.

WICK, 1942.

PREFACE TO FOURTH EDITION

THIS revised edition ends at the definite point of the situation in India on the outbreak of war in 1939, the Postscript, 1939-42, referred to in the third edition having been deleted.

G. D.

CHANDLER'S FORD,
December 1946.

CONTENTS

VOLUME I

CHAPTER ONE

Ancient India

CHAPTER TWO

The Maurya Empire

CHAPTER THREE

Early Hindu India

CHAPTER FOUR

Pre-Mogul Muhammadan Rule

CHAPTER FIVE

Pre-Mogul India

CHAPTER SIX

Mogul India

CHAPTER SEVEN

Akbar

CHAPTER EIGHT

Akbar's System of Government

VOLUME II

CHAPTER TWELVE

The Later Moguls and the Marathas

CHAPTER THIRTEEN

French and English in the Carnatic

CHAPTER SEVENTEEN
British Supremacy

CHAPTER EIGHTEEN
Consolidation of British Rule

CHAPTER NINETEEN
India under the Crown: Part I. Canning to Ripon

CHAPTER TWENTY
British Rule and Indian Nationalism

PART I

PART II

ILLUSTRATIONS

Selected and arranged by Winifred Holmes

My most grateful thanks, for their generous help and advice in selecting the illustrations to this book, are especially due to Mr. K. de B. Codrington, Dr. Randle, Sir John Marshall, Mr. Arthur Probsthain, Mr. F. J. P. Richter, M.A., Mr. J. Allan of the British Museum, Mr. V. P. Bhandarkar, Manager of the Indian Railways Bureau, Mr. A. G. Adams, Director of the Parker Gallery, Mr. Mukul Dey, Director of Government School of Art, Calcutta, and Mr. Robert M. Flaherty.

VOLUME I

xvii

VOLUME II

MAPS

VOLUME I

VOLUME II

A HISTORY OF INDIA

VOLUME I

CHAPTER I

Ancient India

INDIA derives its name from the River Indus and originally [1] meant the country now called Sind with a portion of the Punjab; and it is in the Indus Valley that the earliest traces of civilization in the sub-continent have been brought to light.

Before these discoveries were made the only traces of Man in India in the remote past are easily summarized. They were confined to the quartzite and other hard stone implements of the earliest men (paleolithic), and the stone tools and pottery marking the later improvements of neolithic man, all of which are chiefly found on the Eastern Coast; the gold-mining shafts of a late neolithic settlement at Maski, which are the deepest in the world; prehistoric cemeteries, of which those in the Tinnevelly district possibly hold the burial urns of foreign traders in pearls and conch shell; and, at the dawn of Indian history, the cyclopean walls of Giribbaja in Bihar.

But excavations at Mohenjo Daro and Harappa have proved the existence of a great civilization in the west of India, which is believed to have reached its height between about 3250 and 2750 B.C., a time when famous cities were developing their culture from the earlier stone age on the banks of the Nile and the Euphrates, the Karun and the Helmund.

The Earliest Civilization.

In ancient Egypt and Mesopotamia money and labour were lavished on magnificent temples, palaces and tombs, while the mass of the people lived in mud huts. But in Mohenjo Daro,[2] which looks today like the red brick ruins of some working town

---

[1] Inscriptions of King Darius (521–485 B.C.). Sindhu is the Sanskrit and Hindu the Persian for a river. Hindustan means "The country of the river."

[2] *Mohenjo Daro and the Indus Civilization*, Sir John Marshall, from which this description has been taken.

in Lancashire, the only public structure discovered is the magnificent Public Bath. With this exception the best buildings are the two-storied houses of the ordinary citizens. No temples or palaces, recognizable as such, have been found. The houses had a pipe drainage system from bath-rooms and closets to drains in the street, and rubbish shoots in the walls led down to outside refuse bins. The occupants were merchants and farmers, and the merchants seem to have traded far afield, as five seals of characteristic Indus pattern have been found at Elam and in Mesopotamia. One from Ur and another from Kish are definitely earlier than the Sargonic period. The farmers grew wheat and barley and raised stock which supplied them with beef, mutton, pork and poultry; they also ate quantities of fish and shell-fish. Oxen drew their two-wheeled carts and they kept elephants and camels, but no horses.

Gambling was a favourite amusement, and it is just possible that the oblong bars of copper which have been found represent a metal currency far older than the seventh century B.C. coins of Lydia, which are the earliest known. Their jewellers were skilled workers in gold and silver and ivory. Engraved seals and copper tablets show that their writing was pictographic, but as no bilingual inscriptions have been found, this has defied all attempts to decipher it.

The women spun wool and cotton, and their children played marbles and had little toy carts made of terra-cotta and even of copper.

The warriors took the field with bows, spears, axes and daggers, but without swords, and apparently wore no defensive armour.

Little is known about the religion of the people. The Bull was worshipped, the Mother Goddess held an important place, and there is every indication of Phallic ritual.[1] Sir John Marshall considers certain figurines to be effigies of the Mother Goddess akin to those which have been found from Persia to the Balkans. The Siva-cult of India is composite. One part of it may possibly have been derived from the Indus Valley people, as has been suggested; or they may have derived it from another people, who may again have passed it

---

[1] *Mohenjo Daro*, Vol. I. pp. 49–51.

PLATE I.

FROM THE EXCAVATIONS AT MOHENJO-DARO

(a) Cat's head ; (b) seal ; (c) bronze figurine of woman ; (d) woman's head ; (e) painted pottery jar ; (f) bison ; (g) house

From "Mohenjo-daro and the Indus Civilization," by Sir John Marshall : copyright by the Government of India, reproduced by courtesy of Mr. Arthur Probsthain

PLATE II.

BRONZE GROUP REPRESENTING SIVA, UMA AND SKANDA

Southern India, eleventh century

By courtesy of Indian Museum, South Kensington

on to the Aryans. On the other hand, the fire-pit found in every Aryan home did not exist.

The dead were usually cremated. But at Harappa a few graves have been found, some of them with traces of food and the small personal belongings which primitive man from the earliest times has offered for the use of the dead.

The extent of the Indus civilization is as unknown as its origin. But the municipal life on the banks of that great river the " sea of Sind " was apparently swept away by floods before the Aryan hosts entered the Punjab. At Mohenjo Daro three superimposed cities have been found, and in Khaipur State, on the old course of the Indus, indications of a less advanced civilization were discovered in 1935.

We get our next glimpse of Ancient India from the sacred verses of these Aryans,[1] a people of the same stock as the Persians, and speaking a language akin to Persian, Greek, Latin, Teutonic, Celtic and Slavonic.

The Aryans.

Their ancient literature throws an interesting light upon the life of this Aryan people, although historical events are so generally ignored that not one single reference is made to their irruption into India. The geography of the *Rigveda* is more illuminating and, amongst others, the five rivers from which the Punjab takes its name can all be identified.

Its importance is, however, far greater than this. Religious thought and philosophy have dominated India since the Aryans occupied the country from the Indus to the mouth of the Ganges and south to the Vindhya hills; and in this ancient literature we reach the foundations upon which Indian religion and philosophy are based. But the western world did not make this discovery—as dramatic as the work which Sir J. Marshall and R. D. Banerji began at Mohenjo Daro in 1922—until the days of Warren Hastings. Englishmen in India then realized the immense practical value of the study of ancient Sanskrit literature, and the first translations were made (through Persian into English) in 1776. Ten years later Sir William

---

[1] Aryan denotes a language, not a racial, group.

Jones of the High Court of Calcutta, by his enthusiastic study of Sanskrit, laid the foundations of the modern science of Comparative Philology. Until the vast store of knowledge enshrined in Sanskrit literature and inscriptions could be translated, the story of India, prior to the Muhammadan invasions of the eleventh century A.D., as recorded by the people themselves, remained an absolute blank.

Cut off for centuries by the great wall of mountains barring the entire land frontier, the Indo-Aryans built up a civilization and culture which was entirely their own. They founded two great religions, their national Brahmanism and the far-reaching faith of Buddhism. Neither invasion nor conquest by Persian or Greek, Scythian or Muhammadan could arrest the national development of the Indo-Aryan people. Just as the cultivator in India today farms his land as his earliest ancestors farmed it, and as fire is produced in religious rites, with two sticks, as it was thousands of years ago, so the life and literature of Aryan civilization went on its conservative way until the days of British occupation.

The most ancient Aryan literature consists of the Four Vedas, still preserved in Vedic, the earliest form of Sanskrit. Veda means sacred lore, and Hindus accept the Four Vedas as inspired, while they generally regard all later *samhitas* (collections) as traditional learning. Even after writing was introduced into India, probably towards the end of the Vedic period, the Vedas continued to be learnt by heart, and were transmitted orally with infallible accuracy by the schools of Vedic study down to the present day; and the hymns of the *Rigveda* alone have been calculated to equal in length the surviving poems of Homer.

At the time of the Aryan settlement in India, Vedic does not appear to have been a popular tongue, but a special language handed down by generations of priest singers. This developed into what came to be called Sanskrit, literally " put together," which was stereotyped by the great grammarian Panini (*c.* 300 B.C.). The earliest surviving exegetical work in strictly classical Sanskrit is Yaska's *Nirukta*, a Vedic commentary of the fifth century B.C.,[1]

---

[1] Macdonell, *Sanskrit Literature*, pp. 269–270.

and Sanskrit was undoubtedly spoken in the second century B.C., throughout Aryavarta, the "Land of the Aryans," by the Brahmans and aristocracy.

The lower classes spoke dialects known as Prakrita, the earliest form that has been preserved being Pali. Sanskrit and the Prakrits were therefore current in India much as Norman-French and Saxon were used in England after the Conquest. Sanskrit, the learned language of India, has remained unaltered for more than two thousand years, but the speech of the people has developed into the 222 modern dialects of India. They are based on five parent languages. Austric is the oldest. It is represented in India by the Munda group in Chota Nagpur and the northern districts of the Madras Presidency, and is the language of primitive tribes such as the Gonds. There is no language in the world more widely spread than Austric, for it is traced from Easter Island off South America to Madagascar, and from New Zealand to the Punjab.[1] There is not, however, satisfactory reason to accept Halevy's theory establishing a connection between the Indus Valley script and that of Easter Island, as the characters are quite different.[2] Dravidian is the most important of the Non-Aryan groups of languages spoken in India today. Tamil and Telugu are its chief representatives, and more than 86 million people in Central and Southern India speak Dravida and its seven allied languages. Indo-Aryan is represented by Hindi (the language of one-third of India), Bengali, Marathi, Gujerathi and Punjabi. Semitic was introduced by the later Muhammadan conquerors; and the fifth group is Tibeto-Chinese.

The Vedas were composed in the chronological order given below, though the dates of their composition are *The Vedas.* at best pure conjecture based upon the internal evidence of the development of Aryan civilization and literature. On these grounds the oldest hymn, to Ushas the Dawn, is held to have been composed about 1200 B.C.[3] On the other hand, relying

---

[1] *Indian Census Report,* 1911, Vol. I. p. 524.
[2] Authority Department of Oriental Antiquities, British Museum.
[3] *Camb. Hist. India,* Vol. I. pp. 112–113.

on astronomical data, B. G. Tilak calculates the date of the earliest Vedas to have been about 4500 B.C.[1]

> The Rigveda: 1028 Hymns (including those in the Eighth Book) to accompany the sacrifices to the gods.
>
> The Samaveda: A collection of chants taken from the Rigveda.
>
> The Yajurveda: (1) The Black; sacrificial prayers in verse and the earliest Vedic prose mixed with commentaries.
>
> (2) The White; in which the prose commentaries are separated from the litanies.
>
> The Atharvaveda, which describes the beliefs of the people in evil spirits, spells and incantations over three thousand years ago, was not for some time recognized as canonical and is not now universally admitted by the Brahmans of Southern India.

A definite line cannot be drawn between sacrifices and sorcery in the Vedic religion, in which witchcraft plays an essential part.[2] There is no evidence of totemism, but fetishism is found in the display of an image of Indra in battle. The gods might be thought of as animals, but their direct worship in this shape is hardly found in the Rigveda. Serpent worship has, however, been traced as far back as the third century B.C. by excavation at Rajagriha; and this, in the widespread cult of the snake-goddess Manasa, is still a popular form of belief, especially in eastern India.

Between about 800–600 B.C., there appeared religious manuals in prose to explain to the priest the inner meaning of the sacrifices; they are called Brahmanas. To these were added theosophic meditations for the use of hermits in their forest retreats, and consequently called Aranyakas or Forest Books. There were three of these and each contained an Upanishad, so called because they were taught in secret.

The long series of the Upanishads, the earliest of which must be as old as 600 B.C., closes the second stage of Vedic literature. They are a mixture of half-poetical and half-philosophic speculations

---

[1] Preface to The Arctic Home in the Vedas (Poona, 1903), where European authorities supporting him are cited. Tilak's reasoning in support of the extreme antiquity of Aryan civilization, beginning between 6000 and 4000 B.C., is given in Orion, or Researches into the Antiquity of the Vedas (Poona, 1916).

[2] Macdonell, History of Sanskrit Literature, p. 191.

6

and metaphysical dialogues, and their importance lies in the fact
that they teach what is really a new religion.

The *Rigveda*, with the exception of passages in the tenth and
last book, was frankly polytheistic. But the *Upanishads* speak of a
deity embracing all the gods as well as the forces of nature. This
was Brahma the " holy power," or Atma " The Self, the only
Reality." Their goal is not worldly advantages and eternal happiness
gained by sacrifices, but freedom from the cares of this present
world by the merging of the soul in the world-soul through true
knowledge. This has represented the philosophic side of Hinduism
from that day to this. Although there are over a hundred *Upanishads*,
the most important and probably the oldest being the Chandrogya
of the *Samaveda* and the Brihadaranyaka, the phrase " that art thou "
is held to sum up the entire teaching of what is known as the Vedanta
system.

The third stage of Vedic literature began, possibly about 600 B.C.,
with the first Sutras, which are textbooks regulating the sacrificial
rites, and crystallizing customary law and practice. They are so
compressed that commentaries are necessary to understand them.
As an old Hindu saying puts it, the composers of the grammatical
Sutras delighted as much in the saving of a short vowel as in the birth
of a son; and it must be remembered that a Brahman believes he
cannot gain Heaven without a son to perform his funeral rites.

This Vedic literature and the epics, codes of laws and legends
which followed, are the sole sources of knowledge of the Aryans for
many hundreds of years; and facts can only be gathered by inference.
On the other hand, their religious and social developments can be
clearly traced, the explanation being that their literature was entirely
controlled by the priests to whom political history was nothing, but
in whose eyes religion and philosophy, law, social institutions and
science were alone worthy of consideration. It is not until we come
to the accounts of North-Western India, due to Persian and Greek
invasions, that anything approaching chronology, history, or details
about the country and its inhabitants can be found. The approximate
years of Gautama Buddha's birth and death stand out alone amidst the
shadows. It is the foreigner, in the form of the Persian invader, who

7

supplies us with the first accurate date, relating to the north-western fringe of the country. Accounts of India, some of them very highly coloured, were written by the Greeks from the time of the Persian king Artaxerxes Mnemon, but history only begins with the expedition of Alexander the Great, and the arrival of Megasthenes, ambassador of Seleucus Nicator, at the court of the first Emperor of India.

There are geographical and ethnological arguments [1] in favour
The Wiros. of the theory that the Indo-Aryan race originally came from the fertile plains of Austria and Hungary and the highlands of Bohemia. The people who lived in this country about 2500 B.C. have been given the name of Wiros. It has been put forward that some of their tribes migrated from Europe into Asia, reaching Bactria (Balkh) some time between 2000 and 1500 B.C. Then driven on by the desiccation of Central Asia, which had already begun, they came south over the passes of the Hindu Kush into Afghanistan. From there the Aryans poured down into the plains, the first of a line of conquerors through the gateways of the Kabul, the Kurram and the Gumal rivers.

However that may be, the Aryan movement into India was the
Aryan Invasion. progress of a nation of five peoples divided into a number of tribes in the patriarchal family state.

The Saxon invaders of Britain, after the withdrawal of the Roman garrisons, make an interesting comparison with the Indo-Aryans. The Saxons, too, brought their own women with them. Their society was made up of thanes and priests of gentle blood, farmers who were unfree, and women-servants and menials who were slaves to be bought and sold like cattle. The Saxon kings were hereditary, and were the leaders in war, having also their body-guards of personal retainers. They presided at the great feasts and sacrifices, and were the final source of justice. Their acts, however, had to be confirmed by popular assemblies. Land was allotted to groups of kinsmen. Saxon houses were built of timber with barns, store-houses and sheds clustering about them. The fields were ploughed with oxen, and manured.

[1] See *Camb. Hist. India*, Vol. I. pp. 66–76.

Before the Aryans had absorbed Northern India south-east of the modern Ambala, their life was simple and primitive. The invaders fought their way into the country, forming village settlements on clearings they made in the forest as they went. The villages seem to have been groups of houses and sheds built of wood and bamboo, with the sacred domestic fire burning on every hearth. The family dwellings clustered as a rule round a fortified post.

Social Life.

The families ploughed their allotments with teams of six, eight or even twelve oxen, and grew what may perhaps have been barley on their manured and irrigated fields; the cattle were driven out by the herdsmen to graze in the surrounding forest. Cows were milked, and cakes were made of flour and butter. Vegetables and fruit, then as now, were their staple diet, and butter was used as much as it is today. Oxen, sheep and goats were habitually killed for food and offered in sacrifices to the gods. Horse flesh is supposed to have been eaten only at the horse sacrifices, which were performed by the kings in assertion of their royal power; and eaten with the object of gaining the strength and speed of the animal. The popular beverage was *sura*, which was distilled from grain, and highly intoxicating.

The dress of the Vedic Indians consisted as a rule of two or three garments, generally of wool, but sometimes of skins. They combed and oiled their hair, the women wore it plaited and in some cases the men wore theirs in coils. In the early days the Aryans were on what may be described as the " cow " standard, but gold was highly valued and used by all who could afford it for neck and breast ornaments and ear-rings. Gold may have been obtained from the river beds, for they called the Indus the " Golden River."

The Aryans were great hunters. There are references in the *Rigveda* to the capture of lions in snares, of antelope caught in pits, and of boar-hunting with dogs. They were not a race of fishermen; and when the Vedic Indian took to the waters of the Indus he seems to have relied on a dug-out and a paddle, and never used rudder or sails.

In these early stages of their civilization, the ordinary tasks of life were performed by the free men of the village, all of whom were then grouped together as the Vis class of the community. The man who combined the trades of carpenter, joiner and wheel-wright had the place of honour, for it was he who made the chariot wheels used in war. Next came the smith who hammered out the domestic utensils in copper. The women sewed, wove cloth and plaited mats from grass or reeds.

The point to notice is that none of the occupations given in the *Rigveda* were looked upon as other than honourable; the time was yet to come when some of them would be branded as debasing.

Open-air dancing both by girls and men was a popular amusement, and the people were fond of singing. Their musical instruments were lutes, flutes and drums. But the favourite sport of the Aryans, a horse-loving and chivalrous people, was chariot-racing, closely followed by gambling with a number of brown nuts used as dice. The Aryans were inveterate gamblers, even staking their wives and their personal freedom on a throw. To quote " The Gambler's Lament," which is the oldest secular poem in the Vedas:

> "My wife rejects me and her mother hates me;
> The gamester finds no pity for his troubles.
> No better use can I see for a gambler
> Than for a costly horse worn out and aged." [1]

During the *Rigveda* period the religion of the people was comparatively simple in spite of the host of deities to whom sacrifices were made by the priests. It was the worship of nature personified in its various forms; and from its sacrificial rites Indo-Aryan theological speculation started and developed. First came Dyaus, god of the sky, coupled with Prithivi, the earth; later on Varuna took the place of Dyaus. Varuna, representing cosmic and moral order, to whom the most exalted hymns in the *Rigveda* are addressed, was in turn superseded as the popular deity by Indra. There were five solar gods, and one of them, Vishnu, the personification of the swift-moving sun, was later to become one of the two great gods of India. Siva, his rival, was then

Religion.

[1] *Rigveda*, X. 34.

known as Rudra, the storm god; but in the days of the *Rigveda* the most important deities after Indra were Agni the fire god, and the Soma. Agni was worshipped as the sun in the sky, as the lightning flash and as the fire burning on the domestic hearth. Soma was the sacred intoxicating drink, which formed the most important offering in the Vedic sacrifice. The plant from which it was made has not been identified.

There were no human sacrifices; a substitute was used in the Purushamedha, as this rite was called. The offerings were of flesh and the soma, milk, grain and clarified butter. But although the killing of bulls and cows and the eating of beef (abhorrent in Hindu India for the past two thousand years) is found in the *Rigveda*, the germs of later day Hinduism are apparent. The late tenth book indicates the process of creation as the evolution of " being " from "not being," the unity of the universe is asserted, and the multiplicity of the gods is called in question.

The Aryans peopled the world around them with a host of spirits, from the powerful gods propitiated by the priests, who alone knew the rites which would win favour, down to the elves and sprites in the forest and the streams; beliefs which are reflected in the animism of existing primitive tribes such as those living among the mountain ranges between Assam and Tibet.

The position of the Brahmans, that is to say the priestly class, was already one of assured dignity and importance. It would seem that the tribal kings had almost entirely delegated their earlier functions as regards sacrifice to the Brahmans, the priests; while on the secular side their power was consolidated by the close personal relationship between the ruler and his *purohita*, who was the domestic chaplain of the governing class. Brahmans could marry, and the term Brahmana [1] (descendant of a Brahman) is the only existing evidence as to whether the priesthood was or was not then hereditary.

In the time of the early Vedas there was neither child marriage
Marriage.
nor apparently any prohibition of marriage within the *gotra* (family or clan) other than between near relatives such as brother and sister. The early custom was for a

[1] *Rigveda*, I. 164, 45 ; VI. 75, 10, etc.

widow to marry the brother or nearest kinsman of the dead man,[1] when no son was already born. There is also evidence[2] that a woman was free to marry again if her husband entirely disappeared.

Polyandry was unknown, but a Vedic Indian could have more than one wife, although references to monogamy in the *Rigveda* show that a higher ideal of morality was growing. Speaking generally, men and women had considerable freedom in choosing a wife or a husband.

The wedding festivities included the killing of cows at the bride's house for the entertainment of the guests. The essential part of the ceremony itself consisted in the bridegroom taking his wife's hand, and leading her round her own family fire, before the bridal procession escorted the newly married pair to the bride's future home.

The long hymn,[3] sung during the ceremony, bears witness to the high value placed on marriage, a union which human action could not sever. On her marriage a wife was given in early Vedic times an honoured position in the household and was a regular participator in the religious offerings of her husband.

During the Vedic age the custom known as *sati*, by which the widow was burned on the death of her husband, was not followed; but that this was an ancient custom which had fallen into abeyance is possible from a reference in the *Atharvaveda*.[4]

The dead were either buried, or cremated, and the ashes buried, and as time went on burial became rarer. In the time of the *Rigveda* only vague ideas existed as regards a future state. It was believed that there were dwelling-places for the souls of men with the gods of the world of Yama, first of the dead and their king, or that the spirit departed to the waters or the plants. No idea of punishment after death can be found in the *Rigveda*.

Burial.

At the time of the invasion of India an Aryan warrior meant a man who could handle a weapon, without class distinction. The army was led by the king in person and the members of the noble families (Kshatriyas), who wore helmets, and corselets of flexible armour, and fought in chariots.

War.

---

[1] *Rigveda*, X. 18, 8, supported by Sutra evidence.
[2] *Ibid.*, VI. 49, 8.   [3] *Ibid.*, X. 85.   [4] *Athv.*, XVIII. 3, 1.

The common people (Vis) fought on foot. The principal weapon was the bow. There does not appear to have been the smallest conception of tactics, and the army advanced in a confused mass shouting their battle cry, with flags flying and drums beating.

An Indo-Aryan tribe was made up of three classes—the Brahman, the Kshatriya and the Vis (Vaisya), with a king *Government.* (*rajan*) at the head of it. The kingship seems normally to have been hereditary, but the king may sometimes have been elected from among the Kshatriya. His power was insecure and his acts had to be confirmed by assemblies of the men of the tribe, not unlike the Anglo-Saxon moot. He was the protector of his people and the fount of justice; and in return for his services he received the obedience of his subjects, who contributed towards the upkeep of the royal state. The king was not, in those early days, the recognized owner of the soil, and these contributions were at first more or less voluntary. In the business of government the king was advised by his domestic chaplain, the *purohita*.

The village was not then a recognized legal unit, and it is not known if the office of headman [1] was hereditary, but he presumably had civil and military control over his community. Reference is made in the *Yajurveda* to a village judge, but in the earlier period the punishment of a crime such as theft rested with the person who had been wronged. There is no mention in the *Rigveda* of capital punishment.

At the time of the Aryan invasion the greater part of India was occupied by the Dravidians, whom their conquerors *The Dravidians.* called Dasas or Dasyus. Dravida is the old name of the Tamil country in southern India; Dasyu means " native " as opposed to Aryan in a very wide sense, covering many races and degrees of culture; and the Vedic description—a black-skinned people with broad noses—applies to the Dravidians today.

The northern Dravidians lived in fortified villages, owned large herds of cattle and may possibly have introduced the irrigation of rice fields into the Ganges Valley. Their religion was phallic. The

[1] *Rigveda*, X. 62, 11 and 107, 5.

Anatolian hypothesis [1] credits this race with the colonization of New Guinea about the end of the fourth millennium B.C., while at one time they formed the bulk of the population of Further India and South China. Their earlier movements are still more uncertain. From the evidence of the age of the languages still spoken in India it is in the primitive tribes of the forest, such as the Bhils and the Minas, that the descendants of Indian neolithic man may be found. Consequently, it is possible that the existing outlier of Brahui-speaking people was left behind them by the Dravidians in Baluchistan —assuming that they passed through that country to the first conquest of India.

The Dravidians stood no chance against the Aryans. They were a stout-hearted race but their settlements were overwhelmed by the hosts breaking over them like a rising tide. It was a struggle between the Metal and the Stone Age, and the Aryans carried the earth works and stockades of the Dasas, took their land, and made slaves of the people in droves. Only towards the south was the Aryan invasion checked, and checked for centuries, by the Vindhya Hills and their almost impenetrable forests.

As the Aryans advanced beyond what is now the Punjab, they lost their earlier character of simple, loosely knit communities. The pressure of the hostile race surrounding them, whose country they were conquering, whose colour they despised and whose religion they hated, consolidated the Aryan tribes into small kingdoms and republics.

The lesser chiefs lost their independence and became the leaders of the fighting men, while the Kshatriya class in general rose steadily to a position of great and clearly-defined superiority over the common people, the Vaisya. The Kshatriyas were warriors, though all warriors were not Kshatriyas. Their status was hereditary, but it was probably by no means impossible for a man of the Vaisya class of

Classes of Society.

---

[1] *The Travels and Settlement of Early Man*, T. S. Foster (1929), pp. 243–276, etc.

those times to become a Kshatriya.[1] Later on Kshatriya included the fighting retainers, who increased in numbers with the growth of the States; and in the end the order gave to India that magnificent example of high courage and romantic spirit, the Rajput.

In the confusion and stress of these wars of invasion, which kept the national leaders fighting in the field, the Brahmans seized the golden opportunity to make their position impregnable. Only the priests could ensure the correct performance of the acts of sacrifice, and these rites, vital elements in the national life, became more and more complicated. It was soon recognized that the alliance of the military Kshatriya and the intellectual Brahman was essential for ordered government, while the king's power depended upon popular support in the tribal assembly, the *sabha*.[2] At the same time the importance of the priests was consolidated by the confidential position occupied by the royal chaplain, the *purohita*, who accompanied the king into battle to pray for the success of his arms and cast spells upon the enemy. Behind the spear-head of invasion the mass of the people, the Vaisyas, devoted themselves more and more to farming and trade. Meanwhile a fourth class was added, the Sudra, the name the Indo-Aryans then gave the Dasas, who were originally war captives used as slaves. Later they were peacefully absorbed without loss of liberty, and Sudras included free men of humble occupations. By the law of Manu anyone " begotten by an Aryan on a non-Aryan woman may become an Aryan by virtue." [3]

Brahman and Kshatriya were the two upper classes, but the gap between them and the Vaisya was as nothing to the gulf separating the Vaisya from the Dravidian Sudra. The Aryans were tall and fair, the Dravidians were dark-skinned; and *varna*, which means colour in Sanskrit, was the early barrier between the two races. These were the two original divisions as given in the *Rigveda*, and, eventually, like the Saxon, Dane and Norman invaders of England,

---

[1] *Vedic Index*, Vol. I. p. 207, quoting *Rigv.*, VII. 104, 13.
[2] *Atharvaveda*, III. 4, 6.
[3] *Dharma-Sastra*, X. 67.

the Aryans came to be generally absorbed in the conquered race. This began with social exclusion instead of killing a Dravidian at sight. Today only in Rajputana and a few isolated areas can true Aryan blood be said to survive. The Brahmanas give four colours: white for the Brahman, red for the Kshatriya, yellow for the Vaisya and black for the Sudra; and it has been suggested that this classification came from the colour of the garments worn by them.[1]

With the exception of the Chinese, no civilization now in existence is as ancient as that of India, and the Hindu caste system is its most striking feature. This institution is peculiar to India. Partly from the racial element implied by Brahman and Kshatriya, but mainly upon occupations in different degrees of culture, Brahmanism has evolved the complicated social system of almost innumerable castes and sub-castes. The word caste is, by the way, Portuguese.

Brahmanism is based, unlike the other great religions of India, on the family as the religious unit; and on the *Definition of Caste.* family, with the Brahman priest as its keystone, caste was founded. The fundamental idea of caste is that the individual does not live for himself, and this theory distributes the power, prestige, privileges and goods of this world according to functions.[2]

A caste is a group of families bound to each other by special rules for the observance of ceremonial purity, especially as regards marriage and food. The marriage laws are the most rigid, for caste is an hereditary organization in which a man must marry outside his family and inside his caste. In matters of eating, drinking and touch, the rules are not quite so narrow.

A governing body called a *panchayat*, established by each caste other than the highest, deals with any infringement of its rules, which naturally vary. These offences originally included more than strictly social matters. Immorality, breach of promise of marriage, debt, minor assaults and other cases were dealt with as well. This in effect made each caste a small self-governing society within the nation, as regards its internal affairs.

---

[1] *The Evolution of Caste*, Shamasastry, p. 44.
[2] *Theory of Government in Ancient India*, B. Prasad, p. 338.

PLATE III.

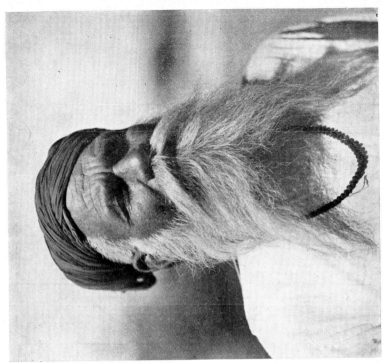

(b) TYPE OF RAJPUT OR " ARYAN " HEAD
By courtesy of Indian Railways Bureau

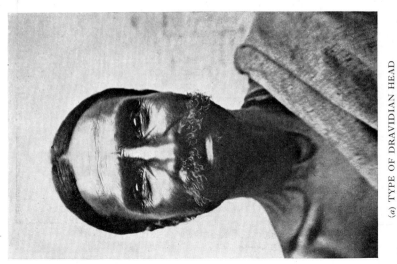

(a) TYPE OF DRAVIDIAN HEAD
A Kota from Nilgiri Hill
By permission of the Secretary of State for India in Council

PLATE IV.

(a) TOY MODEL OF VILLAGE BARBER IN TERRA-COTTA
By courtesy of Indian Museum, South Kensington

(b) WOMAN MILLING FLOUR
By courtesy of Indian Railways Bureau

Caste is not determined by race, religious opinions with certain limits, nor occupations unless they involve caste defilement. The traditional occupation of the caste is naturally the more favoured. A Brahman as belonging to the highest caste would normally live by officiating as a priest (his exclusive right) and by teaching, but he might, if his circumstances were straitened, become a soldier, a mason, or even a labourer. In fact, today, Brahmans may be found in almost any employment other than casual labourer, sweeper and scavenger. But the caste man must follow the set rules governing his own group and avoid giving offence to others.

Admission to an established caste is solely by birth. The social status of a Hindu depends entirely upon the traditional importance of the caste into which it was his lot to be born. It is possible for a ruling prince to belong to one of the low castes, and the touch of his hand would defile the food of a pauper in the streets were that pauper a Brahman.

It is impossible for anyone to rise to a higher caste or sink to a lower one. On the other hand, serious violation of the caste law may, by the vote of the caste assembly, be punished by expulsion from the caste. This sentence means ostracism by members of even the lowest sub-caste in existence, and is social death should the decision be permanent. Except in extreme cases of the violation of caste rules something in the nature of a fine would usually be imposed.

The Hindu rule of life is called *dharma*. This in the *Rigveda* means law or custom. Later it was given a wider meaning. Proceeding from the will of the Creator it included truth, morality, and charity; and became the Law over all human society. All persons who do not follow the Hindu rule of life are regarded by members of that faith as completely outside the pale; and this consequently includes all Europeans, however high their official position in India or their standing in western society.

The orthodox Hindu believes caste to be of divine origin. The *Purusha-Sukta*,[1] the Hymn of Man, divides mankind

Origin of Caste. into Brahman, Rajanya, Vaisya and Sudra. These four orders are there said to have sprung from the mouth, the arms,

[1] *Rigveda*, X. 90, 12.

the thighs and the feet of the Creator, and in this way the primacy
of the Brahman, the strength of the Rajanya (or Kshatriya), the
capacity for useful occupations of the Vaisya and the low position
of the Sudra were derived. These origins are explained in the
Taittirya Samhita of the Black *Yajurveda*. For example the Sudra,
being created from the feet, was to be the transporter of others and
live by the use of his feet.

But there is no evidence that the Aryans were under the caste
system while they were still in the Punjab, where the *Rigveda* was
composed.[1] The *Yajurveda* tells a different story. By this time the
hub of Aryan civilization had shifted from the Indus and its tribu-
taries to Kurukshetra. Here, under the influence of the newly-
developed Brahmanism, caste was evolved from the four orders of
society into its four great divisions.

New castes were originally formed by mixed marriages or in the
following ways, which operate to the present day:

    (i) A tribe or clan of aborigines becoming Hindus under their
        tribal name, or a new one.
   (ii) A change by a body of people from their traditional occupa-
        tion to another.
  (iii) Religious sects forming their own castes.
  (iv) Migration.
   (v) Change of custom, either by neglect or the adoption of new
        ceremonial.

All these methods add greatly to the confusion which exists as
to the precedence of castes. It will be seen that while descent is
undoubtedly a chief factor it is not the only one in the formation of
a caste.

The history of India until the time of British supremacy is a
long story of warfare and confusion broken by periods of peace
under a strong central government. Invaders poured into the

[1] The term Panchanada, " Land of the Five Streams," to describe the Punjab,
does not occur until the epic period. For the opinion that much of the *Rigveda*
was composed further east than the Punjab see authorities quoted in *Vedic Index*,
Vol. I. p. 468.

country, empires rose and fell, but through all these changes and chances the system of caste has held the Hindu steadfast to his social obligations, his religious duties and his economic and civic responsibilities. To this is due the protection of the widow and orphan, the aged and the infirm, for it must be remembered that there are no poor laws in India. It is to this social organization that Hindu India owes its perfections in craftsmanship evolved through countless generations, and to which it is indebted for the steady pursuit of knowledge and culture by the classes marked out as students and teachers. Caste cannot be judged by western standards and ideas, but what it has meant to India is summed up by Monier Williams: " Caste has been useful in promoting self-sacrifice, in securing subordination of the individual to an organized body, in restraining vice and in preventing pauperism."

There is, however, another side to the picture, as the pitiable state of the scheduled classes (the "untouchables"), who numbered about forty-nine million in all India in 1941, still bears witness in many districts. But today social, economic and political influences are gradually weakening the iron rules of a system which touches daily life at nearly every point and presents a philosophy of existence fundamentally at variance with the creeds of the west. The un-avoidable mingling of castes in the trains and the trams, the mills and the mines of twentieth-century India, and the demand of the educated classes for a more democratic form of government are, however slowly, making their impression upon the immemorial social barriers. This movement has the sympathetic support of many of India's progressive leaders, and although the ancient tradition and canons of Hindu orthodoxy held by one-eighth of the population of the globe are not likely to suffer sudden or violent alterations, yet signs are not lacking that an appreciable change in the caste system may be brought about by the people of India.

As the Aryans settled down in the conquered territory life became more complex. The royal household consisted of many court officials. Local government was carried on by the headmen (*gramani*) of the villages as in earlier times, but the status of the industrial classes, and of women in general, was sinking.

No Sudra was ever regarded as Aryan and " twice-born," that is to say, admitted into the religious community by the investiture of the sacred cord; but the Sudras were drawing nearer to the position to which the humbler of the Vaisyas were being reduced, and the Vaisyas were splitting up into a number of divisions by the introduction of the caste system.

This system swept Vaisya and Sudra alike into an ever-increasing number of endogamous [1] hereditary groups which were becoming restricted to a small number of occupations. In this organization of society the Kshatriya was taken as the norm and the other castes were defined according to the relations which they bore to him. An idea of the relative value of the different castes is given in the Sutras. In the matter of private vengeance, tempered by the fining system, a Kshatriya is rated at 1000 cows, a Vaisya at 100, and a Sudra or a woman, at 10; with a bull to the king over and above the fine.[2]

While agriculture remained based upon the village community system of small holdings, the period of the later Samhitas (c. 800–600 B.C.) shows a remarkable advance in industrial life. Houses were still built of wood, as they were in England by the survivors of the great Saxon families up to the time of King John. But Aryan civilization had evolved a host of trades, from jewellers, usurers and weavers to sellers of dried fish and professional acrobats, while two important personages in later village life had made their appearance, the astrologer and the barber. As yet there was no coinage, but gold in necklaces or by weight may have begun to eke out a currency of cattle; and the use of silver was known.

Trades.

The Vedic Indian continued to eat meat, for the doctrine of *ahimsa*, which forbids injury to any animals, had yet to be developed. But already we find an indication [3] of the future renunciation of meat by a whole people.

The practice of medicine, which seems to have reached a relatively

---

[1] Persons who marry only within the limits of a recognized group.
[2] *Camb. Hist. India*, Vol. I. pp. 128, 134.
[3] *Atharvaveda*, VI. 70, 1, where meat is classed with intoxicating liquor as an evil.

high level in the *Rigveda* period, had sunk to the use of spells by the time the *Atharvaveda* was composed. Though as an offset to this the science of Astronomy had made considerable progress.[1]

But the greatest advance is to be seen in religion and philosophy.
Religion. The head of the family still performed the household rites, but public sacrifice of animals and the soma had grown into an elaborate ceremony requiring sixteen or seventeen priests, and prolonged in certain ritual, up to a year or even more. In religious thought a striking development was the doctrine of transmigration. This was foreshadowed in the Brahmanas in the warning that a man may die repeated deaths in the next world, and was definitely taught in the *Upanishads*.

The new doctrine held out the peace of heaven to the ascetic; purgatory in the moon to those who lacked the saving grace of *brahman*, with later birth as a plant or a man; and for the wicked rebirth as outcastes, dogs, swine or reptiles. *Brahman*, " The Holy Power," or *atman*, " The Self," is taught in the *Upanishads* as the one underlying reality. Hinduism holds that the " Absolute " of rationalism and of mystic contemplation is unknowable, and intelligence without thought is ascribed to it. The doctrine of *maya*, as taught by Sarkara, that all existence (with certain qualifications) is mere illusion, did not appear until the ninth century A.D., and it is not universally held by Hindus.[2]

Influenced to some extent by the animist beliefs of the earlier inhabitants of the country (which still survive among the primitive tribes), the doctrine of transmigration came into the national creed with the *Upanishads* about the sixth century B.C. Later there was added the pendent dogma of *karman* (action), which determines on a man's death the nature of his next birth.

While philosophy was developing on these lines the movement towards the religion of modern India had begun. Rudra, with his

[1] For intercalation to correct the more primitive year of 12 months of 30 days see *Camb. Hist. India*, Vol. I. pp. 139, 140.
[2] Sir S. Radhakrishnan, D.Litt., LL.D., in *The Hindu View of Life*, pp. 61-71, examines the theory of *maya* in detail.

accretions from Dravidian sources, especially those connected with sex-worship, became Siva " the auspicious," the dominating national deity, while a relic of the primitive past survived in Kali with her garland of human skulls. Vishnu gained a place of great importance in the sacrificial rites and, contrasting with Siva the Destroyer, Vaishnavism held the idea of a personal god of love, who dwelt among men in his *avatars* (incarnations). Krishna appeared as the god of laughter and song, and the joy of life.

But with all the developments and differences which have been evolved in the comprehensive faith of Hinduism, and to which further reference will be made, the Hindus have remained a distinct cultural unit, with a common history, a common literature and a common civilization.[1] The underlying essentials of Hinduism are what they have been from time immemorial, and the sacred customs of traditional family and caste life, which take the place of the moral law in other countries, have through the centuries been fervently held as inviolable. Add to the sacredness of custom the belief that every god must be worshipped in accordance with what are conceived to be his wishes, and it is possible to understand the Tantric phase of Hinduism with its sexual rites, and the age-long persistence of child-marriage, female infanticide and *suttee*, customs which cannot be regarded as an integral part of the Hindu religion.

The position of the father, the head of the family, grew stronger as time went on. Possibly as early as the eighth century B.C. the rule arose that a man must not eat with his wife, the Satapatha Brahmana pronouncing that " from him who does not a vigorous son is born." About a hundred and fifty years later it was customary for boys of the Brahman, Kshatriya and Vaisya castes to be sent for several years to Brahman schools, where the education was of course essentially religious. No one but a Brahman could teach, and only boys of the " twice-born " castes were admitted. Girls received no education,[2] and even today " literacy has hardly touched the fringe of the female population," [3] in spite of government and non-official efforts.

---

[1] *The Hindu View of Life, passim.*
[2] See *A Primer of Hinduism*, J. N. Farquhar.
[3] *Indian Statutory Commission* (Simon Report), Vol. I. p. 392.

The Hindu religion, as described in these pages, only touches the small literate portion of its adherents in India today. The religion of the overwhelming majority of the people consists in caste customs, family observances and the propitiation of the good and evil spirits of the unseen world around them. Their hopes for a future life are in the care of the village priests, and if they think of a Supreme Being at all His benevolence is assumed as a matter of course.

With their conquests in Northern India consolidated, the Aryan tribes began to make war on each other; and the Kurus to the west of the Ganges and their allies the Panchalas on the left bank of that river, emerge for a time as dominating peoples. Neither these hostilities, nor the lines of tribal kings whose names have survived, in any way affect the course of Indian history. But between the sixth century B.C. and the invasion of the Punjab by Alexander of Macedon, there occurred a series of events of great importance. Two religions were founded; the Indus Valley and part of the Punjab came under foreign occupation; the two famous Indian epics were taking shape; and lastly, this period saw the rise of the kingdom of Magadha, destined to establish two mighty empires.

The second half of the sixth century B.C. was a time of great spiritual activity in Aryan India. A number of schools of religious thought had by this time dissented from the orthodoxy of the pantheistic Vedanta, which is still the dominant philosophy of Brahmanism; and of these two rose to the rank of religions, Jainism and Buddhism.

They followed the same lines as the Sankhya system, a philosophy of considerable influence in India, which taught the complete independence of the human mind and tried to solve its problems by pure reason; and both, in common with the Sankhya system, while acknowledging the lower gods of Brahmanism, denied the existence of a Supreme Deity. But none of the religious systems, other than purely Materialist philosophy, ever denied the theory which has always dominated the belief of the Indian people, that every individual after death experiences a series of new existences in heavens or hells as men or as animals, or in plants, by way of reward or punishment.[1]

[1] See *Sanskrit Literature*, Ch. XV.

23

There were many forerunners, both of Vardhamana Mahavira, the great reformer of the Jain faith, and of Gautama Buddha. Jainism could point to its twenty-three prophets, and twenty-four earlier Buddhas (enlightened ones) had foretold the coming of Siddhartha Gautama, the Buddha.

Vardhamana, the future Mahavira, was the son of the head of *Mahavira.* the warrior house of the Jnatrikas, who lived near Videha, then the capital of a republic, and one of the greatest cities in India. Through his mother Vardhamana was closely related to Bimbisara, King of Magadha, the patron of Buddha and the most powerful ruler in Eastern India.

Born about the year 540 B.C., Vardhamana lived until he was thirty the ordinary life of a man in his position, settled down and married. When his parents died he left his home and his possessions behind him and became a wanderer. For thirteen years he roamed about the country patiently enduring the most abject privations and living a life of meditation and chastity while he fully subdued his senses. In this extreme asceticism he found, as the Jains record, infinite knowledge and was known after this as Mahavira (the great hero) or Jina (the conqueror).

It is believed that his father and mother had been followers of *Jain Doctrine.* the teaching of Parsva, and this was the doctrine which with some additions was taught by Mahavira.

Parsva, who is supposed to have lived about the eighth century B.C., had insisted on four vows: Not to injure life in any form, and the Jains hold that even what is generally considered lifeless matter has a soul; to speak the truth; not to steal; and take the vow of poverty. To these Mahavira added chastity, and nakedness for the ascetic. Laymen were to observe these precepts as far as their occupations allowed.

The austerities of Jainism are of two kinds. One is external, such as fasting even to the length of religious suicide, and the practice of yoga, which consists of prolonged meditation in private in certain recognized postures.

The internal act of discipline is intensive contemplation. In its final stages *karma* is annihilated and the soul leaves the body to be

24

free for ever; *karma* being bondage of works by which the merits and demerits of an individual's previous existence have determined his condition in his present life. For Jainism is a religion of pessimism and looks upon life as an evil perpetuated by transmigration; and it accordingly holds that only the attainment of right knowledge can put an end to the succession of rebirths.

Mahavira spent the remainder of his life preaching his gospel through Magadha and Videha, troubled for a number of years by a rival teacher Gosala, whose colourable imitation of his doctrines had other attractions than stern asceticism. He died, probably about 468 B.C.,[1] at Pawa, near Giribbaja, a place of Jain pilgrimage to this day. He is believed to have survived his great religious rival Gautama Buddha by more than ten years.

Literature. The Jain sacred writings are a mixture of prose and verse called the *Agama*, which was preserved orally until A.D. 454. The non-canonical works are mostly commentaries, poems, legends of saints and religious history. The language of this literature is partly a Prakrit Jain Maharastri and partly Sanskrit; and it is possible that the oldest of the maxims, parables, dialogues, and ballads may have come down from the first disciples of Mahavira. The Jains honour their twenty-four Jinas and venerate the three Jain jewels of Right Faith, Right Action, and Right Morals.

Later History. The later history of this strikingly austere faith, which has remained unchanged through twenty centuries, supporting its religious communities and never attempting widespread missionary effort, is soon told.

The religion won a foothold in the kingdoms of Magadha and Kalinga in the east, and Ujain in Central India became one of its most important centres. But in about 300 B.C. Jainism was losing its hold in Eastern India, and the Jains began their migration westwards to found the settlements in Ajmer and Merwara where they live in slowly decreasing numbers today.[2]

It was at this period that the first signs of schism made their appearance and these came to a head in about A.D. 80, splitting

[1] *Camb. Hist. India*, Vol. I. pp. 155, 156, 163.
[2] *Indian Census Report*, 1931, Vol. I.

45465
LIBRARY
College of St. Francis
JOLIET, ILL.

Jainism into the two sects of Svetambara (white-robed) and Digambara (naked, or sky-clad), of whom only the former admit nuns as well as monks. As the years went on Jainism, which had arisen as a form of protestantism against the authority of the Brahman scriptures, found the force of circumstances too strong, and the caste system was adopted. The vow not to take life prevented the Jains from following professions such as agriculture, so they took to commerce and prosper today as money-lenders.

Jain architecture developed slowly. Its earliest form is to be found in the rock-hewn caves of Orissa, some of *Arts and Sciences.* which are elaborately carved, dating from perhaps the middle of the first century B.C. But it was not until about 900 A.D. that the Jains created a type of their own based on Hindu temples. Great domed roofs magnificently carved with figures and designs, and high towers lavishly ornamented are its most striking features, and these are exemplified at Khajuraho, where Jain and Brahmanical temples are built in similar style.

The Jains have produced valuable works in Sanskrit on grammar and astronomy, and have so influenced the development of southern languages such as Tamil, Kanarese, and Telugu, that they have won for themselves an important place in the literature and civilization of India.

There are superficial points of resemblance in the beginnings of Jainism and Buddhism. Vardhamana Mahavira and Gautama Buddha were contemporaries; both were members of important families; and each had been preceded by a long line of forerunners. Alike they forsook the luxury of their homes at about the age of thirty and sought religious truth by earnest meditation in the midst of extreme hardship and privation. Both faiths deny the existence of an Almighty God, and are religions of pessimism, regarding life as an evil. The two founders equally denied the sanctity of the Vedas, together with the sacrificial ritual and the claims of spiritual superiority of the Brahmans. But they accepted the ascetic practices and the general rule of life decreed by Brahmanism. Monks and nuns are to be found in each religion, but while among the Jains the lay community has always been the more

important element, the religious orders are the dominating factor
in Buddhism.

This is the point at which similarity ends. In every other
respect, and in the doctrines which are the chief notes of the two
religions, Jainism and Buddhism are poles apart.

Gautama was born about the year 563 B.C., at Lumbini, near
Buddha. Kapilavastu, the capital of the Sakiyan republic.
His Life and His father at one time held the elected office of
Doctrine. president of the State assembly and was a man of
considerable importance. Disgusted by the luxury of his home
Gautama, when he was twenty-nine, made his great Renunciation
of the world and went to Gaya, where he lived a life of rigid asceticism
for about six years. Then as he sat in meditation under the sacred
tree the Enlightenment came to him. He had found the Middle
Way and the Eight-fold Path. The Middle Way shunned the
excesses of self-indulgence on the one hand, and avoided on the
other the self-torturing asceticism which he had tried and found
wanting. The Eight-fold Path was to seek what is right in the
eight categories into which thought, word and deed were divided.

Buddha never specifically rejected the general beliefs in the
Hindu gods, and he accepted the theory of transmigration and the
doctrine of *karma*, which is laid down in the *Upanishads*. But
he denied the existence of the soul and taught that *karma* operated
from one birth to the next without this connecting link. Nor was
there anything about a Supreme Deity in Buddha's doctrine.

He concentrated upon a rule of life, not only for his religious
orders but for the laymen to follow. He taught the Four Great
Truths: That human existence is pain, and desire the cause of it,
that release from pain is won by victory over desire, and that this
is achieved by following the Eight-fold Path. He was not a social
reformer. He did not preach against caste; it was simply ignored in
the reception of converts, while his doctrine was taught by those who
had renounced the world as nothing worth.

The new religion of " right conduct " to end suffering spread
rapidly, and within a few years he founded the Sangha, his religious

brotherhood of begging monks. This was soon followed by the order of nuns with its eight rules of obedience to the brethren.

Buddha spent the rest of his life wandering through Magadha and Kosala, and among his Sakiya kinsmen, preaching his doctrine in the simple language of the people, and died at Kusinagara, near the Nepalese border, about the year 483 B.C.

The Buddha's personal teaching is held to be contained in the "Three Baskets," preserved in Pali in Ceylon, Siam and Burma; and in Nepal in the form of Sanskrit from which the translations used from Mongolia to Japan are derived. Buddhism only gradually adopted Sanskrit, but after the sixth century A.D. it was used exclusively. In the Hinayana (Lesser Vehicle of Salvation), Buddhism kept its original form until about the first century A.D., when the Greater Vehicle (Mahayana) was developed.[1] Buddhism then found in Gautama a deity to worship, and there began the evolution of future Buddhas (Bhodisattvas) and their female energies (Shaktis).

The *Jatakas* (birth stories of Buddha) are famous in Buddhist literature and art. A collection existed in 380 B.C., and on the gateways of the great Sanchi *stupa* are bas-reliefs illustrating these legends. The earliest surviving representations of Hindu deities are to be found in Buddhist sculpture, such as the goddess Sri of the second century B.C. Barhut *stupa*. The earliest figures of the Buddha, as distinct from conventional symbols, are the statues dating from about A.D. 100 found in the old Gandhara province.

The Greater Vehicle is the religion of Ceylon, Burma, Nepal and Tibet, but in India the Hindu caste system proved too strong for Buddhism, which was finally swept from the land of its birth by the Moslem invaders. All that survive in India today are the remains of its sculptures and monasteries, its rock-hewn caves and its *stupas*. These last are domes of solid brick or stone surrounded by massive stone copies of wooden post and rail fences, with a relic chamber in the centre of the *stupa*. The smallest *stupas* are miniature

---

[1] Its earliest known trace in Colonial India is in Sanskrit on an early sixth-century *stupa*-tablet in Malaya.

votive models, while the largest, at Anuradhapura, is 250 feet high. *Stupas* were also built by the Jains, and these were identical in form with the Buddhist monuments.[1]

Indian Buddhism greatly influenced the civilized world, both East and West. Contact with China can be traced back to A.D. 67, and by the fifth century Buddhism had fairly established itself in that country. A hundred years later the overland trade route was opened across Central Asia, a flourishing Indian colony sprang up at Loyang, and Indo-Buddhist art was making its profound impression upon China, Corea and Japan.[2] Buddhism has left Europe for ever in its debt. The Buddhist niche of the fourth century B.C. was adopted by Persia, where it became the pointed arch, and so was handed on, with the Persian ribbed vaulting and buttresses, to give birth to the Gothic architecture of western cathedrals.

At the time when Jainism and Buddhism were beginning to make headway in the country of the Ganges, a foreign power, of the same original stock as the Indo-Aryans, was established on the Indus. Cyrus had led his armies into what are now Afghanistan and Baluchistan, and Darius I, about 516 B.C., annexed Gandhara (the modern Peshawur and Rawal Pindi districts) and the lower Indus valley to form the twentieth satrapy of the Persian Empire. Based on the Indian fable of gold-digging ants, Herodotus (III. 94–105) credited the satrapy with an annual tribute of 4680 talents of Indian gold-dust.[3]

About a year later Darius sent a naval expedition under Scylax, a Greek sea captain, down the Indus, from its junction with the Kabul River to the sea. From there the fleet made its way to Egypt, reaching Arsinœ (Suez) two and a half years after it had begun its voyage. Scylax afterwards wrote a book of travel in India, now regrettably lost, in which there figured people who used their enormous feet as

---

[1] *History of Fine Art in India and Ceylon*, 2nd Ed.
[2] *History of Indian and Indonesian Art*, A. K. Coomaraswamy (1927), pp. 141 *et seq.*
[3] *The Greeks in Bactria*, Tarn, pp. 104 *et seq.*, gives Siberia as the source and Bactria the channel of the gold supply ; there was next to none in N.W. India.

sunshades, and others who wrapped their ears round them as blankets while they slept. Quotations from it are made by other early Greek writers such as Herodotus and Ktesias.[1] Ktesias was a Greek doctor attached to the court of Artaxerxes Mnemon, King of Persia from 415–397 B.C., which gave him the opportunity of meeting travellers from India. Only fragments of what he wrote have been preserved, but his *Indika* gave the Greeks the ideas they held about the mysterious land in the East. Unfortunately his imagination knew no bounds.

Persian influence does not appear to have penetrated further into India, but the satrapy was held until its conquest by Alexander the Great. A contingent of Indian troops composed of chariots and mounted and dismounted archers, went with Xerxes when he invaded Greece; and at Arbela, when Darius III made his last stand against Alexander, the Persian army included Indian troops with a detachment of elephants.

The period from about 600–200 B.C. marks the beginning of *The Sutras.* definite Indian history. In literature, it is the era of the Sutras codifying the sacred and legal knowledge upon which the later law-books are based; and towards its close the Indian epics first took shape from the songs of the ancient bards. The Sutra style of classic literature lasted for a thousand years, and may be said still to survive in commentaries of Indian jurists on older works.

The Sutras are the third and last stage of Vedic literature. They consist of:

(i) Ritual: The Crauta Sutras, based on revelation (*çruti*); with the Grihya Sutras, dealing with household rites, attached to them.

(ii) Legal: The Dharma Sutras, which are the oldest sources of Indian law and take, as their name implies, a religious standpoint.

(iii) Subsidiary literature in the shape of grammar and religious commentaries.

[1] *Ancient India as described by Ktesias*, McCrindle, p. 60.

India has its parallel to the Iliad of Homer in two great epics, the *Ramayana* and the *Mahabharata*. These, in vernacular translations and popular editions, are *The Epics.* what no other Sanskrit literature has ever been : a household store throughout Hindu India, to be recited publicly and privately all over the country. For the men and women in these epics, apart from their romantic adventures and the fights of warring nations, lived much the same lives as Hindus do today, although of course there are obvious exceptions. The free choice of a husband which a girl then exercised is one. Another is the marriage of Draupadi in the *Mahabharata* to five brothers at once—a shocking form of incest to more modern Hinduism, but still a custom in countries like Tibet. Lastly, when the epics reached their final form, cow killing and the horse sacrifice were things of the past.

More than this, as Vincent Smith has pointed out, the *Ramayana* has been edited by the Brahmans into a religious book consecrated to the service of the Deity in the form of Vishnu. Rama, the incarnation of the Deity, has become the man-god and saviour of mankind in the eyes of millions of devout worshippers, who have his name in the ejaculation " Ram, Ram " continually on their lips. He is venerated as the ideal man, while his wife Sita is reverenced as the model of womanhood.[1]

Hindus divide epic poetry into *itihasi* and *purana* (tales and legends), and *kavya* (poems). The *Mahabharata* is the best and oldest example of *itihasi* and *purana*, though there are poems in it as well, while the Ramayana is in polished verse.

The *Ramayana*, with the exception of the first and last books (possibly added about the second century B.C., and *The Ramayana.* later), is the work of one author, the hermit Valmiki, who lived in the kingdom of Kosala perhaps before the time of Buddha.

It tells, in seven books running into 48,000 lines, the story of Rama, son of the King of Ayodya. Rama and his wife Sita were driven by intrigue from the court, to meet with many adventures amongst giants and demons. In the end Rama and Sita came home safely to reign in triumph.

[1] *Oxford History of India*, V. A. Smith, pp. 27, 28.

Unlike the *Ramayana*, the *Mahabharata* is the work of many
The   authors. In its present form with its legends and
Mahabharata.   disquisitions on law, philosophy, religion and the
duties of the military caste, it consists of about
200,000 lines, and is the creation of centuries. It was probably built
up from much older legends between about the fourth century B.C.
and the third or fourth century A.D., and gives the first clear and
more or less consistent account of Hindu political thought.

The main story of the *Mahabharata*, like the *Iliad*, is founded on
the traditions of a great war, into which the feud between the Kurus
and the Pandus is held to have dragged every nation in India. The
decisive eighteen days' battle was fought near what is now Delhi, and
both sides were almost annihilated. The war may be taken as an
actual event, fought in the country of Kurukshetra, "the field of the
Kurus," the centre from which Indo-Aryan culture eventually spread.
Hindu tradition gives 3102 B.C. as the date of the war, but Professor
Rapson calculates that it was fought some time about 1000 B.C.[1]

In an early scene the Pandu king is challenged to play against the
most expert dicer at the Kuru court, and stakes in succession his
treasure, his army, his kingdom, his four brothers and then his wife,
Draupadi (to whom they were equally married), only to lose them all.
His final throw sends him into banishment with his family for twelve
years. When his time of exile is over the Pandu king returns and
begins the war of retribution which ends in the total destruction of
the Kurus.[2]

One of the oldest and most popular tales in the *Mahabharata* is
the story of Nala and the beautiful princess Damayanti whom he for
long deserted. Dice again play their part, but in this case it is to
bring about a happy ending.

The kingdom of Magadha comes definitely into history with the
fifth king of its Sisunaga dynasty, Bimbisara. The line had been
founded by a warrior chief who made Giribbaja his capital, and when

---

[1] *Camb. Hist. India*, Vol. I. Ch. XIII.

[2] For fuller details of the Epics see Macdonell's *History of Sanskrit Literature*,
and the lively account of the gambling scene, in which the old men looking on
play the part of the chorus, given in *Camb. Hist. India*, Vol. I. Ch. XI.

PLATE V.

BUDDHIST CHAITYA CAVE (SIXTH CENTURY)
By permission of the Secretary of State for India in Council

PLATE VI.

(a) FROM THE GANDHARA FRIEZE, SHOWING A BIRTH STORY OF BUDDHA
By courtesy of Indian Museum, South Kensington

(b) SANCHI STUPA WITH STONE POST AND RAIL
By permission of the Secretary of State for India in Council

Bimbisara ascended the throne in 543 B.C., at the age of fifteen, his dominions were about one-seventh the size of Kosala, which was at that time the chief power in Northern India, as head of a confederation of clans and republics.

Bimbisara, the friend of Buddha, although himself a convert to Jainism, was a progressive ruler. He built a new and larger capital at Rajagriha, and by conquering the neighbouring State of Anga took the first step towards the future greatness of the kingdom.

Ajatasatru, his son and successor, who lies under the suspicion of having murdered his own father, added Kasi, Kosala and Videha to his dominions, and built the fortress which eventually developed into the famous capital of Pataliputra, on which site Patna now stands.

Nothing survives but the names of the Kshatriya kings of the Sisunaga House who followed him. The last of the line married a Sudra woman and founded the Sudra dynasty of the Nine Nandas, of whom very little is known. One of them, believed to have been a Jainist called Dhana Nanda, was on the throne in 326 B.C., when the Macedonian army refused to cross the Beas and Alexander turned back towards the Indus.

Until he became involved in a plot against the throne and had to fly for his life, the commander-in-chief of the Magadha army in the reign of Dhana Nanda was a young man called Chandragupta, the founder of the first Empire of India.

CHRONOLOGY

B.C.

1200–1000.	Earliest hymns of *Rigveda* (Chhandas period).
	Kuru-Pandu War (*vide Camb. Hist. India*, Vol. I. p. 307). The date by Indian tradition is 3102 B.C.
1000–800.	Later hymns of *Rigveda*, and three later Vedas (Mantra period).
800.	Death of Parsva, precursor of Mahavira.
600–200.	Sutra period.
563–483.	Siddhartha Gautama, founder of Buddhism.
558–530.	Cyrus, King of Persia; conquered Gandhara.
543–491.	Bimbisara, King of Magadha.
540–468.	Vardhamana Mahavira, founder of Jainism.

C

521–485. Darius I, King of Persia.
518. Conquest by Darius of Indus Valley.
517. Naval expedition of Scylax.
491–459. Ajatasatru, King of Magadha.
413–321. Mahapadma to Dhanananda.

The dates of Cyrus and Darius I are historical, those of Buddha, Mahavira and the Persian campaigns are approximate, the others are conjectural. The discrepancies in the accounts of the Nandas in the Puranas and in Jain and Buddhist records make definite history impossible. Indian history first becomes accurately dated by the identification of Chandragupta Maurya with Sandracottus of the Greeks.

BIBLIOGRAPHY

Mohenjo Daro and the Indus Civilization, 3 vols., Sir John Marshall, Archæological Survey of India (London), 1931.
Translation of Rigveda and Samaveda, 5 vols., R. T. H. Griffith (Benares), 1889–1893.
History of Sanskrit Literature, Macdonell, 1925.
Ancient India, Rapson, 1914.
Theory of Government in Ancient India, B. Prasad (Allahabad), 1927.
Evolution of Indian Polity, Shamasastry (Calcutta), 1920.
Caste and Race in India, S. G. Ghuriye (London), 1932.
Cambridge History of India, Vol. I., 1922.
The Dravidian Element in Indian Culture, G. Slater, 1924.
Brief View of the Caste System, J. C. Nesfield (Govt. Press, Allahabad), 1885.

INDIAN MEDICAL SCIENCE. Ayurveda, the science of long life, goes back to the *Atharvaveda* and the *Kausika Sutra* which give the methods of the magician-doctor (held to be an impure calling), an exact detail of the human skeleton and a treatise on embryology and hygiene. The surgeon Susruta (3rd cent. A.D.) knew the value of dissection. He stressed the high moral standard of his profession and held that relatives, friends, widows, the poor and travellers should have free medical attendance, but hunters and outcastes were entitled to none at all. Ayurveda includes incantations against demons as sources of disease, prescriptions of vegetable medicines (the first known MSS. being Buddhist, c. A.D. 340) and drugs to give health, beauty and longevity. The system was unchallenged until Arabic medicine spread east and west in the eleventh and twelfth centuries. Modern European surgery took rhinoplasty from India in the eighteenth century. (See *Hymns of the Atharvaveda*, Sacred Books of the East Series, and *India's Past*, Macdonell.)

CHAPTER II

The Maurya Empire

In the winter months of 327 B.C., Alexander secured his line of communications through Afghanistan.[1] His army of 30,000 men had as many nations in its ranks as the *Grande Armée* of Napoleon, enlisted from countries as far apart as Thrace and the Hindu Kush, with the stout Macedonian phalanx and the magnificent Greek cavalry as its backbone.

He had overthrown the great Aryan Empire of Persia, and in the spring of 326 B.C. he began his campaign in a country made up of rival kingdoms and a number of smaller states fighting to keep their independence.

As soon as Alexander crossed the Indus, Ambhi, King of Taxila, at that time the chief seat of Brahmanical learning, sent him a present of elephants, silver, and droves of sheep and oxen, inviting him to his capital as its overlord. Ambhi was threatened by the Purus and he saw that the invincible Yavana[2] army, far from meaning his own destruction, could be turned to account against his aggressive neighbours.

From Taxila Alexander advanced to attack the Purus, who were preparing to defend the line of the River Hydaspes (Jhelum) under their king, whom the Greeks called Poros; and Ambhi, when he sent 5000 of his troops to fight their fellow countrymen, indicates how foreign nationalities in the centuries to come were enabled to rise to power in India.

[1] For Alexander's route see Robinson's *Ephemerides*. Also see *Ancient India as described in Classical Literature*, McCrindle.

[2] Lit. Ionian, the name given to the Greeks in Indian literature and inscriptions from the third century B.C. to the second century A.D., *e.g.* Greek terms in astronomy and references to Greek girls sent as attendants on Indian princes.

In the engagement which took place at Jalalpur [1] on the banks of the Jhelum, Alexander's tactics in that most difficult operation, crossing a river in the face of strong opposition, were crowned with success. In the battle which followed, the army of Poros occupied a four-mile frontage, with 200 elephants in the centre and 300 chariots on the wings forming the first line, and 30,000 infantry in support, with 4000 cavalry on their flanks. The Macedonian phalanx withstood the charge of the Indian elephants, Alexander's cavalry outflanked their enemy's line and Poros was completely defeated. But his dignity and courage so impressed his conqueror that Alexander with wise magnanimity gave Poros back his kingdom, to be held under Greek suzerainty.

Partly by fighting, aided by his Indian allies, and partly by diplomacy, Alexander advanced to the Hyphasis (Beas). But he was not destined to measure himself against the powerful kingdom of Magadha, beyond the Sutlej, on that great plain, the historical focus of all India, upon which a succession of Delhis have stood and where the fate of India has so often been decided. His Macedonians refused to go a step farther, and Alexander turned back. He reached his newly founded city of Bucephala,[2] planned with Nicæa to form Greek colonies on the fringe of his Empire, and sailed away down river to the coast of the Persian Gulf, in the year 325 B.C. Nearchus, the commander of the fleet, subsequently wrote an account of the Indian expedition, which is largely quoted by Arrian. Twenty Greek chroniclers wrote histories of the campaign, but all these are lost, except for quotations in the works of later writers.[3]

Within two years Alexander lay dead in Babylon, and six years later the short-lived European rule of his satraps had disappeared. All that remained was the definite contact between India and Europe made by the Greek kingdoms established in Western Asia after the disruption of Alexander's Empire. European intrusion in India was at an end until Vasco da Gama crossed the Arabian Sea and set up his marble pillar at Calicut in 1498.

[1] *Vide* Sir Aurel Stein, *The Times*, London, 15th April 1932, but compare *Early History of India*, V. A. Smith, pp. 71–78.

[2] Named after Alexander's charger Bucephalus, which was buried there. The site of the city is probably Jalalpur.

[3] *The Invasion of India by Alexander the Great*, McCrindle.

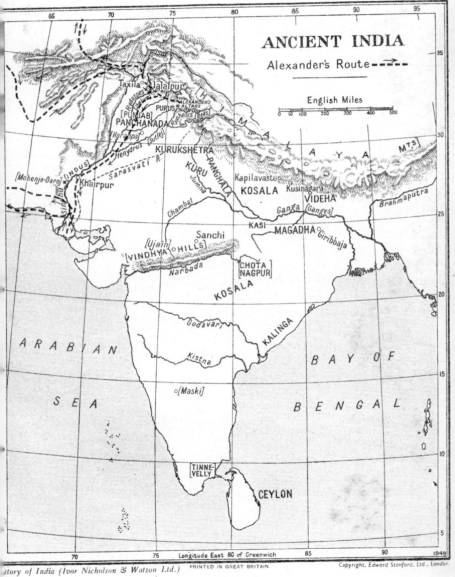

ANCIENT INDIA

Alexander's Route ------->

English Miles

0 50 100   200   300   400   500

Alexander's Route ------->

Labels on map:

Taxila, Jalalpur, [PUNJAB], PANCHANADA, [Harappa], ALEXANDER'S ALTARS, PURUS, Hydaspes (Jhelum), Hyphasis (Beas), [Mohenjo-Daro], [INDUS], Hesudrus (Sutlej), Khairpur, Sarasvati R., KURUKSHETRA, KURU, PANCHALA, Jumna, Kapilavastu, KOSALA, Kusinagara, VIDEHA, Ganga [Ganges], Brahmaputra, Chambal, KASI, MAGADHA, Giribbaja, Sanchi, [Ujain], [VINDHYA] HILLS, Narbada, CHOTA NAGPUR, KOSALA, Godavari, KALINGA, Kistna, [Maski], TINNE-VELLY, CEYLON, MALAYA MTS, HIMALAYA, ARABIAN SEA, BAY OF BENGAL

Longitude East 80 of Greenwich

1949

Shortly after Alexander's withdrawal from India, Chandragupta, with the help of his able adviser, the Brahman Chanakya (Kautalya), seized the throne of Magadha and became the first of the Maurya dynasty to reign at Pataliputra. He may have belonged to the house of Nanda but he made certain of the kingdom by killing Dhana Nanda and his entire family. He then ruthlessly pursued his ambition to extend his suzerainty over the whole of India north of the Narbada. State after State became feudatory to him until his own dominions were threatened in their turn by invasion.

Seleucus Nicator, satrap of Babylon, King of Syria and conqueror of Bactria, in the middle of his turbulent career *Seleucus Nicator.* crossed the Indus, about the year 305 B.C., to conquer Hindustan. Chandragupta advanced to meet him, and it is stated [1] that he could take the field with 9000 war-elephants, great strength in chariots, 30,000 cavalry and 600,000 infantry. There is no record of what followed. But by the terms of peace between the two kings, Seleucus Nicator, in return for 500 elephants, ceded territory to Chandragupta, the Sandracottus of the Greeks, which carried the frontiers of the Indian king to the Hindu Kush in the north and westward to the highlands above Herat.

In India itself the western provinces (now Sind, Kathiawar, Gujerat and Malwa) fell under the overlordship of Pataliputra, and the first Empire of India, the dominion of the Maurya kings of Magadha, was established. These provinces were probably absorbed during the reign of Chandragupta; they were certainly in the possession of his grandson Asoka. Seleucus treated Chandragupta on terms of equality and sent an ambassador to the court of Pataliputra. The ambassador was Megasthenes to whom we are indebted for the wonderfully vivid picture of India two thousand two hundred years ago. His own writings are lost, but they are quoted at some length by Arrian (a Greek official of the Roman Empire of the second century A.D.) and by other writers.[2]

Pataliputra was a wooden city built on the tongue of land at the

---

[1] By Pliny. See *Ancient India as described by Megasthenes and Arrian,* McCrindle.

[2] *Ancient India, Megasthenes and Arrian,* McCrindle.

junction of the Sōn with the Ganges, and forming an oblong of about 9⅕ miles by 1¾. It was defended by a continuous stockade work of heavy timber, with 570 towers and pierced by 64 portcullised gates. Beyond the walls ran a deep moat about 200 yards wide, filled from the River Sōn. The palace, which Megasthenes considered as magnificent as the royal residences of Susa and Ecbatana, stood in a beautiful park, where there were fish-ponds, peacocks and pheasants. The king is recorded to have lived in a state of barbaric splendour in his timber-built palace with its gilded pillars, being served at his table with golden dishes six feet across. When he appeared in public it was either in a palanquin of gold or mounted on an elephant.

The king had his crown lands which were partly cultivated by slaves, but the bulk of the revenue on which the royal state was maintained came from the taxation of the agricultural class, a form of taxation which has always been the foundation-stone of Indian finance. All land ultimately belonged to the king and he was paid a land tax by the holders, who also gave him one-fourth of the produce of the soil, a payment that was made partly in kind and partly in labour.

Civil Administration.

When Megasthenes represented Seleucus at the court of Pataliputra, the government comprised a very large number of officials, magistrates, local governors and royal advisers. It is not possible to determine how far the organization about to be described had been evolved by the Nanda kings; but they undoubtedly possessed a very powerful army to support their authority.

In the Maurya Empire, and indeed throughout Indian history, agriculture has remained the outstanding industry of the country; and the practical unit of administration was naturally the village, under its headman (*gramani*), then an official nominee. The headman dealt with the revenue and supervised the farming, having as his advisers the village council of elders (*panchayat*). The policy of the Maurya government was to provide for the even distribution of the agrarian population by systematic plantation of villages in thinly occupied tracts. For the general improvement of agriculture officials were appointed by the government to " superintend the rivers, measure the land, as is done in Egypt, and inspect the sluices by which water is let out from the main canals into their branches so that everyone may have an equal supply of it." [1] The government water-rate was, however, a heavy burden, varying from one-third to one-fifth of the produce of the land.[2]

Groups of under a dozen villages were under the control of a *gopa*, above whom were placed higher officials, and in the reign of Asoka we find *rajukas* responsible for hundreds of thousands of people.

The district officials, who formed the first of the three categories of government servants mentioned by Megasthenes, were responsible for irrigation and land measurement, hunting, agriculture, woods and forests, metal-foundries and mines, roads and the distance stones maintained on them.

Chandragupta organized the management of his capital in six boards of five persons each, and these town officials formed the second category of government servants. The respective functions of the boards were:

(1) Supervision of factories.
(2) Care of foreigners (control of the inns, charge of the sick and burial of the dead).
(3) Births and deaths, for purpose of taxation and record.
(4) Trade and commerce, supervising weights and measures and generally controlling the markets.
(5) Inspection of manufactured articles and provision of distinction between new and second-hand goods.
(6) Collection of the 10 per cent. tax on sales.

The six municipal boards formed a general council to superintend temples, public works, harbours and prices, and in both town and country there were officials who kept complete registers both of property and the population.[3] The superintendent of passports issued these on payment for the use of all persons entering or leaving the country.[4]

[1] Strabo quoting Megasthenes (see pp. 86–89, McCrindle, *op. cit.*).
[2] *Arthasastra* of Kautalya, Book II. Ch. XXIV. (p. 140 of the translation by Shamasastry).
[3] *Ibid.*, Book II. Ch. XXXVI. p. 175.
[4] *Ibid.*, Book II. Ch. XXXIV. pp. 171, 172.

The organization of the government machine was wonderful, but no scale of punishments could check the corruption which was rife in its offices. Kautalya observes " just as with fish moving under water it cannot possibly be discerned whether they are drinking water or not, so it is impossible to detect government servants employed on official duties when helping themselves to money." He believed that about forty methods of embezzlement had been elaborated.[1]

The third category of officials constituted the War Office. This

Military Administration.

department also consisted of six boards of five, each being provided with a large secretariat:

(1) Admiralty. (2) Quartermaster-General.
(3) Infantry. (4) Cavalry.
(5) Chariots. (6) Elephants.

The forces of the Empire were made up of hereditary troops, representing the old Kshatriya division of society; feudatories who possibly included others besides the warrior caste; guild levies who may have been a kind of corps of armed commissionaires; and forest tribes, who appear to have been used for minor expeditions.[2] The four arms of the service were elephants, four-horsed chariots, cavalry and infantry. The equipment of an army included fixed and mobile engines of war, such as " hundred slayers." The use of advanced guards and reserves was known; and the deployment of an army for battle can be studied in the dispositions made by Poros when he engaged Alexander on the Jhelum. Fighting was no longer a confused mêlée of armed rabbles; organized formations had taken their place. The art of war was systematically studied, and it may be noted that wounded prisoners were supposed to be spared. In addition to chapters on military engineering and organization, five books of the *Arthasastra* lay down the principles of war with the detail of a field service manual.

The royal capital was scientifically defended, and was provided with salients, covered ways and a wide street round the inner side of

[1] *Arthas.*, Book II. Ch. IX. pp. 77 and 72.
[2] *Camb. Hist. India*, Vol. I. p. 489.

the city wall. The frontiers were guarded by forts, and strongholds were built at other strategic points.

The principal Ministers of State included the Treasurer, the Minister of Works (whose responsibilities ranged *The Central* from the maintenance of public buildings to the *Government.* rain gauge); the head of the Judiciary; the Minister of Correspondence, who issued the royal decrees; the Court Chamberlain; and the Commander of the Body-guard.

Over and above the government offices was the king's Inner Cabinet of four: his *Diwan* (chief minister), his *Purohita* (religious adviser), the *Senapati* (commander-in-chief) and the *Yuvaraja* (heir apparent).[1]

Election of a king had by this time entirely disappeared, and primogeniture had not been evolved. The reigning sovereign chose his heir from among his sons, with the concurrence of his people. A most rigorous intellectual and moral training was prescribed for the selected prince.

A number of the chief offices of State were hereditary and, with the exception of the *purohita*, who of course had to be a Brahman, the natural course would have been to select these high officials from the superior castes. But the Nanda line of kings and the Maurya emperors of low extraction who followed them created a standpoint which would have been unthinkable in earlier times. Birth remained a strong qualification, but ability was now held to override it; and the rise of a low-born man to power is not rare in the history of India.

Indian conquerors, whether foreign or of the country itself, have not for the most part, from Alexander's local and short-lived dominion onwards, actually displaced the rulers they subdued. In Chandragupta's time the principles of the central government were, doubtless, loosely imposed upon the tribal system which still survived in the Punjab, but the king's writ ran, and was obeyed, to the farthest limits of his empire; an empire made up of a confederation of States. The independent feudalism and oligarchy of a number of rival States had been replaced by the highly organized bureaucracy of one

[1] *Theory of Government in Ancient India*, B. Prasad, p. 124.

paramount government, supported by a huge standing army and buttressed by swarms of secret agents and informers of both sexes, whose counterpart can best be found in the police of modern Russia.

Over this structure of administration was the King; and *The King.* Kautalya's enunciation [1] of the general principles of foreign policy and the daily time-table of the sovereign make the counsels of Machiavelli on statecraft and of Stockmar on royal duties appear almost feeble.

In the *Arthasastra* the benefit of the State knows no law, and justifies any means to ensure it. Foreign policy as regards neighbouring powers is summed up in the "four expedients" of war, conciliation, bribery or dissension, all of which gave full play to the highest refinements of treachery, propaganda and diplomatic manœuvre.

The royal day was divided into periods which allowed four and a half hours to sleep, three to baths, meals and private study, one and a half hours to religious exercises and an optional hour and a half for recreation. Thirteen and a half hours were to be devoted to affairs of State, from his *purohita's* greeting before dawn, the reports of the secret agents at nightfall, up to the last audience of ascetics and physicians, in the chamber of the sacred fire. [2] In the great palace, with its secret passages and staircases and hollow pillars, and the walled quarters of the queens and concubines, every fantastic precaution was taken for the king's safety; and when he retired for sleep to the strains of music, his room was continually changed for fear of assassination. [3]

How far Chandragupta adhered to the rule of life laid down by his mentor is not known. But Megasthenes records that the king used to hear the causes of his subjects during his daily massage,

---

[1] In the *Arthasastra* (Manual of Politics) already quoted which is attributed to the Maurya statesman Chanakya (Kautalya) and so dated about 300 B.C. But even if the accepted traditional date is too early the *Arthasastra* is a clear statement of the Hindu theory of government of that time, and it had the strongest influence on the thoughts and ideas of future generations. (*Camb. Hist. India*, Vol. I. Ch. XIX., and *Theory of Government in Ancient India*, B. Prasad, Ch. V.)

[2] Kautalya's *Arthasastra*.   [3] *Ancient India, Megasthenes and Arrian*, p. 70.

an illustration of the personal touch which has always characterized Indian rulers.

In the administration of justice moderation and fairness were recognized in theory, but in practice were heavily discounted by caste favouritism. For instance, a Sudra lost the limb with which he assaulted a Brahman, but the reverse did not hold good. If a warrior defamed a priest he was fined 150 *panas*, but if a priest defamed a warrior the fine was 50 *panas*, or if he defamed a slave only 12.

Legal Procedure.

The basis on which the laws were founded were sacred precept (*dharma*), agreement, the custom of villages, guilds and families, and royal edicts.

Civil law dealt with marriage and dowry, inheritance, housing, trespass, debt, slaves, labour, contracts, and sales. Divorce was permitted with the consent of both parties and widows could remarry.

The penal code was very severe and apparently effective, for Megasthenes is quoted by Strabo [1] as noting that with 400,000 men in the camp of Sandracottus the thefts reported on any one day did not exceed the value of 200 drachmæ. In addition to the more obvious charges, the penal code included adultery, defamation, coining, serious violation of caste rules, boycott and other acts of employees, combinations to affect prices and fraud in connection with weights and measures, together with political offences and misconduct of officials.

Cases might be tried by local assemblies, by judges in the towns and, if necessary, on appeal through the higher courts by the king himself. Three Brahmans were attached to the benches of three judges to explain the sacred law. Witnesses took the oath before Brahmans, vessels of water or fire, and underwent close cross-examination. They were given travelling allowances which were paid by the losing party in a civil suit, but on the other hand they were fined if they committed perjury. In a criminal case the accused, if not a Brahman, could be tortured to obtain a confession.

Except for treason, when the invariable punishment was death,

---

[1] *Ancient India, Megasthenes and Arrian*, p. 68.

sentences were adjusted, as has already been noticed, according to the status of the offender and of his victim. These awards ranged in severity from fines to death by impalement, but instead of imposing a death sentence on a Brahman he was outcasted or sent to the mines for life. The law, however, gave some protection to the weak. The honour of women was carefully guarded from the point of view of motherhood; and the abduction, hurt or outrage of a prostitute, her mother, daughter or maidservant was severely punished. But it must be remembered that prostitution was under State supervision; and the fees and expenditure of the women were checked by a superintendent who levied on their income a tax of one-fifteenth. In one instance [1] the rule of increased fines was reversed for, where a common man would be fined the equivalent to a penny, the king (who should know better) would be fined a thousand.

Trial by ordeal, which in earlier days had been only by fire or water, was now developing into nine forms to suit various accusations. Another method of invoking justice, usually to recover a debt, is known to this day as *dharna*. The injured person sits on the doorstep of his opponent and fasts until he dies, or the offender yields.

The capital city of Pataliputra was organized in four districts subdivided into wards and controlled by regulations ranging in scope from precautions against fire to the official report on lost property.

Crafts had greatly developed, especially those dealing with precious metals and textiles. In the big trading communities, clubs and guilds, in some ways not unlike the London city companies, had been established and the wealthy merchants at their head were given official recognition.

Trade.

There was a volume of internal and external trade, controlled, as to distribution and regulation of prices, by the Superintendent of Commerce. Imports were encouraged by favourable tariffs, but all goods, whether they were skins from Central Asia or muslins

---

[1] Laws of Manu, see *Institutes of Menu* (edited by G. C. Haughton, London, 1825), Vol. II. Ch. VIII. 336.

from China, were subject to duties at the frontier and octroi dues at the city gates. Customs duties (export and import) varied from one twenty-fifth to one-fifth of the value of the goods. Articles for religious use were admitted free. Country produce also paid octroi on the way to market, and to prevent evasion of the dues, purchases from local farms were forbidden. Smuggling was dealt with as it is in modern civilized countries.

The king was himself a commercial magnate warned, however, in the *Arthasastra*, not to profiteer. His warehouses throughout the country were filled with the output of his factories, workshops and prisons, and the produce of his personal domains, forests and mines. The higher classes in the State, unlike the feudal land-holding nobility of the west, had a recognized official status; the revenue of an estate, or even of a town, being assigned to them for their maintenance.

In addition to the various sources of revenue already mentioned, the king, when badly in need of money, was entitled to levy benevolences with the active help of informers from all except Brahmans and subjects employed on special service to the State, such as colonization and road construction. Kautalya mentions that those who freely or to do good offered their wealth to the king, should be given a rank at court, or some other honour, an early example of the purchase of a title.

Taxation, under the Maurya emperors, was exceedingly heavy and ingeniously comprehensive, but the cost of Chandragupta's elaborate system of government was enormous, and he maintained a huge army which had successfully defended the country from a formidable foreign invader. Benevolences were not unknown at one time in England, and comparing the financial methods of the Hindus and later the Mogul emperors with modern taxation, it must be remembered that no such expedients as a national debt or long-term Government loans were open to them.

Coining was a State monopoly, and the Royal Mint turned out the *Coinage.* small curved punch-marked ingots of silver and copper which represent the earliest strictly Indian currency. In the north-west an Indian ruler, Saubhuti, who had made friends with Alexander, issued a silver coinage with a Greek legend. Saubhuti (Sophytes) is definitely identified with the Sopeithes of Arrian and Strabo. All the other coins up to this period which have been found in India were apparently brought in from Central Asia. Gold coins were not minted in India until the first century B.C.

With the rise of the Maurya Empire came the growth of luxuries, chiefly in dress; and stone and brick were beginning to displace wood as building materials. But the real test of the civilization of a people is the position of its women.

Social Life.

Both the regular and irregular recognized forms of marriage could be dissolved by mutual consent or, automatically, by prolonged desertion. A wife owned private property in the shape of her dowry and ornaments, and this was to some extent at her own disposal on widowhood. The custom of *sati* was recognized, but until a later date seems to have been confined to royalty. Ill-usage by either husband or wife was punishable, and offences against women were dealt with severely. The time was still to come when foreign invasion was to force Hindu society in self-defence to follow the custom of *purdah*.

Caste had now greatly developed. Megasthenes, in his references to the inhabitants of the country, is misleading on the subject, but the seven categories he describes undoubtedly classify the occupations of the people he saw around him. Kautalya, on the other hand, classifies the nation in the four original castes, although at this date there must have been a considerable number of sub-castes. The ambassador stated that the second caste, the husbandmen, were by far the most numerous and added that, " being exempt from fighting they devote the whole of their time to tillage; nor would an enemy coming upon a husbandman at work on his land do him any harm." [1] The fifth caste, according to Megasthenes, " is the military. It is well organized and equipped for war and holds the second place in point of numbers. The entire force are maintained at the king's expense." [2] An Indian military establishment then consisted of four arms, and the forces of Magadha were

[1] *Ancient India, Megasthenes and Arrian*, p. 39.   [2] *Ibid.*, pp. 40, 41.

reported to Alexander to reach a total of 3000–4000 elephants, 2000 chariots, 20,000 cavalry and 200,000 infantry.

Village life, apart from the exactions of the tax-collectors, was quiet and happy. Inns, eating-houses and licensed gaming establishments (where the State took 5 per cent. of all winnings) were common, and travelling companies of actors, singers and dancers gave performances in the village hall, a form of entertainment deprecated by the author of the *Arthasastra* as being too great a distraction from the fireside and work in the fields.

The staple food of the villagers, except in the north-west, was rice. Vegetarianism had not yet been established and Brahmans are said to have been accustomed to eat meat, excepting apparently that of horned cattle.[1] The popular drink was rice beer, and the people were abstemious except on holiday, when heavy drinking and much eating characterized the festival.

Light is thrown upon the subject of the royal table by the first of Asoka's rock edicts. The emperor forbade the slaughter of animals for sacrifice as being against his principles. He went on to say " formerly in the kitchen of King Priyardarsin, beloved of the gods, many hundreds of thousands of animals were every day slaughtered to make curry. But now . . . only three lives have been killed for curry, namely two peacocks and one deer, but even that deer not regularly. Even these three animals shall not be afterwards killed." [2]

The king riding on an elephant and surrounded by women, some of them holding the royal umbrella, fan and golden pitcher and some of them armed, went in state to hunt in the royal preserves. Men with drums and gongs headed the procession with its escort of spearmen, while the road was kept clear with ropes, which it was death to cross. Another royal amusement was a gladiatorial show, and the animal fights which still survive in some of the Indian States.

[1] *Oxford History of India*, p. 70, where V. A. Smith quotes Quintus Curtius (*c.* first century A.D.).
[2] *Asoka*, Dr. D. R. Bhandarkar, p. 297. Priyardarsin literally means " one of amiable look," and this is how he almost invariably describes himself in his edicts. Asoka always calls himself Raja, the terms Maharaja and Rajadhiraja not having as yet come into use.

The three faiths, Brahmanism, Jainism and Buddhism, lived side by side. Brahmanism represented the established order, and the two great popular deities were Siva and Vishnu under the form of Krishna. But the age had grown tired of elaborate ritual, and Buddhism was challenging Brahmanism. The Brahman was no longer primarily an officiating priest, although the king's private chaplain was one of the principal officers of State. The priest's most obvious function had become that of the professor, and his dwelling the forest hermitage. But in person he was sacred and exempt from taxation, confiscation and torture.[1]

Religion.

Apart from the *Arthasastra* no Indian literature can be definitely associated with the reigns of Chandragupta and his son Bindusara.

Literature.

Jainist tradition affirms that Chandragupta abdicated and became a Jain after he had overrun all India north of the Narbada. He was followed by his son Bindusara, who succeeded in holding the newly won territories, but little else is known about him. He wrote to Antiochus I wishing to buy sweet wine, figs and a sophist to teach him to argue, to be told that sophists were not in the market; and he sent his son Asoka to quell a rebellion at Taxila. The only other recorded event is the presence of an ambassador named Deimachos at his court, sent by the King of Syria.

Reigns of Chandragupta and Bindusara.

Bindusara died about 274 B.C., and the empire passed to one of his hundred sons, Asoka Vardhana. The system of government which Asoka inherited has already been described, and for some years the new emperor lived the life of a normal Hindu king, feasting and hunting to lighten the burden of State affairs. Then came a change as dramatic and far-reaching in its consequences as the conversion of Saul on the road to Damascus.

Asoka.

Asoka, to enlarge his empire towards the south, made war upon the Dravidian kingdom of the Kalingas, and conquered it. But a campaign in which " one hundred and fifty thousand were there slain and many times

Kalinga War.

[1] *Arthas.*, Book IV. Ch. VIII. p. 270.

PLATE VII.

(*a*) COIN OF ALEXANDER THE GREAT
(*b*) POROS MEDAL, THE OBVERSE SHOWING CONTEMPORARY METHODS OF WARFARE
By courtesy of the British Museum

(*c*) CAPITAL FOR PILLAR (*c.* A.D. 50) OVER RELICS OF BUDDHA AT MATHURA
By courtesy of the British Museum

PLATE VIII.

ASOKA PILLAR
By permission of the Secretary of State for India in Council

as many died," [1] filled him with a horror and remorse which changed his entire outlook on life, and had a lasting effect upon the world-history of the great religion to which he turned in his distress.

Asoka, the Buddhist. The Kalinga War was fought in about 262 B.C., and Asoka's conversion to Buddhism immediately followed. Two and a half years later, after his novitiate as a lay disciple, he entered the *sangha*, and in his religious habit made what he has himself described as a strenuous tour of the country.

State and Religion. His position as a Buddhist monk whose vocation was in the outside world is paralleled in Christendom by two western kings in the thirteenth century A.D., Saint Louis of France and Saint Ferdinand of Castile, the liberator of Spain from the Saracens, who both were members of the Third Order of St. Francis. While as regards the relationship between spiritual and temporal authority in India, Hindu society, as Dr. Beni Prasad has pointed out,[2] included in itself what were Church and State in the West, and the clash between the religious and secular powers in medieval Europe had no counterpart in Ancient India.

The Brahman priest, by the time of Chandragupta, no longer exerted his old influence in a State which had evolved a huge civil secretariat. But Asoka impregnated his government with the spirit of Buddhism.

He had abolished the royal hunt and transformed the gay progresses of his predecessors into religious tours; and in the fourteenth year of his reign Asoka impressed upon his administrative officers the duty of inculcating religion and morality in addition to their normal work. A year later he appointed high officials whose sole business it was to teach the law of piety to his subjects of both sexes irrespective of their creed, from the inmates of the palace downwards, these officials being also instructed to redress wrongs and organize charitable endowments.

---

[1] Rock Edict, XIII., *Asoka*, Bhandarkar, pp. 329–334.
[2] *Theory of Government in Ancient India*, B. Prasad, pp. 8, 9.

Missionary Activities. Buddhism, which had pursued its quiet way since the death of its founder three hundred years earlier, was galvanized into a church militant by the marching orders it received from the emperor. Not content with seeing the faith preached throughout the Empire of India, Asoka developed a most effective organization for foreign missions. About the time of the third Buddhist Council, which was held at Pataliputra about 253 B.C. and lasted nine months, missionaries were sent far and wide: to Kashmir where Srinagar was founded, and to the ranges of the Himalaya; to Ceylon, where it is said Asoka's son the monk Mahendra and his daughter the nun Sanghamitra converted the people of the island; and as far afield as the dominions of Antiochus Theos King of Syria and Western Asia, Ptolemy Philadelphos King of Egypt, Magas King of Cyrene in North Africa, Antigonos Gonatas King of Macedonia and Alexander King of Epirus,[1] a record of astounding enterprise.

Darius left behind him the cuneiform inscriptions which blazon the triumphs of the Persian arms as far east as the Western Punjab and Sind. Asoka proclaimed the greatest conquest to be the conquest of duty, and that his wish for all animate beings was security, self-control, peace of mind and happiness. His devotion to religion and morality are recorded on granite rocks and sandstone pillars from the Yusafzai country in the north to Siddapura in the south, and from Kathiawar in the west to Cuttack on the Orissa coast. The might of Persia crumbled into dust before the Macedonian phalanx and the military genius of Alexander, but today the Buddhism of Ceylon, Burma, Siam and Cambodia, of China, Korea, Japan, Mongolia and Tibet, is the harvest of the seed sown by the Emperor Asoka.

Asoka's Character. At the same time, in the spirit of the more enlightened rulers of India, Asoka showed complete tolerance for other faiths. As he said himself, " the sects of other people all deserve reverence." Trust in Buddha's guide to conduct, in the law and in the priesthood, summed up

[1] Rock Edict, XIII. (*Asoka*, Bhandarkar, pp. 329–334); 258 B.C. is the latest date in which all these Greek kings were alive together (*Asoka*, V. A. Smith, p. 43).

the faith Asoka urged upon his subjects. He did not speculate about *nirvana* and left all points of difference between the sects severely alone. *Dharma* was the essence of his religion.

Kingship is the predominant type of government in Indian history, and although restrained in Vedic times by the wishes of the popular assembly, the divine source of the royal authority was emphatically acknowledged. The king's first duty was to protect his people and do justice, and Asoka's edicts show his extreme conscientiousness as a ruler. Accessible at all times to his subjects, he felt that he had never done enough. His favourite maxim was " let small and great exert themselves," and he lived up to this himself. His home and foreign missions were a colossal religious achievement and a widespread influence for good. This he balanced on the material side by establishing hospitals for men and for animals throughout his own country and even in Syria, while he saw to the systematic cultivation of medicinal herbs and plants.

The royal kitchens became vegetarian soon after Asoka was converted to Buddhism, and in the twenty-six years of his reign he published a series of stringent regulations restricting the slaughter and mutilation of animals and birds and making fifty-six days of the year close times for fish.[1] Respect for animal life was then far from universal in the Hindu world, and the enforcement of this law must have seemed a most oppressive innovation. Yet it undoubtedly prepared the way for the future acceptance by all Hindus of the idea of the sanctity of animal life. His care for the aged and the poor,[2] and his rules concerning revision of capital and lesser punishment;[3] the three days respite to those under sentence of execution to allow for an appeal or failing that to make preparation for death;[4] all these are recorded in the edicts which throw so wonderful a light upon his character, and show the kindness of heart which was allied by Asoka with the undoubted severity of the Maurya system of government.

---

[1] Pillar Edict, V., *Asoka*, Bhandarkar, pp. 347–350.
[2] Rock Edict, V., *Ibid.*, pp. 308–315.
[3] Rock Edict, V., *Ibid.*, pp. 308–315.
[4] Pillar Edict, IV., *Ibid.*, pp. 341–346.

Asoka directly governed the dominions centred upon Pataliputra, and was supreme through his viceroys in Taxila, Ujjayina and Kalinga. To the rest of the empire he was the head of a commonwealth of States whose internal administration was their own concern. He pacified the primitive tribes of the interior by bringing the Brahman gods to their knowledge. In his dealings with the frontier tribes, which in the Maurya empire were on the southern as well as the north-western borders, Asoka's primary object was to gain their trust by kindness,[1] and his policy was one of non-interference. It is interesting to note that nearly two thousand two hundred years later the following declaration of policy appeared in the Gazetteer of India: " The policy of the Government of India is to permit no sudden restrictions that may alter the accustomed mode of life of these tribes but rather to win confidence by kindness."

Broken only by the Kalinga war the thirty-seven years of the emperor's rule seem to have been a time of profound peace, " instead of the sound of the war drums the sound of the drum of piety (was) heard." [2]

In the course of his reign Asoka is traditionally believed to have built an immense number of Buddhist shrines; and he erected a pillar in the Lumbini garden when he and one of his queens went on pilgrimage to the reputed birth-place of the Buddha.

Asoka died about the year 237 B.C.,[3] and, with the passing of one of the greatest kings in history, India headed straight for disruption, internal war and foreign invasion.

The latest book of the Three Pitakas, the *Katha-Vatthu*, was almost certainly written by Upagupta (Moggliputta) Tissa, while the great Buddhist Council at which he was a commanding figure was being held at Pataliputra. But the most celebrated author in the reign of Asoka was the emperor himself, who wrote his autobiography in his edicts on the white

Literature.

[1] Kalinga Edict, I., *Asoka*, Bhandarkar, pp. 361–366.

[2] Rock Edict, IV. Translation given by V. A. Smith, *Edicts of Asoka* (Essex House Press), 1909.

[3] *Camb. Hist. India*, Vol. I. p. 503, Dr. F. W. Thomas gives 237–236 B.C., Vincent Smith puts the date at 231 B.C.

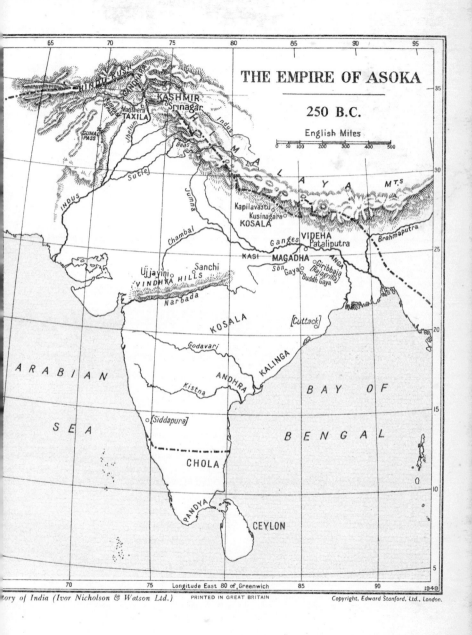

THE EMPIRE OF ASOKA

250 B.C.

English Miles

0   50 100   200   300   400   500

ARABIAN

SEA

BAY   OF

BENGAL

HINDU KUSH
GANDARA
KASHMIR
Srinagar
Manshera
TAXILA
GUMAL
PASS
Kashgar
Indus
Jhelum
Beas
Sutlej
INDUS
Chambal
Jumna
Kapilavastu
Kusinagara
KOSALA
VIDEHA
Pataliputra
Ganges
KASI
MAGADHA
ANGA
Girribaja
(Rajagriha)
Buddh Gaya
Sōn
Gaya
Brahmaputra
MTS
Ujjayini
Sanchi
VINDHYA HILLS
Narbada
KOSALA
[Cuttack]
Godavari
ANDHRA
KALINGA
Kistna
[Siddapura]
CHOLA
PANDYA
CEYLON

1949

ory of India (Ivar Nicholson & Watson Ltd.)   PRINTED IN GREAT BRITAIN   Copyright, Edward Stanford, Ltd., London.

quartz and granite faces of the rocks in the distant provinces and on monoliths of sandstone along the well-beaten tracks in the heart of the empire.

These inscriptions, the earliest records of non-pictographic writing in India, are not in Sanskrit, but in three different Prakrits, that of Magadha being the most usual; and for centuries after Asoka's death official decrees and documents were written in the Middle Indian dialect. But Sanskrit remained the language of culture. Asoka used two characters in his inscriptions. At Shahbazgarhi all the fourteen rock edicts are inscribed in Kharoshthi, and this character is employed for the same form of proclamation at Manshera. But all Asoka's other inscriptions are written in the Brahmi character.

Writing.

Although there is no mention of writing in Indian literature earlier than the fourth century B.C., and Megasthenes has been mis-understood by Strabo to affirm that it did not then exist, there is evidence that writing was, at that time, no recent innovation in India. In Asoka's reign it must have been in common use in public business, in the law courts and in the book-keeping and registration of the secretariats. Moreover, the elaboration of the full Brahmi alphabet of forty-six letters from the twenty-two borrowed Semitic symbols must have taken a considerable time to evolve.[1] The marks used in Brahmi to denote vowels when attached to consonants are not of Semitic origin and may be derived from older Indian scripts. It is within the bounds of possibility that these may go back to the still undeciphered Mohenjo Daro script. In this script some characters have appendages which resemble the Brahmi vowels,[2] but as they cannot at present be read the connection has not yet been established.

The two ancient forms of writing were Kharoshthi and Brahmi; and the Semitic symbols [3] from which they in common with the European alphabet are derived, may have been introduced as early as 800–700 B.C., by traders between Babylon and the western Indian

[1] *Sanskrit Literature*, Macdonell, pp. 16, 17.
[2] Letter from the Department of Oriental Printed Books and MSS., British Museum, 14th November 1934.
[3] Based on the oldest Northern Semitic or Phœnician type as seen on the Moabite stone of King Mesha (*c.* 890–850 B.C.).

ports. Kharosthi, which was written from right to left, was a variant of the Aramaic script used in the fifth century B.C. by the Persian Government of Western Asia. Kharoshthi inscriptions are not found in India later than the fifth century A.D. Brahmi, from which all later Indian alphabets are derived, was first written from right to left, then from left to right, which became the usual method. The earliest known writing materials were birch bark or palm leaves, ink and a reed pen or stylus, the ink being rubbed in afterwards, as in Ceylon today. Strabo (who died about A.D. 24), in Book XV. of his Geography, quotes Nearchus as saying that the Brahmans wrote letters on very closely woven cloth; but added that other writers contradicted their use of written characters.[1] The actual use of ink is proved for the second century B.C., by an inscription from a Buddhist relic mound.[2]

Arts. Maurya art, when uninfluenced by Persian or Mesopotamian culture, could only produce rough terra-cotta reliefs, and it may be noted that no form of china has ever been made in India. But the work of the jeweller and the lapidary show very high technical skill, as the perfectly polished rock-crystal Buddhist reliquary found in the Piprahwa Stupa exemplifies. The earliest known Indian work in ivory is an inscription at Sanchi dating from about 200 to 150 B.C.[3] The punch-marked currency, with its conventional designs, has no artistic merit.

Architecture. Bricks were only just coming into use, and those in the ruins of such places as the Buddhist university at Sarnath, are crude and unwieldy. In spite of the reputation for building gained by Asoka, the existing monuments which can be attributed to him are few in number, and range from the great pillared hall at Patna to the Buddhist chaitya caves cut in solid rock. From the standpoint of history, art and engineering skill the monolithic pillars of highly polished sandstone set up by the emperor are the most striking feature; and their dignity and massive simplicity are typical of the architecture of the period. They may be

[1] *Ancient India*, McCrindle, p. 72.
[2] *Sanskrit Literature*, Macdonell, p. 19.
[3] See *The Arts and Crafts of India and Ceylon*, A. Coomaraswamy, p. 175.

attributed to Persian influence and so can be traced back to the original Assyrian models. With Asoka begins the use of stone in India for building, sculpture and decorating, as the rail at Sarnath and the throne at Buddh Gaya, each cut from a single block of stone, bear witness.

The Maurya dynasty did not long survive the death of its great emperor. Contradictory lists of kings given in Brahman and Buddhist literature are historically useless, but the empire was eventually divided, about the third generation after Asoka, into an eastern and a western kingdom. This was the beginning of the end.

Fall of the Maurya Empire.

The Arsacid power of Parthia rose in the third century B.C. and Bactria with its virile Greek colonies threw off Seleucid authority to reach its zenith under Euthydemus the Greek and his son Demetrius. Asoka's armies had secured the Indian frontiers, but a divided Maurya empire could not resist invasion, and Bactria annexed most of Afghanistan. Between 212 and 206 B.C. Antiochus III, by force and diplomacy, temporarily asserted Seleucid supremacy over Parthia and Bactria. Parthia was beaten, Bactria made peace with honour and Antiochus after an " in and out " raid into India went westwards to his disastrous campaigns against the legions of Rome.

About 184 B.C. Demetrius I crossed the Hindu Kush with the vaulting ambition of reviving under Grecian sway the great empire of Asoka. He took Gandhara, Taxila and Sind, and his lieutenant, Menander, penetrated deep into Upper India. Then the vision faded in the Bactrian rebellion, headed by the able Seleucid sub-king Eucratides, who led his army to the Indus after the defeat and death of Demetrius in 167 B.C. It was left to Menander to withstand Eucratides and establish Greek rule from Gandhara to Mathura over vassal states in what had been the Maurya Empire.

In the eastern kingdom the dynasty came to an end about the year 184 B.C., in a dramatic repetition of history. The country of the Indus lay under the shadow of Yavana rule as it had a hundred and thirty-seven years before, and once again a commander-in-chief of the Magadha army slew his master and founded a new dynasty. Brihadratha was the last of the Maurya kings, and with his murderer Pushyamitra, first of the Sunga line, the kingdom of Magadha sank into obscurity. It was to emerge five hundred years later as an empire, and the founder of its second supremacy bore the historic name of Chundragupta.

CHRONOLOGY

B.C.

327–326. Alexander the Great, King of Macedon, invaded India.
326 (July). Retreat from the Beas.
325. Alexander left India.
323. Death of Alexander.
321. Accession of Chandragupta (Sandracottus), first Maurya Emperor.
305. Indian expedition of Seleucus Nicator and treaty of peace with Chandragupta.
300. Megasthenes at the court of Chandragupta.
297. Accession of Bindusara Maurya (Amitrocrates).
274. Accession of Asoka.
270. Coronation of Asoka.
262. Conquest of Kalinga, and conversion of Asoka to Buddhism.
260. Asoka became a monk and began active propaganda.
259. Asoka issued his first edict ("The Fruit of Exertion," Brahmagiri).
258–7. Issue of the fourteen rock edicts and dedication of cave dwellings in Barabar Hills.
253. Council of Pataliputra.
250. Establishment of kingdom of Parthia by Arsaces and of Bactria by Diodotus.
246. Conversion of Ceylon to Buddhism by Mahendra, the son of Asoka, in the year of the coronation of King Devanampiya Tissa.
243–2. Issue of Asoka's pillar edicts (V. Smith, *Asoka*, p. 146, places the pillar and minor pillar edicts between the 27th and 38th regnal years; *Camb. Hist. India*, Vol. I. p. 503, assumes Asoka's reign to have lasted thirty-six or thirty-seven years, as the Puranas and Pali books affirm).
237–6. Death of Asoka, followed by Maurya kings, beginning with Kunala.
c. 220. Establishment of Andhra kingdom (Satavahana line), and Kalinga (Cheta dynasty).
212–206. Antiochus III, the Great, King of Syria, invaded Parthia and Bactria and made a raid into India.
c. 184. Demetrius I invaded India.
c. 184. Pushyamitra, first Sunga king of Magadha, murdered Brihadratha, last of the Mauryas.

c. 169. Accession of Kharavela of the Cheta dynasty of Kalinga.
c. 169. Eucratides seized Bactria : invaded India prior to 162 B.C.
c. 166. Beginning of Menander's rule in N.W. India.

Dates in Asoka's reign are based on the regnal years given in the royal edicts, and are approximate. The dates of the establishment of the Andhra and Kalinga kingdoms are conjectural. For the dates and text referring to Bactria, Parthia, and Menander the value of Dr. W. W. Tarn's work is here acknowledged.

BIBLIOGRAPHY

Ancient India as described by Ktesias, McCrindle (Calcutta), 1882.
Hindu Civilization, R. K. Mookerji (London), 1936.
Early History of India, Vincent Smith, 1923.
Invasion of India by Alexander the Great, McCrindle (London), 1896.
Ancient India, Megasthenes and Arrian, McCrindle (Calcutta), 1877.
Sanskrit Literature, Macdonell, 1925.
Kautalya's Arthasastra, R. Shamasastry (Mysore), 1923.
Theory of Government in Ancient India, B. Prasad (Allahabad), 1927.
Asoka, D. R. Bhandarkar (Calcutta University Press), 1932.
Asoka, V. A. Smith, 3rd Edn. 1920.
    (Dr. Bhandarkar's *Life of Asoka* goes more into detail; but Vincent Smith's book is easier reading.)
Cambridge History of India, Vol. I., 1922.
The Greeks in Bactria and India, W. W. Tarn, 1938.
History of Fine Art in India and Ceylon, V. A. Smith, 2nd Edn. 1930; revised by K. de B. Codrington. Chapter II. Maurya period.

CHAPTER III

Early Hindu India

THE two main features of the rule of Asoka had been the strength
of the central government and Buddhist missionary
Results of
Maurya Decline. activity. The first, which bound together in security
and peace the commonwealth of States within the
empire, was inherited, but the emperor had the necessary force of
character to maintain it. The second was due to his own personal
fervour. The predominance of Buddhism did not long survive
Asoka, for his death was followed by a strong reaction in favour of
Brahmanism, and Pushyamitra, the founder of the Sunga dynasty,
figures in Buddhist literature as a relentless persecutor of Buddhism.

Peace and security disappeared throughout India directly the
imperial government at the centre failed in its primary duty, which
was to govern. Pataliputra remained for about three hundred years
the capital of a kingdom of some size,[1] first under the later Mauryas
and then under the Sungas; but the empire fell back into the pieces
from which it had been built up, a number of States fighting for
supremacy or struggling to survive. In the Dravidian south Kalinga
asserted its independence soon after Asoka's death, and the Andhras,
who had apparently acknowledged the emperor's supremacy, created
a kingdom, possibly before 200 B.C., which stretched from the Bay of
Bengal to the Western Ghats and north to the Narbada River.

A disunited India was powerless to resist attack from without, as
the conquests made by the Yavana invaders immediately demon-
strated. The decline of the Maurya power was the fatal prelude
to successive waves of foreign conquest.

These invasions all followed the same routes. The barrier of the

---

[1] For the possible extent of the kingdom of Magadha under the Sungas, see
the review of this uncertain point on p. 527 of *Camb. Hist. India*, Vol. I.

Himalaya with the bleak tableland of Tibet behind it, presents an insurmountable obstacle and the only irruption into Hindustan directly from the North has been made from the southern slopes of the main range by Nepal. But along the North-West border open the mountain passes through which conqueror after conqueror has led his armies into India.

For a long period of history, the ocean remained a protection as sure as the Himalaya. Rulers of Egypt from the days of Sesostris in the twentieth century B.C., had tried in vain to cut the Suez Canal, and the coast of India was inviolate until European adventurers rounded the Cape of Good Hope.

When the Seleucid and Maurya Empires were at the height of their power, free intercourse and trade had flourished between Pataliputra and the western world. But the successful revolts of Bactria and Parthia, and the events which followed, completely changed the situation in West-Central Asia, and had a profound effect upon India itself. Two hostile States were established upon the great waterway of the Oxus and upon the most important trade routes of Central Asia which all converged in Bactria. North-Western India was overwhelmed by a series of invaders, and the whole sub-continent became isolated from the West. The intercourse with the western world which still survived was maintained by sea commerce with Mesopotamia and Egypt.

The rival Bactrian houses of Eucratides (in Gandhara and Taxila), and of Euthydemus (to the east of the *Menander.* Jhelum), held sway with varying fortunes until they, in their turn, were invaded in the first century B.C. But with the exceptions of Eucratides, and Euthydemus I, and his son, Demetrius I, Menander is the one ruler of historical importance, and the only Yavana celebrated in ancient Indian literature. He is the Milinda of the *Milindapanha* (Questions of Milinda), and was probably a Buddhist. In this Pali treatise of Buddhist philosophy it is recorded that " as a disputant he was hard to equal, harder still to overcome; the acknowledged superior of all the founders of the various schools of thought. As in wisdom, so in strength of body, swiftness and valour there was found none equal to Milinda in all India. He was rich too, mighty in wealth and prosperity, and the number of his armed hosts knew no end." [1] His fame lived on after his death and beyond the border of his own country, for Plutarch two centuries later refers to the honour in which his memory was held in India.

From the evidence of his coinage, Menander ruled over a number of kingdoms, from what is now Kabul to the Punjab, and in the western districts of the United Provinces. He waged ceaseless war with his rival and contemporary Eucratides and was almost certainly the Yavana who made an enterprising raid eastwards and threatened, if he did not actually take, Pataliputra. But he took Sakala from the Sunga Pushyamitra and held it, making the place his capital.

None of the other Bactrian rulers in Northern India have left behind them more than the inscriptions on their varied and abundant coinage. These coins have, however, two points of interest. Certain specimens struck in Bactria before 200 B.C. are of nickel, a metal which was not known in Europe until its discovery by Swedish scientists about the middle of the eighteenth century A.D. The other interesting feature is to be found in the series of bilingual coins, the first of which were struck by Demetrius I, or possibly by another king of the same name who came soon after him, early in the second century B.C.

Coinage of Bactrian Rulers.

The coins of these Eurasian Greeks were at first strictly Hellenistic, and of almost incomparable artistic beauty; later they deteriorated. But the bilingual coinage struck for the use of conquerors and conquered in India has been of the greatest value quite apart from the names of kings made known by the superscriptions, and the extent of their rule as indicated by the localities where the coins have been chiefly found. The obverse of these coins bears a Greek legend, and the reverse an Indian Prakrit translation in Kharoshthi characters. The clue to that alphabet which this provides has made it possible to translate long inscriptions on stone and copper plates found in different parts of India.

[1] *Sacred Books of the East*, Vol. XXXV., T. W. Rhys Davids, pp. 6, 7.

Yavana rule in India did not long remain unchallenged. Scythians,
known as Sakas, under pressure of Chinese nomads
The Scythians. called Yueh-chi behind them, moved steadily
westward across Central Asia and conquered Bactria. The Yavana
kings were driven out by the Sakas about 135 B.C., and the unwarlike native inhabitants of the country, preoccupied by trade,
exchanged one set of rulers for another. Taking the line of least
resistance, through what is now Western and Southern Afghanistan
and Baluchistan, the Sakas went on and poured into the country
of the Lower Indus. With these invaders the Pahlavas (Parthians
of Seistan and the Kandahar district) were so closely associated
as to be almost indistinguishable. The house of Eucratides,
however, kept their hold on the country south of the Hindu
Kush and in the Kabul Valley until conquered by the Pahlavas
about 25 B.C.

The conquests of the Sakas and Pahlavas, extending as far east
as the region of the Jumna, drove a wedge between the rival Yavana
kings. These Scythian territories were governed by satraps, the
system instituted by Persia and continued first by Alexander and then
by the Maurya emperors. Sakas and Pahlavas alike, these rulers, in
common with the Parthian monarchs, claimed on their coinage the
suzerain title of King of Kings. The house of Euthydemus continued
to rule in the Eastern Punjab until the Saka King Azes I conquered
their territory about 58 B.C.

These invasions, and the huge expansion of the semi-barbaric
power of Parthia under Mithradates I to the Hindu
Results of the Kush on the east and westward to the River
Invasion. Euphrates, isolated India by land from the west,
and her intercourse with the outside world swung eastward to China.
This orientation was brought about by the coming of the Yueh-chi,
who had followed hard upon the heels of the Sakas; and for centuries
foreign descriptions of the country, once the monopoly of the Greek
ambassador or adventurer, are to be found only in the reports of an
envoy from the Court of China, or the diary of one of the many
Chinese pilgrims who came to visit the holy places of Buddhism in
India.

While invader followed invader through the passes to bring chaos into North-Western India, the more powerful of the Dravidian States in the south were steadily expanding into important kingdoms.

Before the Maurya period the Dravidians had a definite culture of their own, which was entirely independent of Brahmanism and the caste system. This civilization and the languages of the people remain predominant in Southern India to this day; and there can be no doubt that Dravidian culture has very greatly influenced Aryan civilization and Aryan religion in the north. It is to the work of the Jain monks that the growth of this civilization and the literary development of the Kanarese and Tamil languages, some centuries after the Christian era, are largely due.[1]

Dravidian Society.

At the time of the Maurya Empire a Dravidian king had supreme control subject to the advice of his " Five Great Assemblies," which are said to have represented ministers, chaplains, generals, commissioners and secret agents. It is possible that the Dravidian local-government system of village representation is their equivalent to the Anglo-Saxon " shire moot," and had already been evolved. The highest social class in a Tamil [2] community were the sages, and next to them the landowners. Herdsmen, hunters, artisans and soldiers ranked next, with fishers and scavengers at the bottom of the scale.[3]

Long before Asoka came to the throne some of the Dravidian States were exporting by sea to Western Asia, Egypt and Greece, pepper [4] and ginger, cinnamon and rice, as well as such luxuries as spices, precious stones and tortoise-shell. This trade was enormously increased when the Roman Empire became all-powerful in the Near East, and reached its height in the time of Nero. Golden *aurei* as well as silver and copper coinage poured into India to an extent which, according to Pliny, greatly strained Roman finance. One of the numerous Roman

Oversea Trade.

[1] *Ancient India*, Rapson, pp. 9, 29, 66.
[2] *Dravida* is *Damila* in Pali.
[3] See *Camb. Hist. India*, Vol. I. Ch. XXIV.
[4] The English word " pepper " is derived through the Greek *peperi* from the Tamil *pippali*, and other Indian commodities such as ginger have a similar derivation.

coins found in Southern India makes the first introduction of the British Isles to the country in the shape of a gold piece struck by the Emperor Claudius (A.D. 41–54) to commemorate the Roman conquest of Britain.

Hippalus, a sea-captain, is credited with the discovery in A.D. 45 of the monsoon-winds, and the long coast voyage of the Greek vessels was exchanged for a direct sea passage. This brought Alexandria within about two months of the Indian coast. The record [1] for the crossing of the Arabian Sea appears to have been made by a ship caught in the monsoon off the Arabian coast and blown to Ceylon in fifteen days; Scylax, in the days of Darius, had taken two and a half years to sail from what is now Attock on the Indus to Suez.

Andhra Conquests. The Andhras, or Telugus as they are now called, who had asserted complete independence after the death of Asoka, are said by Pliny [2] to have possessed thirty fortified towns and maintained an army of 1000 elephants, 2000 cavalry and 100,000 infantry. The Andhra dominion was extended about the middle of the second century B.C. to Ujjayina (Ujain), then, as now, one of the seven holy places of Hinduism, and later, when the Sunga dynasty came to an end, to Videsa.

Nor was this the only blow dealt at the heart of what had been the Maurya Empire by the Dravidian people of the south. The Kalinga power had greatly increased after they won their independence, and King Kharavela, about 150 B.C., claimed a population of 350,000 in his capital. This ruler invaded Northern India time after time, and at some unknown date the Kalinga army heavily defeated the king then reigning at Pataliputra.

The Sunga dynasty is noteworthy only for the strong probability that Patanjali lived during the reign of Pushyamitra (178–142 B.C.). This author wrote the *Mahabhashya*, the great commentary on Panini's grammar of about three centuries earlier, incidentally making the earliest references to the acted drama in the " Slaying of Kamsa " and the " Binding of Bali," episodes in the story of

[1] See *India and the Western World*, Rawlinson, pp. 109–111.
[2] History, VI. 19 (22).

Krishna.[1] The end of the Sungas came about the year 72 B.C. They were originally feudatories of the Maurya emperors, with their headquarters at Videsa, and this remained their western capital after Pushyamitra, the first of the Sungas, seized the throne. They had become puppets in the hands of their Brahman ministers, and the dissolute Devabhuti, last of the Sungas, was murdered at the instigation of his mayor of the palace, a Kanva Brahman. According to the Puranas, in their present form, this minister Vasudeva started a line of Kanva kings, afterwards destroyed with what was left of the Sunga power by the Andhras.[2]

Amongst the numerous obscure independent States scattered over India at this period, there were two groups of clans, some under kings, but the majority ruled by tribal oligarchies, that were destined later on to take an important place in the history of Northern India. These communities living in the north of the Punjab, east of the Ravi, and at the junction of the Indus and the Sutlej, were Kshatriya, and the ancestors of the Rajputs, so-called after Rajputana, the cradle of the race. Two of their States issued coins as early as the first century B.C.[3]

This brief survey of India, from south to north after the fall of the Maurya Empire, brings us back to the north-west frontier, where yet another invasion was about to inundate the country and engulf Yavana, Saka and Pahlava alike. Mention has already been made of the Yueh-chi and their movement across Central Asia. About the year 165 B.C. this people, living between the mountains of Kan-su province and the Great Wall of China, were defeated by the Huns and driven from their own country. They numbered probably more than half a million souls, and in their westward march pushed on before them the other nomads in their way. When

---

[1] *Sanskrit Literature*, p. 347. For Patanjali's date see *Collected Works*, R. G. Bhandarkar, Vol. I. p. 81.

[2] *Camb. Hist. India*, Vol. I. p. 522, states the argument against the existence of a Kanva dynasty. But Sir R. G. Bhandarkar observes that the Sungas may well have been reigning while the Kanvas were ruling just as the rajas of Satara reigned while the Peshwas held the true power. *Collected Works*, Vol. I. p. 513.

[3] *Camb. Hist. India*, Vol. I. p. 528, together with Plate V. (13).

PLATE IX.

IRON PILLAR AT DELHI
By courtesy of Indian Museum, South Kensington

PLATE X.

(a) EARLY BAS RELIEF FIGURE OF BUDDHA
(IN TALCHOSE SCHIST), GRAECO-BUDDHIST
From the Malakand

(b) HEAD OF BODHISATVA, GRAECO-BUDDHIST

the Chinese envoy Changk'ien visited the Yueh-chi in 126 B.C., they were still north of the Oxus River; but from this point it becomes hopeless to fix the chronology of their movements. Probably about 70 B.C. the five Yueh-chi tribes absorbed Bactria, and a little later than A.D. 25 the chief of the Kushanas gained complete supremacy and united the hordes into a kingdom under the name of his own tribe. Once again Bactria became the base for an invasion of India, and the Kushanas soon made themselves masters of modern Southern Afghanistan, then under the rule of the Pahlava suzerain, who was possibly Gondopharnes. This conquest took place about the middle of the first century A.D.

Gondopharnes had begun to reign in A.D. 19. He was suzerain over Eastern and North-West India, and during his sovereignty, which certainly lasted until A.D. 45,[1] the Pahlava power was at its height. But it is not on the extent of his reign, or of his authority, that interest is focused, at least from the standpoint of Christianity. Gondopharnes is the Gudnaphar " King of India " to whose court St. Thomas the apostle is said to have gone during his traditional mission in the country before suffering martyrdom at Mylapore, near Madras. All that is definitely known of St. Thomas is to be found in the Fourth Gospel. All that can be said for the tradition is that the *Acta Thomae*, preserved in Syriac and Greek, on which the legend is founded, was written at the beginning of the third century A.D.; that a granite cross with a seventh-century inscription marks the place where strong local tradition affirms that the apostle was martyred; that a bishop " from India and Persia " was present at the Council of Nicæa in A.D. 325; that, on the Malabar coast, a body of Christians still use a form of Syriac for their liturgical language; and that the date is historically possible.[2]

Gondopharnes was followed by Pasores, but by A.D. 79 the Kushanas were ruling in Taxila. Their victorious leader, V'ima Kadphises, " Great King, Supreme King of Kings, son of the Gods,

---

[1] Takht-i-Bahi monument, in the Peshawar district, dated the twenty-sixth year of his reign.

[2] Father H. Thurston, S.J., who is a rigid critic, sums up against the tradition; *vide Catholic Encyclopedia*, Vol. XIV. pp. 658, 659.

the Kushana," had, it is assumed, already been succeeded by Kanishka, the third of their kings. By the year A.D. 89 the suzerainty of the Kushanas seems to have been extended to the country of the Lower Indus. The domination of the new invaders of Northern India was secure. But the confusion of an obscure period is worse confounded by the name of Saka being given to the chronological era founded by Kanishka in A.D. 78.

Sakas and Pahlavas continued to rule their own States in the country of the Lower Indus, under Kushana suzerainty,[1] which did not, however, prevent them from making war on each other.

Under the leadership of these satraps the Kushan Empire was extended to Surashta and Malwa in Western India, and from the second century to the end of the fourth this region was governed by Saka princes, until its conquest by the Guptas a hundred and fifty years or more after the extinction of the Kushan Empire. This gave the name of Saka in Indian literature and inscriptions [2] to what is really the Kanishka era. The Sakas had rapidly become Hinduized, and by the second generation most of them had Indian names. An inscription in which one of them describes his exploits is composed in a mixture of Sanskrit and Prakrit,[3] neither of which was the language of his forefathers.

The collision, in about A.D. 90, of the Kushan power with China, did not affect the rest of India. But in the reign of Kanishka, when Buddhism came to be enthusiastically supported by that ruler, the empire formed a connecting link between China and India. This brought Buddhism to China and the Far East, and an Indian culture, Indian alphabet and languages found their way into Chinese Turkestan. Kanishka himself appears to have combined other cults with his devotion to the primitive form of Buddhism, although the theology of the Mahayana, which closely corresponded to Hindu ideas, had by this time developed.

The Gandhara school of art had come into existence in the days

---

[1] Sue Vihara inscription (Bahawalpur State) dated the eleventh year of King Kanishka (A.D. 89).

[2] *Camb. Hist. India*, Vol. I. p. 585.

[3] Macdonell, *Sanskrit Literature*, pp. 322, 323.

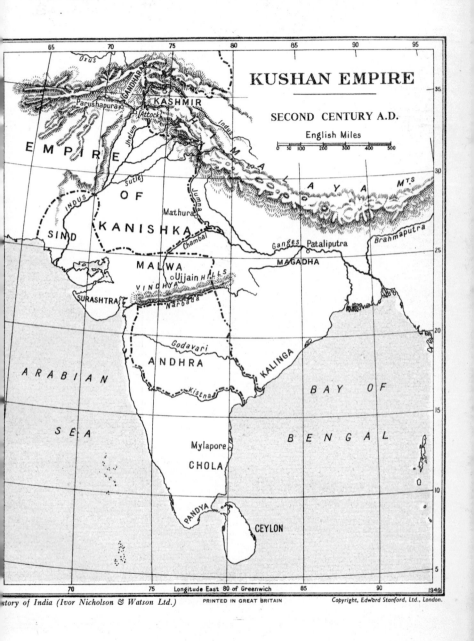

KUSHAN EMPIRE

SECOND CENTURY A.D.

English Miles

0 50 100   200   300   400   500

Oxus

GANDHARA

Parushapura

KASHMIR

(Attock)

Jhelum

Indus

H I M A L A Y A   MTS.

EMPIRE

Sutlej

INDUS

OF

SIND

KANISHKA

Mathura

Jumna

Chambal

Ganges Pataliputra

Brahmaputra

MALWA

Ujjain HILLS

MAGADHA

VINDHYA

SURASHTRA

Narbada

ARABIAN

Godavari

ANDHRA

KALINGA

BAY   OF

SEA

Kistna

BENGAL

Mylapore

CHOLA

PANDYA

CEYLON

1949

story of India (Ivor Nicholson & Watson Ltd.)   PRINTED IN GREAT BRITAIN   Copyright, Edward Stanford, Ltd., London.

of the Saka supremacy in the north; and now, stimulated by Kushan enthusiasm, it developed those conceptions of sculpture which have left an indelible mark on Buddhist art throughout the East. In earlier days the figure of Buddha had not been directly represented; it now became the central idea of Buddhist sculpture.

Kanishka built a great monastery at his capital, Purushapura (Peshawar), which was still a famous seat of Buddhist learning up to the ninth or tenth century. He died after a reign of from twenty-five to thirty years and was succeeded by Huviska.

Huviska seems to have kept intact the Kushan Empire in India, together with the Chinese States of Kashgar, Yarkand and Khotan, which his predecessor had won. He, too, was a Buddhist, and founded a magnificent monastery at Mathura. Vasudeva followed him, and his Hindu name, coupled with the fact that his coins almost invariably have on them the Indian god Siva and his bull, with the insignia of the noose and trident, show that he had absorbed the civilization and the religion of the conquered people.

End of Kushan Empire.

The empire broke up some time about the close of Vasudeva's long reign (c. A.D. 226), but Kushan kings continued to rule in Kabul until the Hun invasion of the fifth century. The north-west now relapsed into a number of independent States like the rest of India.

In the Deccan the Andhra power had declined about the end of the second century, after Rudradaman, the western satrap, annexed Surashtra, Malwa and other districts; and, towards the middle of the third century, what had been the Andhra kingdom of the Satavahana dynasty, disappeared altogether.

Nothing within historical times in India is more uncertain than the chronology of the Kushan period. The dates given in the *Cambridge History of India* have been followed in this account; but it must be noted that Mr. V. A. Smith [1] puts the accession of King Kanishka at A.D. 120–125, while Sir R. G. Bhandarkar considers

---

[1] *Early History of India* and *Oxford History of India* (as revised by S. M. Edwardes), 1928 impression. In the latter, which is the latest edition of Vincent Smith's work, it is considered that Kadphises I died about A.D. 77–78 and that the era dates from the succession of his son Kadphises II (see pp. 127, 128).

that Kanishka's reign began about A.D. 260 and that his successors held North-West India to Mathura until Chandragupta II took it from them.[1]

Chaotic darkness had fallen upon India with the disruption of the Maurya Empire, and it lasted until the beginning *Chandragupta I.* of the fourth century, when it was dispelled by the rise of another great Indian Empire with its capital at Pataliputra. Chandragupta Maurya had ascended the throne of Magadha over the dead body of his murdered master, and secured it by wiping out the entire royal family.

Chandragupta, first of the Gupta dynasty, founded his fortunes upon his marriage, which he freely acknowledged when he issued his coinage in the joint names of himself, his queen, and the historic Lichchhavi clan to which she belonged. It would seem that the Lichchhavi had taken Pataliputra when the Sunga rule decayed, and Chandragupta now succeeded to the power held by his wife's family. His alliance in about 308 with Kumara Devi was the stepping-stone by which he rose from the insignificance of a local chieftain to the height of a paramount sovereign, and the founder of a new era. Year I of the Gupta era, the year of Chandragupta's coronation as heir to the imperial power of Pataliputra, has been fixed between A.D. 318 and 320. This era, one of more than thirty instituted by different Indian rulers, was in use for several hundred years and has been of the greatest value in turning conjectural dates into definite historical sequence.

Chandragupta I enlarged his kingdom by conquest up the Ganges Valley to its junction with the Jumna, and ruled what are now Tirhut, Bihar and Oudh. He was succeeded by the son of his choice, Samudragupta, the greatest king of the dynasty, after a reign of about six years.

Samudragupta on his accession began at once to make himself master of Hindustan. The series of successful *Samudragupta.* campaigns, which brought under his direct control the country between the Jumna and the Chambal rivers on the west,

[1] R. G. Bhandarkar, *Collected Works*, Vol. I. pp. 40, 520.

the Hooghly on the east, and the foothills of the Himalaya and the line of the Narbada River to north and south, have been described by his court poet Harishena. Eleven kings of the south, nine kings of Aryavarta (the most fertile and thickly populated country of Northern India), the chiefs of the primitive forest tribes, and the rulers of the frontier kingdoms and republics, were forced to acknowledge his power. The itinerary of his southern campaign alone must have involved more than three thousand miles of marching for a period of at least three years. The probable date of this great military enterprise is about A.D. 340.[1] Samudragupta made no attempt to bring the southern kingdoms within his empire. He fought his way through South Kosala, defeated the Pallava kings of Kanchi (Conjeeveram) and Palakha (Palghatcherry), exacted the temporary submission of the States he invaded, and then returned through the western part of the Deccan.

Samudragupta was the most able soldier of a line of fighting kings, and although his suzerainty did not reach the Punjab, and the Saka Satrap Rudrasinha still ruled in Ujjain over the country from Malwa to Sind, he was overlord of the one Indian Empire there had been for more than five hundred years. The kingdoms on the east of the Ganges and upon the southern slopes of the Himalaya were under his protection, and he maintained friendly relations with the Kushan King of Kabul and with the King of Ceylon.

When his fighting days were over he had Harishena's panegyric cut in stone, and with cynical humour selected one of Asoka's pillars (now standing in the fort at Allahabad) on which to record his military achievements. This (with the Eran inscription in the Sagar district), helped out by his coinage, have enabled archæological research within the last hundred years to rescue Samudragupta from complete oblivion.[2] For these thirty lines of poetry and about an equal length of prose are the only surviving accounts of Samudragupta's wars. To celebrate one of his triumphs and to proclaim his suzerainty, the emperor, an orthodox Hindu, revived the rite

---

[1] *Early History of India*, V. A. Smith, pp. 248–250, *ibid.*, p. 245, gives 326 as the date of Samudragupta's accession.
[2] *Ibid.*, p. 253.

of the horse sacrifice which had probably not been performed in Northern India since Pushyamitra asserted his paramountcy after the defeat of the King of Vidarbha.

The later years of Samudragupta's long reign seem to have been spent in the peaceful encouragement of the arts. The emperor was himself a poet, and a patron of poets, and in Harishena he found his poet laureate. The Gupta supremacy and the reign of Harsha are the golden age of Hindu literature, and this is surveyed as a whole at the end of the period.

The date of Samudragupta's death is uncertain.[1] He was *Chandragupta II.* succeeded by the son he had made his heir, who, by Hindu custom, took the name of his grandfather, adding to it the title of Vikramaditya (son of power).

Like his father before him, Chandragupta II was an ambitious soldier, and he extended his empire in every direction but the south. The campaigns in Bengal are recorded on the famous Iron Pillar at Delhi, which, as an example of early Indian metallurgy, is itself an achievement. Not only is the mass of iron larger than any which European foundries could handle until the latter part of the nineteenth century, but the pillar, though fully exposed to the weather, has never rusted and the inscription remains today as clear as when it was cut.[2] It commemorates the king's war against the Vanga countries and a campaign in which he crossed the " seven mouths of the Indus " and conquered an unidentified people called the Vahlika. There is a still larger iron column at Dhar, over 42 feet in length, which was cast about the year A.D. 320.

But by far the most important operations undertaken by Chandragupta II were his western campaigns. These are known to have taken place between A.D. 388–401,[3] and resulted in the overthrow of the western satraps. Malwa, Gujerat and the peninsula of Surashtra (Kathiawar) were annexed, and the western ports which fell into Chandragupta's hands brought his empire into direct commercial intercourse by sea with Egypt.

[1] V. A. Smith puts it at about 375 (*Early History of India*, p. 254).
[2] *The Arts and Crafts of India and Ceylon*, A. Coomaraswamy, p. 137.
[3] *Early History of India*, V. A. Smith, p. 255.

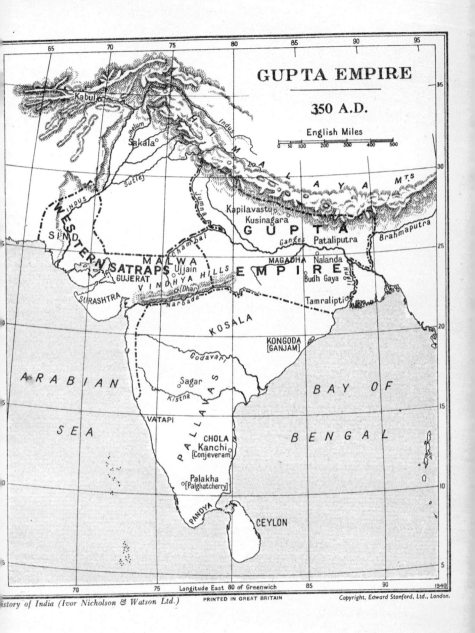

GUPTA EMPIRE

350 A.D.

English Miles

0 50 100   200   300   400   500

Kabul

Sakala

Jhelum

Indus

Sutlej

WESTERN

SINDH

INDUS

Kapilavastu
Kusinagara

GUPTA

Ganges Pataliputra   Brahmaputra

MALWA

SATRAPS

GUJERAT

Ujjain

VINDHYA HILLS

[Dhar]

SURASHTRA

Narbada

Chambal

Jumna

MAGADHA Nalanda

EMPIRE

Budh Gaya

Tamralipti

Sone

KOSALA

KONGODA
[GANJAM]

ARABIAN

Godavari

Sagar

Kistna

P
A
L
L
A
V
A
S

BAY OF

SEA

VATAPI

CHOLA
Kanchi
[Conjeveram]

Palakha
[Palghatcherry]

PANDYA

CEYLON

BENGAL

1948

During the reign of Chandragupta II, a Buddhist monk Fa-hien
came through Central Asia from his home in China
Fa-hien. and visited India between 399 and 414. He crossed
the Indus by a suspension bridge, as travellers in Kashmir and
Southern Tibet swing their way over rivers to this day, and finally
reached the Hooghly. His one object, which he secured at Pataliputra,
was to obtain the Disciplinary Rules for monks which form the
second part of the *Tripitaka*. Fa-hien saw everything with the
eyes of a pious pilgrim, and his account is almost entirely made up
of Buddhist legends and descriptions of sacred relics. He failed
to realize that in spite of the many monasteries, with monks who
might be counted by thousands, whose hospitality he enjoyed,
Buddhism was losing its hold upon India. But in his occasional
observations on the outside world he has given to posterity a
valuable description of life under the Guptas as he saw it.[1] The
book would be well worth reading for its irrelevant final chapter
alone, which vividly describes the storm during Fa-hien's home-
ward voyage with his precious manuscripts, and he is regarded
as a Jonah.

Fa-hien says of the " Middle Kingdom," by which he means the
country of the Ganges Valley: " The people are numerous and
happy; they have not to register their households or attend to any
magistrates and their rules; only those who cultivate the royal
land have to pay (a portion of) the gain from it. If they want to go,
they go; if they want to stay on, they stay. The king governs without
decapitation or (other) corporal punishments; criminals are simply
fined, lightly or heavily, according to the circumstances. Even (in)
cases of repeated attempts at wicked rebellion, they only have their
right hands cut off. The king's body-guards and attendants all have
salaries. Throughout the whole country the people do not kill any
living creature, nor drink intoxicating liquors; the only exception
being the butchers (*chandalas*),[2] who are wicked men living apart.
In that country they do not keep pigs and fowls, and do not sell live

[1] *Fa-hien's Record of Buddhist Kingdoms*, Legge.
[2] Dr. Legge in a footnote (p. 43, *ibid.*) refers to Dr. Eitel's *Handbook for the
Student of Chinese Buddhism* (pp. 145, 146) on this point.

cattle; in the markets there are no butchers' shops. In buying and selling commodities they use cowries." [1]

At Pataliputra, Fa-hien was greatly impressed by the stone palace with its carving, which had been built by Asoka, and by the two big monasteries, one Mahayana and one Hinayana, in each of which lived from six to seven hundred monks. [2]

In his account of the kingdom of Magadha he goes on to say: " The heads of the Vaisya families establish in the cities houses for dispensing charity and medicines. All the poor and destitute in the country, orphans, widowers and childless men, maimed people and cripples, and all who are diseased, go to those houses and are provided with every kind of help, and doctors examine their diseases. They get the food and medicines which their cases require and when they are better they go away of themselves." [3]

The only danger to travellers mentioned by Fa-hien was from the large numbers of lions, tigers and wolves,[4] and the reader is reminded of a verse in Fitzgerald's "Omar Khayyam," by the observation that Gaya was by this time utterly deserted and the once great and wealthy city of Svagasti then held about two hundred families, while Budh Gaya, Kapilavastu and Kusinagara, all of them holy places of Buddhism, were desolate.[5] The whole countryside had not shared in the prosperity he saw on his journey through India.

These are the main points of social interest in the Diary. When *Yajnavalkya.* comparing them with conditions under the Mauryas, it must be remembered that Kautalya was a prime minister laying down his theory and method of government, while Fa-hien was a Chinese pilgrim observing the working of what must have been a more easy-going rule. The official view of government administration under the Guptas may be taken from the *Dharma Sastra* of Yajnavalkya (the most influential Indian lawgiver, with the exception of Manu), who probably lived in Videha State about A.D. 350.[6] Yajnavalkya says that " to inflict punishment or death

---

[1] Fa-hien, Ch. XVI. [2] *Ibid.*, Ch. XXVII. [3] *Ibid.*, Ch. XXVII.
[4] *Ibid.*, Ch. XXXIII. [5] *Ibid.*, Chs. XX., XXII., XXIV., XXXI.
[6] *Sanskrit Literature*, Macdonell, pp. 428, 429.

on those who deserve it is to perform many sacrifices and bestow the finest gifts." But punishment is never to be arbitrary.[1] Yajnavalkya agrees in general with Kautalya, but it seems certain that the application of the penal code was much less strict than it had been in the Maurya Empire.

Kumaragupta. Chandragupta Vikramaditya was followed, between 411 and 414, by his son Kumaragupta I, who celebrated some long-forgotten triumph in the horse sacrifice.

Skandagupta and the Huns. His son Skandagupta, who succeeded him about the year 454, at an unknown date subjugated a tribe called Pushyasmitra. But at the beginning of his reign he had to face the same catastrophe which was simultaneously threatening Europe, in the form of Hun invasion. This devastating menace to civilization poured in two streams from the steppes of Central Asia. One body went westward and fought their way through the Eastern Roman Empire and across the Rhine into Gaul. The remaining hordes, known as the White Huns, turned south and burst into India through the north-western passes. Western Europe was saved at Chalons in 451 by the allied armies of Romans and Visigoths; and some years after this date Skandagupta, by a great victory over the Hun invaders of India, postponed the impending disaster to his empire.

It would seem from inscriptions[2] that for nearly fifteen years the country was at peace, although the debasement of the coinage in latter years discloses the financial difficulties of the government. In about 465 the Huns appeared again, swept the Kushans out of Kabul, and occupied Gandhara. Five years later they invaded India for the second time and overthrew the empire. What was left of the dominions of the Guptas split up into petty kingdoms, and the last representative of the dynasty reigned in Magadha at the beginning of the eighth century.

The Hun leader in India was Torama, and he rapidly established

[1] See *Theory of Government in Ancient India*, B. Prasad, pp. 174-176, for a summary of Yajnavalkya's principles.
[2] Detailed in *Early History of India*, pp. 268, 269.

himself in the north and west,[1] before his death in about 510. His son Mihiragula, who is known in Indian tradition as a revolting and bloodthirsty tyrant, succeeded him, and made Sakala (Chuniot or Shahkot) his Indian capital. But the Hun domination, with its savage cruelty, was of short duration. About the year 528 Mihiragula was defeated by a confederacy of Hindu princes under Baladitya (possibly Narasimhagupta), King of Magadha, and Yasedharman, a Central Indian raja; and the country was cleared of the invaders, with the exception of some settlements in the north, which were dealt with later by the kings of Kanauj and Thanesar.[2] Nor did the dominion of the White Huns last long in Central Asia. Some time between 560–570 Khusra Anushirvan, King of Persia, joined forces with the Turkish tribes and destroyed this peril to civilization in the East.

The remainder of the sixth century is an absolute blank in the history of India. But in 606 an event, destined to be of the greatest importance, took place when a youth of sixteen, named Harsha-vardhana, became ruler of the State of Thanesar.

Accession of Harsha.

Harsha at once began, deliberately and systematically, to make himself master of Northern India. His father, Prabhakara-vardhana, who was possibly a Vaisa Rajput [3] and through his mother had Gupta blood in his veins, had made his State a power by successful war with the Huns and with his neighbours. Harsha consequently had at his command a formidable army of 5000 elephants, 20,000 cavalry and 50,000 infantry with which to realize the traditional Kshatriya dream of bringing the whole country, as far as possible, " under one umbrella." With this force of three arms, chariots being regarded as obsolete, Harsha brought the " Five Indias," stated to have been Svarastra

His Conquests.

---

[1] For inscriptions showing the progress of the Hun invasion see *Early History of India*, footnotes 1 and 2 to p. 274.

[2] Aphsad inscription. See *Harsha*, R. Mookerji, pp. 13 (footnote) and 51.

[3] Cunningham's opinion, quoted by Walters, who, however, observes that the Chinese Buddhist pilgrim Yuan-chwang, with ample opportunities for learning the antecedents of the royal family, states that Harsha belonged to the Vaisya caste. (See *Yuan-Chwang*, Walters, Vol. I. pp. 343–345.)

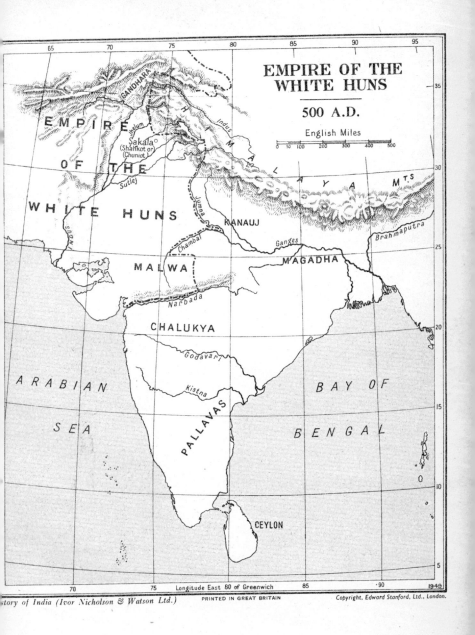

EMPIRE OF THE
WHITE HUNS

500 A.D.

English Miles

0 50 100   200   300   400   500

GANDHARA

EMPIRE

OF   THE

WHITE   HUNS

Indus

Sakala
(Shahkot or
Chuniot.)

Sutlej

Jumna

Indus

Chambal

Narbada

MALWA

KANAUJ

Ganges

Brahmaputra

MAGADHA

CHALUKYA

Godavari

Kistna

ARABIAN

SEA

PALLAVAS

BAY OF

BENGAL

CEYLON

story of India (Ivor Nicholson & Watson Ltd.)   PRINTED IN GREAT BRITAIN   Copyright, Edward Stanford, Ltd., London.

(Punjab), Kanyakubja, Ganda (Bengal), Mithila (Darbhanga) and Orissa, under his allegiance. In six years,[1] "while the elephants were not unharnessed, nor the soldiers unhelmeted," he conquered the northern plains from the Sutlej to the Hugli, and Central India to the banks of the Chambal and the Narbada; while away to the east Kamarupa (Assam) acknowledged his supremacy. In the north the most powerful State was Kashmir, whose ruler was overlord of a considerable part of the Western Punjab. This king was a Buddhist, and the only recorded intercourse between him and Harsha is the forcible removal by the latter of a tooth relic of Buddha when he came on pilgrimage to Kashmir to see it, the relic being subsequently enshrined at Kanauj. With China Harsha maintained friendly relations, sending a Brahman envoy to the Chinese court in 641 to open the exchange of embassies. Yuan-Chwang, who visited Harsha in Kanauj city during his travels in India between 629–645, states that when he had enlarged his territory he increased his army, bringing the elephant corps up to 60,000 and the cavalry to 100,000, and reigned in peace for thirty years without raising a weapon; a way of putting an army on a peace footing which recalls the Roman proverb and the methods of King Solomon.

Harsha met with only one check in his victorious career. The feudatory princes under him had optimistically represented that "the Saka realm is but a rabbit's track, the Deccan easily won at the price of valour," but the powerful kingdom of the south, ruled by Pulikesin II, greatest of the Chalukya kings, was too strong for him. The battle between the suzerains of Northern and Southern India took place on the border between their respective dominions, the banks of the river Narbada, and Harsha was completely defeated. The issue was apparently decided by Pulikesin's great superiority in elephants,[2] in spite of Harsha's troops drawn from " the Five Indias

---

[1] The reasons for believing that Harsha's continuous wars of conquests were concluded by 612, and the authorities for the statement, are given by Mookerji in a footnote to pp. 36, 37 of *Harsha*. But see *Early History of India*, pp. 286, 289, where Harsha is said to have engaged in thirty-seven years of warfare before he sheathed his sword, and the war with Pulikesin is dated about 620. There is no difference of opinion about the Ganjam campaign of 643.

[2] Walters, Vol. II. p. 239.

and the best generals from all countries." Yuan-Chwang informs us that Pulikesin's elephants were doped before battle and that the troops were issued with the Maharashtran equivalent to a rum ration, which made them invincible.

The only recorded result of the battle, beyond Harsha's abandonment of a southern invasion, was the assumption of a second title by the victor. Harsha fought his last campaign in Kongoda (Ganjam) in the year 643, and annexed this territory. He died about five years later.

The deities of Harsha's family were Siva and the Sun, but, like the greatest of the Maurya emperors, he became a Buddhist. Asoka's religion had been of the simplest, but Harsha was an enthusiastic follower of the Mahayana sect, and in addition to what may be called his missionary tours through his dominions, eagerly pressed his Chinese visitor Yuan-Chwang into the service of propaganda.

Harsha's Rule and Character.

The Buddhist monk has recorded of Harsha [1]: "He was just in his administration and punctilious in the discharge of his duties. . . . He was indefatigable, and the day was too short for him. The king's day was divided into three periods—one to affairs of government and two to religious works. . . . He caused the use of animal food to cease throughout the Five Indias and he prohibited the taking of life under severe penalties. He erected thousands of topes, . . . and established travellers' rest-houses all through his dominions, which were provided with food and drink, doctors being appointed to them, who supplied medicine free to the poor. Harsha also built Buddhist monasteries at sacred places. [2] He regularly held the quinquennial convocation and gave away in religious alms everything except the material of war. . . . At the royal lodges every day viands were provided for 1000 Buddhist monks and 500 Brahmans." Harsha, even on his administrative progresses, when he had only a greenwood hut to live in, kept up considerable state,

[1] Walters, Vol. I. pp. 343, 345.

[2] Mookerji, basing his calculations on Rhys Davids, estimates a total of 5000 monasteries and 212,130 Buddhist monks (of all sects) in India during Harsha's reign. (*Harsha*, pp. 124–127.) However inaccurate, Yuan-Chwang's census demonstrates the still surviving strength of Buddhism at the time.

and like Chandragupta Maurya was accompanied by his women attendants. The *Harsha Charita* of Bana,[1] the court poet who wrote a biography of his master, tells us that with his " necklace of pearls and other ornaments he looked like a jewel mountain with its outstretched wings of jewels spread on both sides."

Civil Administration. The offices of the chief councillors of State seem to have been the same as in the Maurya administration, although the rank of the ministers appears to have been that of chiefs and feudatory rulers. The State revenue was mainly derived from one-sixth of the produce of the crown lands, other sources including light octroi and ferry dues, and a percentage on goods sold. Yuan-Chwang observes that families were not registered, and taxation was very light. Land settlement was clearly defined, with government surveyors and arbitrators to assess the revenue. All government officials were paid in grants of land and not in money. Public works were carried out by conscripted labour, for which payment was made.[2]

Penal Code. For treason the sentence was imprisonment for life, which, in the conditions of the times, might mean death by starvation. Lesser offences were punished by mutilation or banishment; and in minor cases fines were imposed. In addition to the ordinary procedure Yuan-Chwang mentions trial by ordeal.[3]

Religion. Buddhism, although losing its hold, was still a vital force. The great university of Nalanda, with its six-storied monasteries and thousands of inmates, gave the students who entered it free education, board, lodging, bedding and medicines out of the income of its estates.[4] One of the chief strongholds of Buddhism at the time was Sind, then under a Sudra king. But many of the great monasteries in Central and North-Eastern India, even the splendid buildings of Sanchi itself, were deserted and falling into decay.

Brahmanism was the religion of the mass of the people; and the

[1] From which this account is largely taken.
[2] Walters, Vol. I. pp. 176, 177.
[3] *Ibid.*, pp. 171, 172.
[4] *Harsha*, pp. 129–132.

Vedanta was studied by scholars in the forest retreats of the hermits. The most popular deities were Vishnu, Siva and the Sun. Yuan-Chwang noticed temples dedicated to all three at Kanyakubja, then a centre of both Brahmanism and Buddhism. Benares, in those days as it is now, was the most important place of Siva worship; and there were many other Hindu temples in different parts of the country.

From the fourth century A.D. Indian colonists carried their civilization and the Buddhist faith (later replaced by Hinduism) to Cambodia, Malaya and Java. In Malaya the stone remains of Siva temples of the seventh and eighth centuries proclaim the greatness of Pallava expansion.[1] About A.D. 600 there began the plantation of self-contained colonies in Java from Gujerat; and in Harsha's reign ocean-going ships taking 200 passengers plied regularly between Tamralipti, Ceylon and Java.[2] The Hindu arts flourished in these colonies until the coming of Islam between the twelfth and fifteenth centuries.

The reigns of the Guptas and Harsha-vardhana, that is to say between the fourth and the seventh centuries, cover the greatest period in Hindu culture.

In technical literature the metrical Code of Manu, the most
Literature.   important of all the Sanskrit law books, had probably
taken its present form not much later than A.D. 200.
The great epic, the *Mahabharata*, with which that code is closely connected, was certainly completed by the middle of the fifth century,[3] if not more than a hundred years earlier at the beginning of the Gupta era; while during this period the earlier Puranas, the literature which deals with the creation, the exploits of gods and heroes, the genealogies of solar and lunar kings, and the conduct of religious duties, were recast into the shape they are today. Bana's *Harsha Charita* gives a flowing and poetical account of Harsha's

[1] Authority, H. Q. Wales, Field Director Greater Britain Research Committee, 1937-8.
[2] For Chola expansion see p. 201.
[3] See Sir R. G. Bhandarkar's *Collected Works*, Vol. I. pp. 79-93.

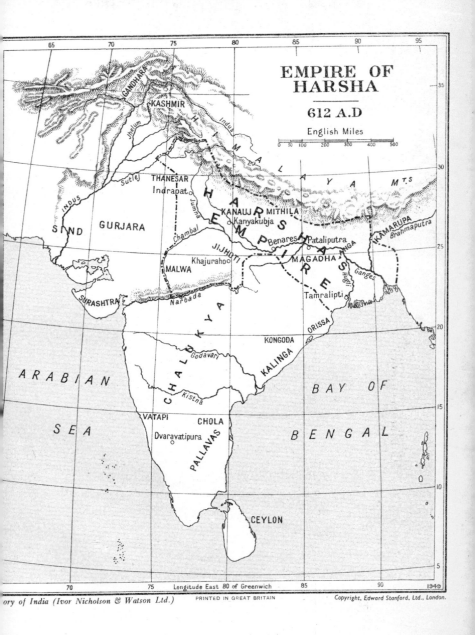

EMPIRE OF HARSHA

612 A.D

English Miles

0 50 100   200   300   400   500

GANDHARA

KASHMIR

Indus

Jhelum

H I M A L A Y A MTS

Sutlej

THANESAR
Indrapat

INDUS

SIND

GURJARA

Chambal

Jumna

KANAUJ MITHILA
Kanyakubja

Benares Pataliputra

IKAMARUPA
Brahmaputra

GANGA

Ganges

JIJHOTI
Khajurahoo

MALWA

MAGADHA

Sugli

SHRASHTRA

Narbada

Tamralipti

ORISSA

KONGODA

C H A L U K Y A

Godavari

KALINGA

ARABIAN

Kistna

BAY OF

SEA

VATAPI
Dvaravatipura

CHOLA

BENGAL

PALLAVAS

CEYLON

Longitude East 80 of Greenwich

1949

ory of India (Ivor Nicholson & Watson Ltd.)   PRINTED IN GREAT BRITAIN   Copyright, Edward Stanford, Ltd., London.

life, but it cannot be called historical biography. No definitely historical work appears in Sanskrit literature until the *Chronicle of the Kings of Kashmir* was written in 1148.

The technical works mentioned above, all of them of the highest importance, had been the growth of centuries, but *Kalidasa and the Drama.* in the realm of poetry and the drama this period can claim for its own the greatest of all Indian poets.

Indian drama developed from the " song and dance " performances of strolling players into the religious plays representing the history of Krishna and Vishnu; and plays were certainly being acted when Pantajali wrote his *Mahabhashya*.

By the Gupta period the theatre had become the amusement of the princes and nobles. The performances were given at the palaces before aristocratic audiences, by highly competent companies, who relied on practically no scenery and only the simplest of stage properties. After an overture on flutes and other instruments by the orchestra, the manager, acting as *compère*, and the leading lady would open with a scene like a sketch in a modern revue, by way of prologue. The play followed, with its dialogue interspersed with songs and ballet.

The greatest of the Indian plays were all written between about the beginning of the fifth and the end of the eighth century A.D., and by far the most celebrated of these dramatists is Kalidasa, who in all probability lived in Malwa at the beginning of the fifth century. Three of his plays have been preserved, the *Sakuntala* (The Fatal Ring), *Vikramorvasi* (Urvasi won by Valour) and *Malavikagnimitra* (Malavika and Agnimitra), and they justly entitle their author to a place amongst the greatest of dramatists. His plays are full of beautiful lyrics, while in " The Cloud Messenger " and " The Four Seasons " Kalidasa has written the two most perfect lyric poems in Sanskrit. In Indian epic poetry with its rigid rules of construction Kalidasa's are the two most famous examples,[1] while in romantic drama his tenderness and sincerity stand pre-eminent. The cele-

---

[1] For Kalidasa's works see *Sanskrit Literature*, Chs. XI., XII.; for reference to his influence on Goethe, see *Life of Goethe*, J. G. Robertson, p. 214.

brated sixth-century play, " The Little Clay Cart," [1] is a mixture of drama and comedy. The amusing scene in the third act, where the burglar must do something " to astonish the natives," could not be bettered. Though attributed to royalty the author may have been Dandin, whose poem, " Adventures of the Ten Princes," mirrors the sixth-century under-world of thieves, gamblers and ladies of easy virtue. After Krishnamisra's allegorical Vaishnavist play, " Rise of the Moon of Knowledge " (c. 1100), Indian drama dwindled under Moslem invasion into mystery plays on village greens and the low-life monologues of southern India.

One of the most important works on astronomy was written in the fourth century A.D., and this was put into concise and practical form by Aryabhata, who was born, as he states himself, at Pataliputra in A.D. 476. He maintained the rotation of the earth round its axis and explained the causes of eclipses of the sun and moon. The early Indian astronomers, in the chapters they give to algebra, reach a far higher standard than anything ever attempted by the Greeks.[2]

Science.

In the Kushana and later Andhra period of art (A.D. 50–320) sculpture was massive and primitive. But in the Gupta period which followed, taste had been definitely created and types and compositions were now standardized in forms whose influence extended far beyond the Ganges Valley. This influence spread not only throughout India and Ceylon, but well outside the confines of India proper, and survives to the present day.[3] At the beginning of the Gupta period we find the earliest examples of Hindu temples, decorated with carved bricks. These early stone temples, planned to resemble saitya caves, were barrel-roofed buildings, built with an apse. The entrances to the Mahayana halls of about A.D. 500 are elaborately ornamented with figures of Buddha and rose-lotus decorations, while the interiors are painted.

Architecture and Sculpture.

[1] For a description of the early drama and the modern development of the Indian stage under European influences see *The Indian Theatre*, R. K. Yajnik (Allen & Unwin), 1933.

[2] *Sanskrit Literature*, pp. 434-5, and see Note at end of this chapter.

[3] *History of Indian and Indonesian Art*, A. K. Coomaraswamy, pp. 71, 72.

PLATE XI.

(b) HEAD OF BUDDHA IN RED SANDSTONE
Mathura (non-Hellenic) fifth century A.D.
By courtesy of Indian Museum, South Kensington

(a) RED SANDSTONE FIGURES FROM MATHURA
Early Kushan period, second century A.D.
By courtesy of Indian Museum, South Kensington

PLATE XII.

(b) DETAIL FROM AMARAVATI
BAS RELIEF (GUPTA)
By courtesy of the British Museum

(a) AMARAVATI BAS RELIEFS (GUPTA)
By courtesy of the British Museum

At the great university at Nalanda in South Bihar, founded about the year 470, the monastery buildings were six storeys high, and the great brick temple rose to a height of over three hundred feet, with richly adorned towers and turrets. Yuan-Chwang has described it " with its dragon-like projections, coloured eaves, pearl-red pillars carved and ornamented, richly adorned balustrades and roofs covered with shining tiles."

But with the death of Harsha the golden age came to an end. His minister Arjuna, who usurped the throne, was utterly incompetent to keep the empire together. His first act was to murder the escort to the Chinese embassy under Wang-hiuen-tse which had just reached the court, the envoys themselves escaping to Nepal. Wang-hiuen-tse returned with a combined force of Nepalese and Tibetans and, aided by Kumara, King of Assam, the feudatory and personal friend of the late emperor, the allies completely defeated Arjuna, who was sent as a prisoner to China.[1] The country which Harsha had ruled so firmly and well relapsed once more into the chaos of endless war between petty States.

In the hopeless confusion of the next five hundred years, kingdoms occasionally emerged under strong and determined rulers, none of whom, however, were powerful enough to found an empire and turn chaos into coherent history.

The arts were still encouraged at various courts, especially temple architecture. Temples were built in honour of all three religions, but there are no Buddhist, Jainist or Brahmanical styles of architecture; they all were built in the Indian style of their respective periods. Sculpture remained at a high level, and the latest and best paintings at Ajanta belong to the eighth century.[2] At the beginning of the medieval period of art, in about the ninth century, the brick temple of Laksmana, unsurpassed in the richness and refinement of its ornament, was built

Arts.

---

[1] *Early History of India*, pp. 298–299, gives a full account of the incident.
[2] See *Ajanta* (published under the special authority of H.E.H. The Nizam, Oxford University Press, 1931–1934), a magnificent publication with many reproductions in colour.

at Sirpur; and the magnificent temples of Orissa and at Khajuraho, were built about the year 1000.

Hindi, Bengali, Gujerati and other present-day languages were forming to give birth to the vernacular literatures.

Chess was probably played in India as early as A.D. 700.

The history of the Deccan [1] from about 550 to 750 centres upon the fortunes of the Chalukyas, a line of kings pos-

The Deccan.

sibly of Hun origin, who had settled in Gujerat and become Rajputs. Their greatest representative, Pulikesin II, greatly enlarged his kingdom of Vatapi at the expense of his neighbours until, as the most powerful ruler south of the Narbada, he repelled the invading armies of Harsha. In the course of his victorious career Pulikesin drove the Pallava king of Kanchi out of the country between the Kistna and Godavari rivers, and so began a conflict of alternating fortunes which resulted in his defeat and death in 642. The rule of the Chalukyas ended for the time being about the middle of the eighth century when Dantidurga of the ancient Indian family of the Rashtrakutas came down from the Maharashtra country and overthrew Kirttivarmana II. The overlordship of the Deccan then passed into Rashtrakuta hands for more than two centuries. The famous rock-cut shrine of Kailasa at Ellora was made during the reign of Krishna I, the second of their kings.

In 973 the Chalukyas came into their own again, and the last of the Rashtrakutas was dethroned by Tailapa II, founder of the second Chalukya dynasty. Tailapa succeeded in regaining most of the old territory of his house, and his descendants ruled at Kalyani for over two hundred years. But simultaneously with the overthrow of the Rashtrakutas and the return of the Chalukya dynasty, a powerful and aggressive State, the kingdom of the Cholas, arose south of the Kistna to make a bid for supremacy in the south and west of the Deccan. The succession of frontier wars between these two equally matched States was begun by the greatest Chola king, Rajaraja the Great, who invaded the Chalukya country about the year 1000 and annexed a large part of what is now Mysore. Rajaraja had already made considerable conquests in the south, and subsequently

[1] For further details see Ch. XV. of the *Early History of India*, V. A. Smith.

extended his sovereignty over Kalinga and Ceylon. But about the year 1080, in the reign of the enlightened King Vikramaditya Chalukya, Rajaraja's conquests in Mysore were won back from the Cholas.

The Chalukya kings of Kalyani continued to hold their supremacy until they were crushed between their former feudatories the Hoysalas of Dvaravatipura and the Yadavas of Deogir before the middle of the twelfth century. The Cholas were themselves overthrown about the year 1220 by the Pandyans of Madura, by which date their supremacy had passed away; for the Chola-Pandya hostilities had, as one of its results, the dominance of the Hoysala power above the other warring states, under their greatest King Vira Ballala II. From the chieftainship of a small hill tribe in the Western Ghats the Hoysala family had risen in just under two hundred years to the paramount position in the Deccan. They achieved this in 1192 after a succession of conquests which concluded with the defeat of the Yadavas. Their supremacy, however, was brief. Shaken to pieces by Muhammadan invasion in 1310, when the capital Dvaravatipura was sacked, the kingdom was wiped out on the return of their conquerors sixteen years later.

In the country between the Narbada and the Jumna the Chandel kings of Jijhoti enjoyed for about three centuries a less chequered existence than their neighbours to the north and south. Early in the ninth century they had established themselves as a state to be reckoned with south of the Jumna; and between the years 950 and 1050 they built the groups of magnificent Hindu and Jainist temples at their capital of Khajuraho. After the Moslem invasion the Chandel dynasty continued to reign as feudatories of the Ghaznavids until, after an unsuccessful revolt, the kingdom was annexed in 1203 by the Muhammadans.

Further to the north Kanauj once more found a strong

The Pala Dynasty. ruler in Bhoja (Mihira Parihar), a Rajput chief who usurped the throne and created a powerful kingdom which he ruled for nearly fifty years, until his death about 890. His descendants were still kings of Kanauj when Mahmud of Ghazni made his descent upon Northern India.

The country we now know as Bengal felt to the full the anarchy which swept over Northern India after the break-up of Harsha's empire. But in about 750 the people in sheer desperation elected a king to restore peace and security. In choosing a Buddhist named Gopala they made a fortunate choice, for his son Dharmapala, second king of the Pala dynasty, proved himself to be a strong ruler and a successful soldier, who made himself master of much of Northern India about the beginning of the ninth century. The dynasty met with various vicissitudes of fortune, but it succeeded in surviving until there came upon it that inevitable ending to all the kingdoms north of the Deccan, destruction by Muhammadan invasion before the middle of the thirteenth century.

But the fortunes of ambitious princes in Hindustan and in the Deccan during this time of confusion of States and distress of the people are of little historical importance. The centre of interest had long since moved from Pataliputra and Ajodhya, the later capital of the Guptas, to Kanauj; it now comes still further west and is focused upon Rajputana, Sind and the Punjab.

This wide belt of territory on the west is to India what eastern England and parts of Scotland are to the rest of Great Britain, the zone which has been exposed in the past to foreign raids and more permanent invasion. The inhabitants are therefore of mixed descent, and the people of Southern India, like the inhabitants of the western fringe of England and the Principality of Wales, are the descendants of the earlier owners of the soil.

Broadly speaking, the Rajput clans represent the old Kshatriya *The Rajputs.* order of Indo-Aryan society, with whom Brahmans had to some slight extent intermarried. By tradition the Rajputs claim descent, as Suryavamsa, Chaudravamsa and Agni-kula, from the Sun, the Moon, and the Sacrificial Fire. The Rajputs, among the hills and valleys of their country remote from the rich plains, are to India what the Highlanders are to Scotland, a proud people boasting a common origin with their chiefs, sudden and quick in quarrel, and split up into clans, which never could unite to form an empire. The minor Rajput baron, " with a pedigree as long as his sword and a sword as long as the village street," held his fief on military tenure. The Rajputs showed to their women a respect unusual in the East, and for their enemies a chivalry unsurpassed in the annals of history. The women of the race jealously guarded a tradition which matched the courage of their men. In the face of irretrievable disaster, as at Manaich when besieged by Mahmud of Ghazni, they could show that their spirit at least was unconquerable in the terrible rite of *jauhar*, when the women and children destroyed themselves by fire while the defenders of the place rushed out in saffron robes upon the enemy, sword in hand, to die to a man.

But not all of the Rajput clans are of Indo-Aryan origin. A number of the most distinguished clan-castes of Rajputana are descended from the upper class of later invaders of India, such as the Gurjaras and White Huns, who, it must be noted, were a tall fair race and unlike the inferior type who tried to conquer Europe. These foreigners became absorbed in the country they subdued, and established themselves amongst the true Kshatriyas in what are now Rajputana and Gujerat, the district which is named after the most powerful of the clans of Saka stock. From one of these, the Parihar sept of the Gurjaras, came the line of kings who captured Kanauj about the year 840 and transferred their capital from Bhilmal to the imperial city of Harsha, while Rajput dynasties rose to power in Malwa and Bundelkhand.

Approximate Dates	CHRONOLOGY
B.C.	
135.	Saka invasion of Bactria.
70.	Yueh-chi conquered Bactria.
58.	Azes I Saka conquered Euthydemian kingdom of Eastern Punjab.
25.	Pahlava conquest of Kabul.
A.D.	
19–50.	Gondopharnes "King of India."
50.	Yueh-chi (Kushanas) took South Afghanistan and began conquest of N.W. India.
c. 78.	V'ima Khadphises Kushana reigned in Taxila.
c. 89.	Foundation of Kushan Empire.

85

A.D.

150. Rudraman the Western satrap defeated the Andhras.

180. Decline of the Andhra power.

226. Death of Vasudeva Kushana and break-up of Kushan Empire.

318–319. Accession of Chandragupta I.   Rise of Gupta Empire.

326–375. Samudragupta.

340. Campaign in Southern India.

375–411. Chandragupta II.

388–401. End of the Western satraps.

400–450. Kalidasa, poet and dramatist.

c. 400–1400. Hindu colonization in South-East Asia.

411–454. Kumaragupta I.

454. Skandagupta.   First appearance of the White Huns in N.W. India.

465. White Huns took Kabul and occupied Gandhara.

470. Torama and the White Huns conquered N.W. India.

528. Confederacy of Indian kings defeated the White Huns under Mihiragula.

550. Rise of Chalukya dynasty in the Deccan.

560–570. Khusru Anushirvan King of Persia destroyed the White Huns.

606. Harsha-vardhana became King of Thanesar.

612. Conquered Northern India, but was defeated in his invasion of South India by Pulikesin II.

609–665 Pulikesin II.   Chalukya.

622. The Hijra : flight of the Prophet Muhammad to Medina.

648. Death of Harsha and break-up of his Empire.

BIBLIOGRAPHY

Cambridge History of India, Vol. I., 1922.

Sacred Books of the East, Questions of Milinda, Vol. XXXV., T. W. Rhys Davids, 1890.

Ancient India, Rapson, 1914.

Intercourse between India and the Western World, Rawlinson, 1926.

History of Sanskrit Literature, Macdonell, 1925.

Early History of India, V. A. Smith, 1904, 3rd Edn.

Fa-hien's Record of Buddhist Kingdoms, tr. J. Legge (Clarendon Press, Oxford), 1886.

Theory of Government in Ancient India, B. Prasad (Allahabad), 1927.

Harsha, R. Mookerji (Oxford University Press), 1926.

Yuan-Chwang, T. Walters, Oriental Translation Fund, Royal Asiatic Society (London), 1904.

History of Fine Art in India and Ceylon, V. A. Smith as revised by
K. de B. Codrington (1930).
(For specialized information on the dawn of Indian architecture
from cave temples, see the magnificent work *Ancient India from the
Earliest Times to the Guptas*, with 76 plates, K. de B. Codrington
and William Rothenstein, 1926.)

NOTE. Mathematics, astronomy and astrology were always closely associated
in India. Trigonometry, probably learnt from the Greeks, was used in astronomical calculations. Geometry (including Euclid's I, 47) was used to lay out
sacrificial ground in squares and circles and transform plane figures into others of
equal area ; this may well go back to the time of the Vedic hymns. In the works
of the great astronomers Brahmagupta (early seventh century A.D.) and Bhaskara
(b. 1114) Indian mathematics reached their highest form. Simple arithmetic
included cube root, rule of three, calculation of interest and other practical mathematics. The algebraical treatises of both these mathematicians go beyond the
solution of equations with more than one unknown quantity. A method of solving
indeterminate equations of the second degree had been discovered which the high
mathematical authority Hankel has declared to be the most delicate operation in
the theory of numbers achieved before the time of the great eighteenth-century
French astronomer Lagrange. (See *India's Past*, Macdonell, on which this Note
is based.)

CHAPTER IV

Pre-Mogul Muhammadan Rule

Rise of Islam.

PREVIOUS invasions had come from the north-west, but the first warning to India of the storm which swept across Asia, North Africa and Southern Europe about the beginning of the eighth century was to fall upon Sind.

When we consider the overwhelming success of the Muhammadan conquerors of India, it must be borne in mind what took place in the west. As Sir Wolseley Haig points out,[1] the rise of Islam is one of the marvels of history, and the relentless force of its expansion by the sword was almost irresistible. In A.D. 622 a prophet, unable to gather together more than a dozen disciples, fled from his native city of Mecca to what is now known as Medina. Little more than a century later the successors and followers of the fugitive were ruling an empire which extended from the Atlantic to Afghanistan and from the Caspian to the Cataracts of the Nile.

The Arabs in Sind.

By the beginning of the eighth century the Arabs had carried the banners of the Prophet into Gedrosia, the modern Baluchistan; and an act of piracy by nominal subjects of Dahir, the Brahman king of Sind, who had ousted the Saka ruler of the country, led to the Arab invasion in 711 by the youthful Muhammad Qasim.

Muhammad, with his heavy siege engines to support his picked troops, took one fortified town after another. By the year 712 he had penetrated into the heart of Sind, where he met Dahir in a pitched battle. The Hindu king was killed, his army was routed, and the victor organized the government of Lower Sind under local administrators. In 713 he advanced upon Multan and took it.

The Arabs now were in possession of Sind and the Lower Punjab,

[1] *Camb. Hist. India*, Vol. III. p. 1.

and their conquest marks a new stage in Muhammadan policy. The Koran lays down that Christians and Jews on account of their inspired scriptures belong to a more favoured class than other "unbelievers." Consequently when conquered their lives should be spared and their religion tolerated so long as they made their submission and paid a poll tax, while the early interpretation of the Koran allowed to other unbelievers only the choice between Islam and death. But the conquest of Sind was not a holy war, and Muhammad's policy of arousing as little general hostility as possible led him to apply to Damascus for an amnesty to Hindus, which spared their temples and allowed them religious freedom.

The religion of Islam reduced to its simplest terms consists of the formula " There is one God and Muhammad is his Prophet," while its beliefs are bounded by the Shari'at, the sum total of the natural, ethical and social laws taught by its founder. The Moslem sects differ only in their interpretation of these laws, which are binding on the whole Muhammadan world.

The control exercised by the Caliphs of Baghdad over their Indian dependency gradually weakened. In 871 it practically disappeared altogether with the creation of two independent States under chiefs of the Prophet's own tribe of the Koreish at Multan and Mansurah.

The Arabs made no serious attempt to break the power of the Rajput kings to the north and east, and their conquest of Sind and the Lower Punjab left the rest of India untouched. Their authority was supported by Arab soldier-colonists who settled down and made local marriages, while the actual administration was largely left in the hands of the people of the country and the taxation of the Hindu population was eminently fair. Invasion of a very different character was to descend upon India with Mahmud of Ghazni and his Turki armies.

The rise of the Turks to power is a remarkable story. To make
Rise of the Ghaznavids. their own position secure from the growing Persian influence and the risk of Arab revolt, the Caliphs of Baghdad formed a personal guard of Turki slaves captured in war. But the Turki guard gradually acquired the chief

offices of State, got control of the provinces and, becoming the masters of the Caliph, made the Turkish race predominant throughout the Moslem world.

The occupation by slaves of the highest positions in the State occurs over and over again in the history of Moslem India. The enslavement of the vanquished in war was in those days the only alternative to wholesale massacre, and the Koran laid down that slaves who say their prayers (*i.e.* embrace Islam) are brothers and must be clothed and fed as their masters, with permission to ransom themselves if they were in a position to do so. Moreover, if a slave woman bore a child to her master, the child was free and the mother emancipated, which contrasts favourably with conditions in the American plantations many centuries later.

By the end of the tenth century Islam had lost its political unity. The power had slipped from the hands of the Arabian successors of Muhammad and was now divided amongst a number of independent dynasties to whom the Caliph at Baghdad was simply the spiritual head.

One of these independent states was Ghazni, to whose throne a slave called Sabuktigin succeeded in 977. This ruler rapidly enlarged his kingdom to the Oxus on the north, the present frontier of Persia on the west, and after two successful campaigns against Jaipal, the Hindu king of the Punjab, took from him, in 988, an extent of territory which included Kabul. Six years later he was given the governorship of Khorasan (Eastern Persia) by the ruler of Bokhara. Sabuktigin died in 997 and a year later his younger son Ismail, who had succeeded him, was dethroned by his elder brother Mahmud.

Mahmud was twenty-seven when he took over the kingdom *Invasions of* which his father had built up, and in the following *Mahmud of* year he added the province of Sistan to his dominions. *Ghazni.* The Caliph al-Qadir Billah formally recognized his sovereignty, conferring on him the title of Yamin-ud-Daula, from which Mahmud's successors are known in the East as the Yamini dynasty. It was then that Mahmud is said to have vowed to make a yearly expedition to carry the Crescent in a holy war into India. These campaigns cannot be followed with certainty, but there were not less than twelve of them, and they may have numbered as many as seventeen.

Mahmud had not to deal with a united empire in Northern India, but with a number of States too suspicious of each other, and even hostile, to offer the resistance of more than a brief and half-hearted alliance. Apart from the small Brahman State of Und on the Indus, which was immediately obliterated, the fury of the Moslem storm fell upon the kingdom of the Punjab, whose capital was Bhatinda. Its kings, Jaipal I, Anandpal, Jaipal II and Bhimpal the Fearless, bravely but fruitlessly resisted Mahmud's invasions. But the end came in 1021, and Bhimpal had to take refuge in Ajmer.

The first invasion took place in 1001. Mahmud with a force of 15,000 cavalry advanced on Peshawar, where at the end of November he found Jaipal barring the way with an army of 12,000 cavalry, 30,000 infantry, and 300 elephants. The Indian troops were routed by the Muhammadan cavalry, with a loss of 15,000 killed, and Jaipal was taken prisoner. After the Punjab king's release on ransom he abdicated in favour of his son Anandpal, and, overwhelmed with the shame of defeat, perished on a funeral pyre.

The next few years were spent by Mahmud in minor expeditions and in settling a revolt on the Oxus where, it is interesting to note, an Indian contingent formed part of his army. But in 1008 he came down into India to crush Anandpal. The Punjab king, with his allies the rulers of Ujjain, Gwalior, Kalinjar, Kanauj, Delhi and Ajmer, had concentrated the Indian forces to the west of Und. Instead of adopting his former tactics of an impetuous attack, Mahmud took up a defensive position, entrenched his flanks, and for forty days awaited the Indian assault.

It came on the last day of the year, and opened with flank attacks by 30,000 hillmen who carried the Muhammadan trenches. Mahmud's defeat seemed certain when Anandpal's elephant took fright and bolted from the battlefield. The Indian troops, seeing the flight of their leader, broke in disorder, and the Muhammadans won a complete victory. Mahmud pressed on to Kangra, the treasure-house of North-Western India, plundered it and returned with an enormous booty to Ghazni.

Year after year, during the cold weather, invasion followed invasion, and Mahmud went back into his mountain fastnesses laden with plunder and carrying off with his army immense numbers of prisoners to be sold in Ghazni as slaves. Thanesar, the holy city of Muttra, and Kanauj the Hindu centre of India, all fell into the hands of the Muhammadans, and after the raid of 1018–19, when 53,000 captives, 380 elephants and an enormous quantity of treasure were taken, Mahmud founded in Ghazni the great mosque of marble and granite called the " Bride of Heaven " and the college which was attached to it.

With the exception of the campaign of 1021, when Bhimpal was defeated and the Punjab annexed, all Mahmud's military operations had up to this time been either to strengthen his rule on the Oxus and at Multan, or to storm through Northern India bent on plunder and the destruction of temples. But in 1024 he started on his most celebrated expedition, crossed the great India desert with 30,000 camels to carry water for his troops, and took Somnath. The Hindus offered a stout resistance and disputed with the greatest courage every yard of the streets leading to the great temple where a thousand Brahmans served at its shrine and guarded its almost incalculable treasures. Fifty thousand Indians lay dead in Somnath before the temple was taken, rifled of its gold and its jewels, and the great stone *linga* broken into pieces. It was not until the spring of 1026 that Mahmud's army returned with its spoils to Ghazni.

In the autumn of the same year Mahmud made his last expedition into India, against the Jats of the Sind-Sagar Doab who had harassed his retirement from Somnath. He defeated them in a naval engagement on the Indus, in which he employed 1400 boats fitted with spikes and armed his crews with bows and arrows and naphtha hand-grenades. Mahmud died at Ghazni in 1030.

It is not possible to regard him as a king of India, although he founded a dynasty which ruled the Punjab for a *Mahmud's Character.* century and a half. The Punjab was not annexed until late in his reign, and all his interests were centred in his capital of Ghazni. But by his desecration and ruin of Hindu temples he sowed the seeds of hatred and religious bitterness between Hindus and Moslems. The communal feuds of today have their origin in the acts of Mahmud of Ghazni.[1]

Mahmud's incessant raids into India and the appalling massacres which accompanied them were no doubt inspired by his zeal for Islam, for he was a devout and iconoclastic believer; but he certainly looked upon India in the light of an inexhaustible source of plunder rather than a new world to conquer and rule, and attracted to his standards thousands of volunteers eager to share the spoil, from the steppes of Central Asia.

Firdausi and Al-Beruni. Mahmud was the first of the great Moslem leaders who carried the Crescent into the heart of Hindustan. Not only was he a most able soldier, but he was a patron of the arts who enriched his capital with many noble buildings, and he attracted to his court of Ghazni a number of poets, the greatest of whom was Firdausi, author of the *Shah-nama.*

Chief among the scholars and men of letters surrounding Mahmud was Abu-Rihan Muhammad, familiarly known as Al-Beruni (the foreigner). This most gifted scientist and man of letters had been brought to Ghazni as a hostage or a prisoner, from his home in Khiva, by Mahmud. After the annexation of the Punjab he spent some time there, mastered Sanskrit, made a close study of Hindu philosophy and science, and wrote a book usually referred to as " Al-Beruni's India," on the history and customs of the Hindus, which, as Vincent Smith observes, is unique in Moslem literature. From what survives of his treatises on a wide range of subjects, including astronomy and physics, Al-Beruni was undoubtedly a scientist of the very first rank. He died in 1048 at the age of seventy-five.

With all his reputation for avarice, Mahmud founded a university and a library, he paid away large sums in pensions to men of letters and was ever lavish where his religion was concerned. He ruled his great kingdom and kept order and security with a firm hand, but, preoccupied with incessant warfare, he neglected to organize and consolidate his government, and his dominions began slowly to fall to pieces soon after his death.

[1] *The Indian Horizon,* by the Maharajadhiraja of Burdwan, p. 13.

Mas'ud. The succession to the throne in 1030 was a repetition of what had taken place when Mahmud deposed his younger brother. After a short struggle Mas'ud, the elder and abler of Mahmud's sons, took the kingdom from Muhammad, the younger son, to whom it had been left, and carried his ill-starred brother, blinded and a prisoner, to the temporary capital of Balkh.

Mahmud had appointed as Governor of the Punjab a Turkish officer named Ariyaruq who assumed almost independent power, retaining the bulk of the revenue, oppressing the people and refusing them access to appeal to the king. Mas'ud's first act was to remove and execute the Governor and to make an equally unfortunate appointment in his father's treasurer Ahmad Niyaltigin. He gave his Punjab officials, however, strict instructions calculated to prevent a repetition of what had happened under Ariyaruq's administration. No military expeditions beyond the Punjab border were to be made, Turkish officials were not to drink, play polo, or mix socially with the Hindu officers at Lahore, and they were to avoid unnecessary displays of religious bigotry.

Ahmad was not long in quarrelling with Abu-'l-Hasan, who had been sent on a commission of inquiry into Ariyaruq's conduct and to collect the revenue. The commissioner bluntly advised that Ahmad should confine himself to the civil administration and delegate the command of the army to a military officer. But Mas'ud supported the Governor, who in 1034 responded by leading an expedition to Benares, plundered the city and returned to Lahore with an immense booty.

Abu-'l-Hasan reported to Mas'ud that Ahmad was raising a large army in the province and was on the point of throwing off his allegiance. Mas'ud was unable to go to India in person to reassert his authority. Balkh was being threatened by the Saljuqs, the situation in Iraq was critical, and the hourly-expected death of the Caliph al-Qadir Billah was certain to bring fresh disorders. The question arose, who would bell the cat, and as the Muhammadan nobles were most reluctant to make the attempt, the Hindu Tilak stepped into the breach. The son of a barber, he had risen by sheer ability in

94

Mahmud's service, and after Mas'ud's accession had been appointed commander of the Hindu troops, with the rank of a noble.

Tilak at first struck ruthlessly, took Lahore, defeated and killed Ahmad and his son, and then gave a complete amnesty to the Jats who had joined the standard of the late governor. In 1036 Mas'ud made his second son Majdud governor of the Punjab, and in the following year, in spite of the danger of a Saljuq invasion of his northern and western provinces, he entered India to stamp out what was left of the rebellion. In this he was successful, but in the meantime the Saljuqs had overrun Persia and invaded Khurasan.

Mas'ud, after a fatal delay in his capital, moved to meet the enemy, was completely beaten at Taliqan near Merv in 1040 and forced to retire on Ghazni. Khurasan and Persia were lost to the Ghaznavids, and Mas'ud in panic fled from his capital to India with his harem, the brother whom he had blinded and all the treasure he could collect. But long before he could reach Lahore his guards mutinied and acclaimed his brother Muhammad as king.

Within a few months Mas'ud was murdered by a nephew, and his son Maudud hurrying down from Ghazni defeated Muhammad's troops, put that luckless prince to death by torture and was master of the Punjab by the middle of 1042. But neither he, nor the Ghaznavid kings who succeeded him, had the strength and ability of the founder of the dynasty. As early as 1044 Mahipal, raja of the city of Delhi built by his Tomara predecessor fifty years before on the site of Indrapat, invaded the Punjab. He took Hansi, Thanesar and Kangra and laid siege to Lahore, failed to take it and was forced to retire. But it was all that the Ghaznavids could do to hold the Punjab.

The Arab colonies in Sind had as little influence over the rest of India as the Persian satrapy of the Indus Valley twelve hundred years earlier. The irruptions of Mahmud from his mountain fastnesses, even though they led to the annexation of the Punjab, were a succession of raids in search of plunder, with their attendant horrors of wholesale massacre, enslavement and destruction: catastrophes which did not affect the greater part of the sub-continent. But a new era of domination by foreigners from Central Asia and the widespread introduction of Islam was now to set in. The Muhammadan conquest of India came, like the stupendous growth of the Faith itself, from the smallest of beginnings.

In the year 1010 Mahmud, after his return from the sack of Kangra, had marched against the insignificant but independent hill State of Ghor [1] two hundred miles north of his capital, and forced its chief, the Persian Muhammad bin Suri, to acknowledge the overlordship of Ghazni. But the Ghaznavid kingdom grew weaker, while the rulers of Ghor strengthened their position by successful war until in 1151 the army of the vassal State descended upon Ghazni, put its defenders to the sword and burnt the city to the ground. The conflagration lasted for seven days, earning for Ala-ud-din Hussain prince of Ghor the name of Jahansuz, "The world-burner," and of all the magnificent buildings of Ghazni only the tomb of Mahmud and two minarets remained standing.

The Ghoris.

Jahansuz did not long enjoy the fruits of his victory and the revenge for his brother's death which had led to it. Shortly afterwards he fell foul of Sultan Sanjar the Saljuq and was himself defeated. Bahram the reigning Ghaznavid king thereupon regained his capital, which his successor Khusru Shah lost in 1160 to the Ghuzz tribe of Turkmans, the conquerors of Sultan Sanjar. All that now remained to the descendants of Mahmud was the Punjab. But while the Ghaznavids, in the small kingdom which was left to them, were letting their authority fall into the hands of the district governors, the princes of Ghor were again becoming formidable. Ghiyas-ud-din Muhammad, nephew of Jahansuz, was now the ruler of that country and in 1173 he took Ghazni from the Ghuzz Turkmans and made his younger brother Mu'izz-ud-din Muhammad Shihab-ud-din governor of the province.

The two brothers, with a loyalty rare in the story of Moslem dynasties, exercised what was practically a joint sovereignty. Ghiyas-ud-din was content to rule the ancient patrimony of his house, while the younger brother, Muhammad Ghori, the ruler of

[1] *Camb. Hist. India*, Vol. III. p. 16, footnote, gives Ghur as the correct spelling, though Ghor is more usual.

PLATE XIII.

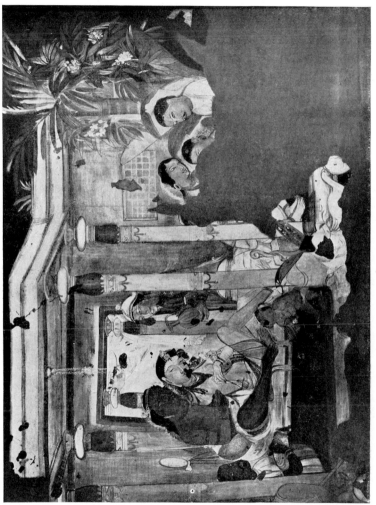

FRESCO FROM AJANTA CAVE

By courtesy of Indian Museum, South Kensington

PLATE XIV.

TEMPLE AT KHAJURAHO

By permission of the Secretary of State for India in Council

Ghazni, set no bounds to his ambition, either eastward to the furthest borders of Hindustan or north-westward to the Oxus.

Muhammad Ghori's primary object was to get possession of the *Muhammad* Muhammadan provinces in India, and in 1175 he *Ghori's* came down from Ghazni and took Multan, the *Conquests.* capital of the Arab colony then in the hands of Isma'ilian heretics. Expedition followed upon expedition. In 1182 the whole of Sind was subdued. Four years later the Punjab to the Sutlej was in his hands, Khusru Malik a prisoner, and the Ghaznavid dynasty at an end.

Muhammad now prepared to conquer the Hindu States of Northern India. In the cold weather of 1190-91 he invaded the kingdom of Delhi, took Bhatinda and appointed a governor over the district. But the Chauhan raja Prithvi Raj was not prepared to submit without a struggle. The country was thoroughly alarmed by this new threat of invasion, and the Rajput king, with an army reinforced by contingents from all the leading States, met Muhammad at Taraori, about thirty miles from the historic battlefield of Panipat. The Muhammadan horse made repeated charges, but they failed to shake the Hindu troops and at last, heavily outnumbered, the Moslem army broke and fled. There was no pursuit. Prithvi Raj contented himself with the investment of Bhatinda which capitulated thirteen months later.

The battle of Taraori was not Muhammad's first defeat in India. During the course of his operations in Sind the Ghori invader made an attack on Gujerat, but was beaten by Bhim the Vaghela, raja of Anhilvara. In 1180 Muhammad occupied Anhilvara, but Bhim's victory two years earlier had the effect of saving Gujerat from serious Muhammadan invasion for more than a hundred years.

In 1192 Muhammad again invaded India, determined to wipe out the defeat of the previous year. Once more he met Prithvi Raj on the field of Taraori, and this time he completely outgeneralled him. Muhammad made feint attacks upon the flanks and rear of the Hindu army until he saw his opportunity to launch his cavalry against his enemy's centre. The effect was decisive, the Hindus were completely routed and Prithvi Raj was killed. This victory gave Muhammad Northern India to the gates of Delhi, which fell into his hands at the

G

beginning of the new year. The victor turned south after the fight of Taraori, plundered Ajmer and carried off many of its inhabitants as slaves. But the place was too isolated for the safety of a Muhammadan governor, and Muhammad appointed a son of Prithvi Raj who undertook to pay tribute. Interesting though this none too successful arrangement was, Muhammad's appointment of Qutb-ud-din as Viceroy of his northern conquests was of infinitely greater importance.

Qutb-ud-din Aibak had in his youth been brought as a slave
Qutb-ud-din *Aibak.* from Turkistan and passed eventually into the hands of Muhammad Ghori. Strong and energetic, a fine rider and a good archer, well enough educated and of lavish generosity, he had risen to the highest rank in his master's service; and Muhammad trusted him as fully as he himself was trusted by his elder brother. Such was the character of the slave who had once been sold to the local governor of Nishapur and was destined to be the real founder of Muhammadan dominion in India.

Aibak, engaged in the task of setting the government within his viceroyalty upon a firm basis, did not make many campaigns. In 1193, however, a year after he became Viceroy at Delhi, he inflicted a crushing defeat at Chandwar (Firozabad) upon the army of Jaichand the Rathor Rajput king of Kanauj. Jaichand was killed at the moment when the Moslem troops were actually wavering and the Hindu army fled in panic.

The highest authorities in the administration as it was now constituted were the Muhammadan holders of military fiefs, but Hindus were employed in the lower official grades; and there were large tracts of country still under Hindu rulers who paid tribute or taxes to the central government. Where Moslem authority was weak the Hindus regained much of their power, but on the other hand they suffered severely whenever the local governors were despotic and indulged their religious bigotry. This state of affairs lasted until the middle of the sixteenth century.

Aibak's conquests in India did not extend further east, and the
Ikhtiyar-ud-din. general who made the Muhammadans masters of Bengal was Ikhtiyar-ud-din Muhammad, son of Bakhtiar of the Turkish tribe of Khalj, whose country lay between

Seistan and Ghazni: a people who were to give a line of kings to India a century later, and finally emerge in history as the Ghilzais of Afghanistan. This adventurous soldier was clumsy and unprepossessing in appearance, while the length of his arms, which enabled him to touch the calves of his legs when standing upright, made him look a positive deformity. But he was resolute and energetic and he swept eastward with his army, leaving a trail of destruction behind him.

In about the year 1193 he invaded Bihar, sacked the capital Odantapuri, destroyed its great monastery and dealt Buddhism in its last stronghold a blow from which it was unable to recover. From that day the Buddhist religion was at an end in Northern India. The monks who succeeded in escaping from the massacre scattered to Nepal, Tibet and the south.

End of Indian Buddhism.

The conquest of Lower Bengal followed about the year 1202. Its capital, Nadia, had been almost deserted by the wealthier inhabitants, terrified by what they had heard of the ruthless cruelty and rapacity of the Moslems, but Lakshman the old Brahman king of the country was still in the city. Ikhtiyar-ud-din left Bihar with a strong body of cavalry and pressed on so rapidly that he arrived at Nadia with only eighteen men. Pretending to be horse-dealers, the Muhammadan general and his party made their way into the city, reached the palace and, cutting down the guards, burst into it. The king, who was eating his meal in the usual undress of a high-caste Hindu, barely escaped by boat with his life. Ikhtiyar-ud-din succeeded in holding the palace until his troops appeared, when the city was plundered and destroyed. This at least is the Muhammadan version. After the sack of Nadia, Ikhtiyar-ud-din retired to Lakhnawati (Gaur), where he established himself as Governor of Bengal and began to found mosques and colleges.

Conquest of Bengal.

At the beginning of 1203 Ghiyas-ud-din died, and his younger brother Mu'izz-ud-din Muhammad bin Sam, overlord of Northern India, became sole ruler of the Ghuri dominions. His Indian kingdom now extended from Sind to Eastern Bengal, and almost the whole of Northern India acknowledged his suzerainty. But

Muhammad was not satisfied. He wished to create an empire in Central Asia and, in about 1203, he invaded Khvarasm, the modern Khiva. The invasion failed and his defeat was so complete as to shake his Indian empire to its foundations. Multan threw off its allegiance, the tribes north of the Salt Range rose in revolt and Lahore was plundered by the rebels. Eager though he was to revenge his defeat at Andkhui, Muhammad came south to quell the rebellion, and with the assistance of Aibak he succeeded in re-establishing his authority early in 1206. But on his way back to Ghazni immediately afterwards, to lead a second expedition into Khvarasm, he was murdered in his tent, probably by fanatical Shiahs of the heretical Isma'ili sect.

Muhammad was an able and successful soldier, and his conquests were more extensive and far more solid than those of Mahmud, who completely overshadows him in history; and he was magnificently served by his Indian Viceroy Aibak.

Ikhtiyar-ud-din, the conqueror of Bihar and Bengal, met a like fate as his master, early in the same year but after a disastrous defeat. Governor of Bengal, it became his ambition to extend his power across the Himalaya, and in the middle of 1205 with a force whose incredible composition was 10,000 cavalry he invaded Tibet. The Raja of Kamrup gave the Muhammadan general the admirable advice at least to wait until the spring. But Ikhtiyar-ud-din refused to listen to reason. He led his troops fifteen marches into the hills and then retired, badly worsted by the inhabitants. When his forces regained the plains the Raja of Kamrup fell on them and turned an unsuccessful expedition into complete disaster. Ikhtiyar-ud-din reached Lakhnawati with a hundred survivors and was shortly afterwards murdered.

After the death of Muhammad Ghori, Aibak became independent and ruled Northern India until his death in 1210, from an accident at polo. The line he established on an uneasy throne has been given the name of the " Slave Kings " from the origin of its founder, in those days not an unusual road to supreme power, as the Turkish slaves about the court of the Caliph, the Mamelukes in Egypt, and the rise of the Ghaznavid dynasty bear witness. The Moslem rulers found these able servants excellent advisers, gave them the highest posts, and at times rewarded them by marriage with their daughters.

Iltutmish. Aibak's death was followed by disorder and revolt among both the Muhammadans and Hindus and, in 1211, the Moslem nobles offered the throne to Shams-ud-din Iltutmish, son-in-law of Aibak, the most outstanding of his slaves and a member of a leading family of the Ilbari tribe of Turkmans.

It was seventeen years before Iltutmish reduced to order a kingdom which he had found in utter confusion, with Hindustan, Multan and Sind all in open rebellion. To add to his anxieties the formidable Chingiz Khan, in the full tide of the merciless conquests which ravaged Central Asia, invaded the Western Punjab in 1221. But, luckily for the inhabitants of Northern India, the Mongolian hordes came no further into the country and retired into Afghanistan.

" The Forty." But while Iltutmish was establishing his rule from the Indus to the mouths of the Ganges, a power was rising in his own capital which was to master his successors. The Turkish slaves of the court formed themselves into a conclave known as " The Forty " and, ousting the free nobility from the more important offices, gradually got the reins of government into their own hands.

Early Moslem Architecture. Although Muhammadan rule in India had been ushered in with the widespread iconoclasm of Mahmud of Ghazni it must be remembered that this leader in war was himself a patron of the arts and that Islam has enriched the world, from Granada to Agra, with superb gems of architecture. It was not art itself which the Muhammadan conquerors hated but the Hindu religion and its expression in erotic images and carvings.

The reigns of the earlier Slave Kings mark the beginning of Moslem architecture in India. Aibak and Iltutmish between them erected within the citadel of Delhi the magnificent buildings known at the Jami Masjid and the Kutb Minar. The mosque was begun in 1191 after the occupation of the capital, and the Tower of Victory was completed in 1232. It is by his buildings at Delhi and Ajmer that Iltutmish is to be remembered.

In the building of these early mosques Hindu masons were employed and they, using the shattered remains of Jain and Hindu temples, breathed into their work the strength and grace which are the most vital characteristics of the old Indian architecture. With these were incorporated the Saracenic features of the dome, the pointed arch, the slender tower and a bold spaciousness of design, together with the detail of flat surface carving and intricate geometric ornament.

In 1236 when Iltutmish, the greatest of the Slave Kings, lay
Queen Raziyya.   dying, he nominated his daughter Raziyya to succeed
him, remarking with prophetic truth that she was a better man than any of her brothers. But the kingdom had to endure Rukn-ud-din Firuz for six months, to the accompaniment of internal rebellion and an invasion from Ghazni which penetrated to Multan, before this weak and licentious ruler was murdered and Raziyya was acclaimed Sultan in Delhi. A contemporary chronicler [1] has recorded of her: " She was a great sovereign and sagacious, just, beneficent and a dispenser of justice, and of warlike talent, and was endowed with all the admirable attributes and qualifications necessary for kings." But, he added, as a fatal bar she was a woman. Yet it was the century in which the slave-wife of Saladin's grand-nephew ruled in Egypt and defeated the Crusade of St. Louis of France, and a princess, the last of the house of Salghar, reigned for nearly twenty-five years in Fars.

For three years Raziyya held her own: by diplomacy as when, at the beginning of her reign, she was threatened by an overwhelming confederacy including Multan and Lahore, and in the field, where she accompanied her troops not merely unveiled, but dressed as a man and mounted on her elephant. But she made one fatal mistake, and it cost her the throne and her life. Instead of relying entirely upon " The Forty " she chose as one of her chief advisers an Abyssinian, Yaqut. The jealous and infuriated " Forty " raised a rebellion, and its leader Ikhtiyar-ud-din Altunya defeated the royal

---

[1] Minhaj-ud-din, who wrote his chronicle the *Tabaqat-i-Nasiri* during the reign of Nasir-ud-din (1246–1266) ; translated by Major H. G. Raverty, Bibliothica Indica Series, Asiatic Society of Bengal, Calcutta, 1880.

troops, took the queen prisoner, and made her half-brother Bahram king in 1240. But Raziyya had not reached the end of her resources. She married her captor Altunya and at the head of a large army marched on Delhi to win back the throne. But the fates were against her. Bahram routed her forces and Raziyya was killed by a rustic for the rich clothes she was wearing while she slept worn out in the forest.

Bahram, after a nominal rule of two years, quarrelled with his masters, "The Forty," and was put to death, the marked event in his reign being a Mongol raid at the end of 1241 in which Lahore was taken and sacked.

Ala-ud-din Mas'ud, the grandson of Iltutmish who came to the throne in 1242, succeeded to a kingdom which was rapidly shorn by revolt of Sind, Multan, the Upper Punjab, Bengal and Bihar. As he was indolent, a drunkard and unbalanced in his gusts of severity, "The Forty" decided in 1246 to make his uncle Nasir-ud-din Mahmud king in his place. Mas'ud was murdered and Nasir-ud-din, then a youth of seventeen, succeeded him.

The new ruler was studious, strictly temperate and deeply religious, while he had in Balban a minister of untiring energy as a military leader and of unbending determination. This member of "The Forty" came from Central Asia where his father was a ruling chief, but Balban, the slave, was to rise to far greater heights than the chieftainship of an obscure Turkman clan.

Within two years Balban reduced the unruly Hindu tribes of the Punjab to order, repelled a Mongol raid and reasserted the authority of the central government among the turbulent Hindus of the Doab. Created lieutenant of the kingdom in 1249 after the marriage of his daughter to Nasir-ud-din, Balban was now the most powerful man in Northern India, and "The Forty" began to plot his downfall. In 1253 Balban was banished to his fief of Nagaur, to be recalled eighteen months later and reinstated in his former position at Delhi. From then onwards he held the kingdom together by the energy and ruthlessness of his campaigns, and when Nasir-ud-din, the last of the male descendants of Iltutmish, died in 1266, he became king as Ghiyas-ud-din Balban. The throne to which he had succeeded was anything but secure, for the ruler of Northern India was exposed to the danger of Mongol invasion and to the possibility of conspiracy and rebellion among the Moslem nobles and ambitious provincial governors.

Conditions in Northern India. The Muhammadans, who were almost immeasurably outnumbered by the far from unwarlike Hindu agricultural population, kept their hold by means of widespread garrisons, while great fiefs were scattered over the country to provide local governors or hold the Rajput and north-west marches. As regards the bulk of the people, the attitude of the Indian peasant towards the government of the country and the religion of his rulers has always been one of complete indifference, provided he is allowed to cultivate his land in peace and without oppression. The Slave Kings were, on the whole, cruel and intolerant only towards rebellion and banditry. All the minor posts dealing with such matters as land assessment and revenue were in Hindu hands, and the normal custom of the central government was to confirm the Indian rulers and landholders, as vassals, in the possession of their inheritances. These Hindus of the upper class did at times rebel, but a general rising against a foreign yoke in India, where no universal national feeling has ever crystallized into united action, was an impossibility.

Balban. Throughout his reign Balban had to put down incessant Hindu disaffection and the rebellion of ambitious Muhammadan nobles, and he did this by what amounted to a reign of terror. Even under the mild Mahmud he had crushed the Meo bandits, at least for a time, with horrible ferocity, massacring the more fortunate men, women and children by the thousand, and publicly putting 250 of the leaders to death by being trampled by elephants, cut into pieces, or flayed alive. As king he was prepared to hang an unsuccessful general to encourage the remainder and did not hesitate to inflict the most terrible punishments as a deterrent to his enemies. It was his life or theirs, and he succeeded in holding his unruly realm until he died at the age of eighty-two. He relied

PLATE XV

(a) BLIND DRUMMER IN MOSQUE
By courtesy of Indian Railways Bureau

(b) DOOR OF QUEEN'S TOMB, AHMADABAD
Muhammadan
By permission of the Secretary of State for India in Council

PLATE XVI.

SCULPTURED FRIEZE FROM SIVA-DURGA TEMPLE AT HALEBID
Hoysala Dynasty, thirteenth century
By courtesy of Indian Museum, South Kensington

on the swiftness of his forced marches when quelling a revolt, kept order by the establishment of forts at important points, and counted, in his internal administration, on that feature of Muhammadan rule in India, an army of spies who were independent of the local governors.

One of the first acts of his reign had been to draw the fangs of "The Forty." Another was to organize the defence of his frontier against the insistent danger of Mongol invasion. He gave his cousin Sher Khan the command of a well-equipped army and made forts at strategic points to bar the way to Delhi. He also cut roads through the jungle to tame the hill tribes.

In 1270 Balban re-established the provincial government of Lahore, and in 1280 he put down a formidable rebellion in Bengal. The Governor, Tughril, was killed and his family and adherents impaled on rows of stakes along the two miles of the main street of Lakhnawati. Balban made one of his sons, Bughra Khan, Governor of Bengal.

Mongol incursions during his reign met with no great success, but in 1285 Balban experienced the greatest sorrow of his life when his promising son and heir Muhammad Khan was killed in action against the Mongol invaders of Multan.

Balban died in 1287. The short unprepossessing slave who had risen from water-carrier to huntsman, from *Balban's Character.* huntsman to general and statesman, and so to supreme power, had held his kingdom together and saved it from foreign invasion. Temperate in his living, for he neither drank wine nor gambled after he came to the throne, Balban was fully alive to the value of the ceremony and state which he maintained. Capable though he was of appalling cruelty to the disaffected, he was otherwise just and tolerant, and for all his severity he was undoubtedly popular with his Hindu subjects.

After his death the Moslem ministers set Kaiqubad the son of Bughra Khan upon the throne. It was an unfortunate selection. The young king, freed from the trammels of a strict upbringing, plunged into the lowest depths of debauchery, and in three years had drunk himself into a state of helpless paralysis. The sword which hung over the head of a worthless and incompetent ruler of those days was unnecessary, and Kaiqubad's assassin despatched him with a contemptuous kick on the head.

Jalal-ud-din Firoz, whom the anti-Turkish section of the Moslem nobility now made king of Delhi at the age of seventy, *Firoz.* was not a popular choice. He was a Khalji, the tribe to which Ikhtiyar-ud-din the ambitious governor of Bengal had belonged, and he was regarded as a foreign intruder and a barbarian. The new king dared not show himself in Delhi, and built a suburban capital at Kilokhri a few miles away from the city. There he reigned for six years with a mildness and a mistaken clemency towards defeated rebels, bandits and murderers which justly exasperated the Khalji officers of the court. Balban had been guilty of inhuman ferocity when he dealt with the Meos, but to capture a thousand thugs, convey them down river in boats and then set them loose in Bengal was an act of culpable folly and injustice.

In 1292, two years after Firoz began to reign, a horde of more than a hundred thousand Mongols invaded the country. Partly as the result of a successful battle and partly by negotiation, Firoz made them withdraw, though some of their number stayed in India as converts to Islam and settled round Delhi. About five years later they rose in rebellion, and Ala-ud-din, who was then on the throne, dealt with the rising by slaughtering all the male settlers in one day, a number estimated at between 15,000 and 30,000.

The only other outstanding event of the reign was the amazing raid into the Deccan made in 1294-95 by Ala-ud-din, Governor of Kara and nephew and son-in-law of the king. Arranging with his deputy for the periodical despatch of news to Delhi which would allay all suspicion of anything unusual, Ala-ud-din with about eight thousand horsemen made a march of two months through the unknown and hostile country of Berar. He defeated the greatly superior forces got together to oppose him, forced Ramachandra, King of Deogiri and the Western Deccan to sue for peace, and returned safely to Kara with plunder and an indemnity amounting to nearly 20,000 pounds weight of gold, 200 pounds of pearls and a great quantity of silver.

Firoz, hearing that his favourite relative was returning with immense spoils from the south, hurried to Kara to meet Ala-ud-din against the advice and warnings of his councillors, and was murdered while welcoming his treacherous nephew.

Ala-ud-din at once marched upon Delhi with his uncle's head on a pike, scattering largesse as he went and buying
Ala-ud-din Khalji. over the army of 120,000 men sent to oppose him, and at the beginning of October 1296 he was enthroned as king. He had gained the kingdom by an act of the vilest treachery and ingratitude, and he at once strengthened his position by putting out the eyes of the murdered king's two sons. A few months later his general, Zafar Khan, completely defeated a large horde of invading Mongols near Jullundur, and his throne was secure.

Ala-ud-din now began the series of repressive measures which were one of the features of his reign, and his first
His Repressive Measures. objective was the Moslem nobility whom he had bribed to win over to his side. He argued that he had reached supreme power by the use of money, and consequently great riches in the hands of his subjects might easily become a danger to himself. He removed that danger by despoiling the nobles, and some were blinded or imprisoned and others killed, while their families were reduced to beggary.

In putting down a revolt due to the discontent aroused by the division of the plunder taken when Gujerat was annexed in 1297, the king established the barbarous principle of making the innocent wives and families suffer for the sins of rebels against the government.

The ease with which success had come to Ala-ud-din unbalanced his judgement. He dreamed over the wine-cup of founding a new universal religion to overshadow Islam and of establishing a world empire greater than the conquests of Alexander. But Ala-ul-Mulk the friend of his youth, and now the fat and level-headed chief magistrate of Delhi, succeeded in bringing him to reason, tactfully pointing out that preaching was for prophets; and as for finding new worlds to conquer, the whole of Southern India was still unsubdued, and marauding hordes of Mongols were an ever-present danger on his frontier. The magistrate had the courage to add that less wine and a closer attention to business would be an advantage to the king and to his subjects. Ala-ud-din instead of resenting this candid advice promised to adopt it and handsomely rewarded his counsellor.

It was not long before the threat of Mongol invasion again came *Zafar Khan.* to a head. An incursion made in 1297 was easily dealt with by Zafar Khan, but two years later a horde of about 200,000 Mongols entered India bent not upon plunder but conquest, and appeared before the walls of Delhi. In the battle which ensued Zafar Khan charged the Mongol line with impetuous fury, routed the left flank and hotly pursued the flying enemy. But the general by his constant successes in the field had aroused the jealousy of his master, and Ala-ud-din, although his kingdom was at stake, saw his faithful servant go to certain death without attempting to support him by an advance upon the weakened Mongol forces. Night fell upon what seemed to be a drawn battle, but in the morning the invaders had disappeared, shaken by the desperate valour of Zafar Khan, and the danger was over.

Ala-ud-din's home and foreign policy can be described in the *Ala-ud-din's Domestic Policy.* two words repression and annexation. He was convinced that the succession of revolts against his authority were due to the general prosperity in which too many people were rich and idle, and he took steps to remedy this.

The Moslem nobles were watched by informers, and kept in hand by restrictions on social gatherings and a law forbidding marriage without the royal consent, while he attacked private property by confiscating all religious endowments and grants of rent-free land, and by making a general seizure of gold. By another ordinance he forbade the use of intoxicating liquors and drugs, a law which, it must be said, he obeyed himself, only to find that private stills and smuggling became general. The drinking habit was too strong for legislation and this enactment had to be relaxed.

These ordinances pressed heavily upon his Muhammadan subjects, but they were light in comparison with the repressive measures

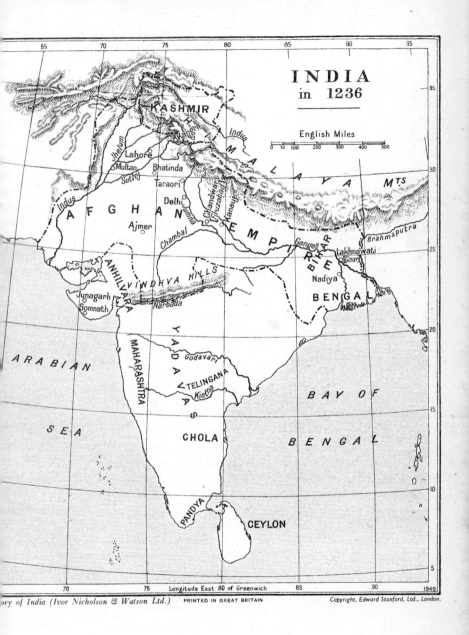

INDIA
in 1236

English Miles

0 50 100   200   300   400   500

KASHMIR

Indus

Jhelum

Lahore
Multan
Sutlej
Bhatinda
Taraori

Delhi
Ajmer
Chambal
Jumna

Chandwar
Firuzabad
Kanauj

MALAVA

MTS

AFGHAN

EMPIRE

Ganges

BIHAR
Lakhnawati
Gauri
Nadiya

Brahmaputra

BENGAL

Junagarh
Somnath

ANHILVARA

VINDHYA HILLS

Narbada

MAHARASHTRA

YADAVAS

Godavari

TELINGANA
Kistna

ARABIAN

SEA

CHOLA

BAY OF

BENGAL

PANDYA

CEYLON

ory of India (Ivor Nicholson & Watson Ltd.)   PRINTED IN GREAT BRITAIN   Copyright, Edward Stanford, Ltd., London.

directed against the Hindus, many of whom were rich and discontented and whose religion he hated. No Hindu was allowed to
ride a horse, or carry arms, and the sumptuary laws were very severe.
Hindu taxation was now raised from the customary one-sixth of all
land produce to a half, and duties were levied upon all cattle, goats
and sheep. The Moslem revenue officials were universally loathed,
and the wretched Hindu hereditary assessors and collectors were
reduced to the level of unwilling slaves. It should, however, be
remembered that, with the exception of the *jizya* (poll tax), these
are the only instances of special laws against the Hindus in Muhammadan legislation.[1]

Apart from his anxiety to curb the spirit of his subjects, Ala-ud-din
unquestionably required money to keep up an efficient and contented
standing army and maintain the forts in a state of repair, as a protection against Mongol invasion. His own defence of his administration is recorded: "Whatever I think to be for the good of the State,
or opportune for the emergency, that I decree."

Ala-ud-din's policy, when not interrupted by Mongol invasion,
was to annex as much of India as he could administer from Delhi.
The more distant States which he was able to subdue were put under
tribute; and at the same time he made his authority absolute over
the confederacy of fiefs which owed allegiance to Delhi.

Mongol invasion was an ever-present danger, and between
1297–1308 [2] six of these incursions succeeded in

*Mongol
Invasions.*
swamping the frontier garrisons and penetrated
some distance into India. The most formidable of
all was made in 1303, when the Mongols took advantage of the
opportunity given by Ala-ud-din's siege of Chitor. The invading
host of 120,000 men laid siege to Delhi, and only the difficulty of
supporting so large an army in devastated country, with the added
pressure of Ala-ud-din's forces as the great fief-holders began to
concentrate, forced them to retire without taking the capital.

---

[1] *Camb. Hist. India*, Vol. III. p. 107.
[2] *Ibid.*, Vol. III. pp. 111, 112 cites an invasion in 1306 and another in
1307–8 (both across the Indus), when the prisoners were in the customary
manner crushed to death by elephants.

Ala-ud-din's Indian campaigns of conquest began in 1297, when he overthrew the Rajput State of Gujerat, the richest kingdom in India, and appointed a Moslem governor in place of the last ruler of the Vaghala dynasty. It was then that the Hindu eunuch, the slave Kafur, came into the king's service to be at first his vicious favourite, then as Malik Naib lieutenant of the kingdom, and finally for five weeks to be regent of India. In 1301 Ranthambhor was taken, after an obstinate resistance ending with the rite of *jauhar*, and Chauhan rule in Hindustan was at an end. Ala-ud-din's next campaign was against Chitor, which was taken and sacked in 1303; but before it fell its Rajput defenders took so heavy a toll of the Moslem army that Ala-ud-din nearly lost Delhi to the Mongols, who were then invading India. Malwa was conquered in 1305, Marwar in 1307, and Ala-ud-din's armies then went farther afield.

Indian Campaigns.

The Telingana country was reduced in 1308, and in 1310 Kafur Hasardinari,[1] now Malik Naib, having established Moslem supremacy in the Deccan, was sent with Khvaja Haji on a great expedition to the south, with orders to plunder the Hoysala kingdom and make their way to the southernmost point of India. The enterprise met with complete success. The capital Dvaravatipura was taken and sacked, and Vira Ballala III was captured. The victorious Muhammadan army went on into the Pandya kingdom, took Madura its capital, destroyed the great temple there and, moving eastward to the coast, founded on what are now the Palk Straits a mosque which Malik Naib named after his master. The victors left Madura on the return march on April 24, 1311, and reached Delhi on October 18, with the huge spoils which included 312 elephants, 20,000 horses and 2750 pounds of gold.

Ala-ud-din was now at the height of his power. The fear of Mongol invasion had gone, rebellion had been crushed, money was cheap on account of the immense plunder that had poured in from the south, and his armies could be easily maintained. The control of the markets kept down the cost of living, no robbers dared to infest the high roads, and the land could be tilled in peace.

Death of Ala-ud-din.

[1] " The thousand dinar slave," the nickname coming from his purchase price.

But from 1311 Ala-ud-din's powers declined rapidly. Excesses had undermined his health, his violent temper became quite uncontrolled, and the tyrannical acts to which he was instigated by Malik Naib caused widespread discontent and open rebellion. Finally he developed dropsy and died at the beginning of January 1316, his end hastened, it was generally supposed, by Malik Naib.

Ala-ud-din has left, in the Alai Darwaza, a monument to his reign which, as Sir John Marshall has observed,[1] is one of the most treasured gems of Islamic architecture; and he built the second of the seven cities of Delhi at Siri as a fortified capital about the year 1303. Indifferent to learning though he was, men of letters were to be found at his court. In Amir Khusru, Ala-ud-din had as his poet laureate the most celebrated of all the Indian poets who ever wrote in Persian. He had started his literary career at the court of Balban, remained at Delhi during the reign of Ala-ud-din, and died in religious retirement at the age of seventy-two in 1325, after writing more than 400,000 couplets. But no poet laureate, however gifted, could wash the blood from the hands of the king who described himself upon his coinage as " The Second Alexander " and dreamt of founding a world-wide religion.

Arts of the Reign.

Malik Naib, on the death of Ala-ud-din, presented himself to the Moslem nobles of Delhi as regent of the kingdom for an infant son of the late king, and with the object of usurping the throne he used his brief authority to imprison, blind or murder every other member of the royal family whom he could get within his power. After a regency lasting thirty-five days he was killed by the palace guard, and Mubarak, Ala-ud-din's third son, a youth of about eighteen, was recognized as regent for his little brother.

Two months later Mubarak blinded the six-year-old king and ascended the throne as Qutb-ud-din Mubarak Shah. He began his reign by releasing seventeen thousand prisoners and abolishing all the taxes and penalties which his father had imposed.

Qutb-ud-din Mubarak.

---

[1] *Camb. Hist. India*, Vol. III. p. 583.

The new king then proceeded to flout his own religion, and plunged for the four years of his reign into the foulest depths of debauchery with an outcast from Gujerat, known as Khusru Khan, as the royal favourite. With profligacy he combined the violent temper and inhuman cruelty of his father. Conspiracies were put down to the accompaniment of wholesale slaughter of innocent children, and when Harpal Deo, raja of Deogir, raised a feeble rebellion in the Deccan in 1317, Mubarak had him flayed alive. In 1320 Khusru Khan murdered his master and proclaimed himself king as Nasir-ud-din Khusru Shah, " The Helper of the Faith."

End of the Khaljis. For a reign of less than five months the usurper and his fellow-ruffians, who had celebrated Mubarak's murder by breaking into the harem, butchering the children of the royal family and outraging the women, defiled the mosques and openly insulted the faith of the dominant power in India. Then the end came. Ghazi Malik, warden of the north-western marches, a loyal supporter of the late dynasty and a strict Muhammadan, came down from the Punjab and marched on Delhi. He defeated Khusru, executed him after the battle, and, finding that the Khalji house had ceased to exist, was proclaimed king under the title of Ghiyas-ud-din Tughlak Shah.

Ghiyas-ud-din Tughlak. The founder of the new dynasty, the son of a Turkish slave in Balban's household who had married a Jat woman, though old in years was both energetic and resolute. He at once began to remedy as far as possible the injustice and follies of the previous months. In spite of the unpopularity it aroused, Tughlak recovered the royal treasure which had been plundered or squandered by Khusru, and allayed discontent by his measures for the welfare of his subjects. He encouraged agriculture by limiting the taxation of the gross produce to a tenth, and he made irrigation one of the public works. Tughlak also instituted a postal service far more efficient than any previously known in India. The news of the arrival, at the mouth of the Indus in 1333, of the Moorish traveller, Ibn Batutah,[1] author of the celebrated

---

[1] See bibliographical note at end of chapter.

account of the first Tughlak kings, reached Delhi by post in five days, a distance between eight and nine hundred miles. This postal service speaks volumes for the security of the country at the time.

In 1321 a rebellion broke out in Telingana, where the Hindu raja of Warangal disavowed allegiance to the new dynasty. This was not put down by Ulugh Khan, the king's eldest son, until 1323, when the Telingana country was annexed as a province of the empire and divided into fiefs and districts under Moslem nobles and officials.

While this campaign was in progress Tughlak beat off a Mongol invasion and then made an expedition to Bengal. Taking advantage of the civil war which was raging in that country Tughlak converted Eastern Bengal, which had been independent for thirteen years, into a province of Delhi. At the same time he reasserted his suzerainty over the kingdom of Western Bengal, where he left Nasir-ud-din, the descendant of Bughra Khan of the house of Balban, as his vassal. On this expedition Tirhut was annexed.

On his return to Tughlakabad, the capital which he had built for himself and his great treasure-house south of Delhi, Tughlak was killed by the fall of a roof treacherously planned by Ulugh Khan,[1] who had already (during the Warangal expedition) shown flagrant disloyalty to his father. Tughlak had been greatly disquieted by his eldest son's undesirable friendship with Shaikh Nijam-ud-din Auliya, whom the king had warned that Delhi would be too small for them both. The Shaikh is recorded to have returned the reply, " Hanuz Dilhi dur ast," which afterwards became famous as the Oriental equivalent to the Highland saying, " It is a far cry to Loch Awe."

Ulugh Khan ascended the throne of Delhi in 1325 with the title of Muhammad Shah over the body of his *Muhammad Shah's Character.* murdered father, the ominous beginning of a reign of rebellion and bloodshed.

There are kings in history who have been overwhelmed by undeserved ill-fortune, but Muhammad Shah Tughlak was not one

---

[1] See note at the end of this chapter.

of them. His fault was not in his star but in the incredible and contradictory character of the man himself, which brought catastrophe after catastrophe upon a peaceful empire extending from the Khyber to the Sunderbunds and from the Himalaya to what is now Mysore. The highly cultured scholar and man of letters, who established hospitals and alms-houses and was capable of boundless generosity to foreigners, was equally capable of the most revolting cruelty to his own flesh and blood and to thousands of his unfortunate people, innocent and guilty alike. The king whose pride, in the words of Barani his chronicler and friend, " was so overweening that he could not endure to hear of a corner of the earth not subject to his sway and whose ambition it was to make all the kings of the earth his slaves," would grovel publicly in embarrassing submission before foreign visitors of distinction. Regular in his devotions, a rigid abstainer from wine, and conforming in his private life to the ritual and moral precepts of Islam, he habitually flung the laws of God and man to the winds when dealing with his subjects, while the smallest infraction of an impracticable regulation of his own and the most flagrant act of rebellion were equally punished, in his unbalanced judgement, by a cruel death. He was a brave and energetic soldier, and his military operations in common with his administrative measures exhibited at times abilities of the highest order and at others were the acts of a madman.[1] " *Omnium consensu capax imperii, nisi imperasset.*"

In 1327, the second year of Muhammad's reign, the king's

Revolts in the Deccan and Sind. cousin Baha-ud-din Gurshap rose in revolt and the rebellion spread throughout the Deccan before it was crushed. Gurshap then took refuge with the Raja of Kampli, who beat off the first attack made by Muhammad's troops, but on the arrival of reinforcements the fall of the place became certain. The raja, no longer able to protect his guest, sent him to Vira Ballala III Hoysala for sanctuary, and then, after the women had all perished in the rite of *jauhar*, led out his fighting men to meet a Rajput death. Vira Ballala weakly surrendered

---

[1] See Firishta's *History of the Rise of the Mahomedan Power*, Vol. I. pp. 409–443 and *Camb. Hist. India*, Vol. III. Ch. VI.

Gurshap, who was taken to Deogir, where Muhammad flayed and roasted him alive, sent his cooked flesh to his family and, after stuffing his skin with straw, exhibited the loathsome trophy in the chief cities of the kingdom.

During his stay in Deogir, Muhammad decided to establish a more central seat of government and decreed that the place, which he renamed Daulatabad,[1] should be the new capital; and a great and spacious city with magnificent buildings was admirably planned and built for the official and trading community. With Daulatabad as his base Muhammad soon restored order in the Deccan, only to learn that Multan and Sind were in revolt, a rising which was crushed with equal success. Later in the year 1328 the Mongols made an incursion which penetrated as far as the Ganges before it was repulsed.

During the first four years of his reign Muhammad's ruthless cruelty had been generally aimed at individuals, not all of whom were guilty, although at the taking of Multan only the prayers of Shaikh Rukn-ud-din had prevented a general massacre of the inhabitants. But in 1329 Muhammad inflicted upon his people the first of the wholesale vindictive punishments which eventually led to the dismemberment of the empire.

Muhammad came back to stay in Delhi, after the retirement of the Mongols, to find himself highly unpopular with *The Delhi Deportation.* its inhabitants, who had been almost ruined by the removal of the court to Daulatabad. The citizens showed their discontent by throwing anonymous letters of abuse into the audience hall at night. The king replied by issuing a decree that every soul was to leave Delhi, a city ten miles across including its suburbs, and go to Daulatabad, more than six hundred miles away, and the miserably inadequate arrangements forbade the transport of their possessions. When the inhabitants hesitated to obey, a second proclamation gave them three days to quit. Then Muhammad went through the deserted streets, and finding a cripple and a blind man still within the walls had them tortured to death.

[1] " The abode of riches." For the marvellous feat of engineering in the fortification of the citadel of Deogir see *Camb. Hist. India*, Vol. III. p. 141.

In the first year of his reign Muhammad had caused a register of revenue and expenditure to be made by all the provincial governments, apparently to establish a uniform assessment, but in 1330 he introduced into the Doab new and heavy taxation, partly to fill a depleted treasury but chiefly to punish the turbulent and disaffected Hindus living in one of his richest and most fertile provinces. The taxation was at least doubled and the peasants, being quite unable to meet the demand, fled to the jungle and took to brigandage. The whole countryside went to wrack and ruin, its inhabitants became the king's open enemies, and by 1333 a state of war existed in the Doab and Kanauj.

Devastation of the Doab.

About the year 1329, in order to raise money, Muhammad tried the expedient of a token currency. The idea of substituting paper for metal was not a new one; it had been used in China with suitable precautions, and also in Persia. But Muhammad believed that, by a decree, he could make copper tokens pass current as gold and silver coins. The king failed to realize the ease with which counterfeit tokens could be made. In four years the scheme collapsed under "mountains" of false tokens, and Muhammad, to his credit be it said, recalled the expensive issue, and although it was impossible to distinguish the counterfeit from the genuine, paid for the tokens presented at the treasury in good money. The gold tanga had risen to the value of a hundred copper tokens, and the king's subjects for once made a good thing out of a government whose farming of the provincial and district taxes was already a scandal which was growing into a source of frequent rebellion.

Token Currency.

Muhammad had by this time revoked his decree against the citizens of Delhi, and a number of them had returned to their homes and a famine-stricken district. The king took prompt measures for their relief, giving a daily issue of grain and cooked food and advancing large sums to the peasants for seed corn, stock and necessary improvements. Partly on account of official dishonesty the loans were not a success, and Muhammad visited the failure upon his starving subjects with an orgy of barbarous

Famine Relief.

executions. Something had, however, to be done for the people
of Delhi, and Muhammad once more ordered the evacuation of the
city, this time, however, for the welfare of his subjects. In 1336
he built a town of booths a hundred and sixty-five miles away at
Sargadwari, and these huts were replaced in the following year by
more permanent buildings. Here, supplied from the fertile province
of Oudh, which had remained prosperous under the wise and kindly
rule of its governor 'Ain-ul-Mulk, the Delhi colony remained for
six years.

The rest of Muhammad's reign is a tale of unbroken and ir-
reparable disaster. In the madness of his dreams
The Tibet Expedition. of world conquest Muhammad resolved to conquer
China through Tibet, and in the year 1337 he sent
an army of 100,000 cavalry and a strong force of infantry, under
Malik Nikpai (who held the honorary post of Chief of the Inkstand-
bearers), to destruction amidst the forests and passes of the Himalaya.
A year later the general himself, two other officers and about ten
men returned to India, the sole survivors of the expedition. This
catastrophe, in which a large army and a huge amount of treasure
were lost, shook the empire to its foundations, and rebellion broke
out against Muhammad's tyranny throughout the twenty-three
provinces.

Whenever Muhammad marched to subdue his subjects in one
part of his empire, rebellion flamed up elsewhere,
Civil War. and by 1339 Eastern and Western Bengal had both
successfully asserted their independence, to be finally united in one
kingdom by Malik Iliyas in 1352.

To the evils of war, which Muhammad tried in vain to end by
frightfulness, were added the horrors of a famine
Famine. in which the people of Northern India were reduced
to eating human flesh. Muhammad's measures, had they been
practical, would, in the words of his chronicler, Barani, have so improved agriculture that " plenty would have reigned throughout the
earth and so much money would have poured into the treasury that
the king would have been able to conquer the world." As it was,
the Ministry of Agriculture and the district undertakers who were

given more than seventy million tangas as an inducement to establish the theoretical rotation of crops, proved a complete failure.

Southern India in the meanwhile was not only throwing off the suzerainty of its Tughlak overlord, but returning to Hindu kings. Vira Ballala III established his independence at Dvaravatipura, and a son of the heroic raja who had protected Gurshap with his life ruled over Kampli, while Krishna Naik, who had expelled the Moslem officers from Telingana, had made himself king at Warangal.

Dismemberment of the Empire.

But the most crushing blow fell in 1347, when a revenue collector, Hasan Zafar Khan, got together a large body of insurgents and inflicted so decisive a defeat upon the royal forces that the Deccan was lost to the kingdom of Delhi. The victorious leader ascended the throne he had won for himself as Abu'l-Muzaffar Ala-ud-din Bahman Shah, founder of the Bahmani dynasty.

The news of this disaster reached Muhammad when he was putting down a rebellion in Gujerat and Kathiawar, and, giving up all hope of recovering the Deccan, he proceeded to restore order in his western provinces. But in March 1351 he died of fever in Sind and " the king was freed from his people and they from their king "; [1] a king who had lavished almost untold wealth upon foreigners who visited his country but who had, in his own words to Barani, " looked upon his subjects as his natural enemies, and the penal laws as a means of visiting his personal displeasure on them."

Death of Muhammad Tughlak.

Muhammad Tughlak was succeeded, at the end of August 1351, by his cousin Firoz, the elderly son of Siparsalar Rajab and a Rajput princess. The new king, indolent, easy-going and kindly except in matters of religion, had one invaluable asset, an unerring judgement of character. Had he not been so faithfully served by the ministers

Firoz Shah Tughlak.

[1] *Muntakhabu-t-Tawarikh*, Vol. I. p. 317, by Ibn-i-Mulk Shah, known as Abdu'l Qadir al Badaoni (Budauni), who wrote his history in the reign of Akbar. For the tremendous indictment upon which the estimate of Muhammad Tughlak's character given in this chapter is based, see pp. 315–317 of *Al-Badaoni's History*, Vol. I.

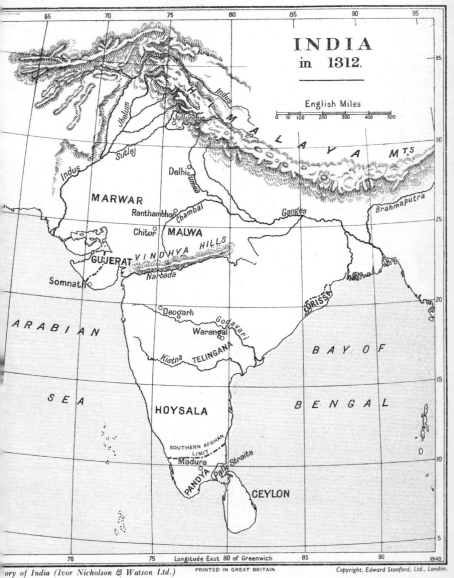

INDIA
in 1312.

English Miles

0 50 100   200   300   400   500

and the viceroys to whom he freely delegated his authority, the kingdom of Delhi would have broken into pieces during his reign. From the day of his accession Firoz had as his chief adviser the able Malik Maqbul, a Brahman of Telingana who had been converted to Islam, and the administration was supported by a large body of loyal officers. But the wholesale decentralization of authority, coupled with a return to the system of paying government officials by assignments of grants of land and their revenue instead of in cash, undoubtedly led to the subsequent collapse of the dynasty. These grants are known as *jagirs*, and Ala-ud-din had abolished the system as liable to cause insubordination and rebellion.

Agricultural Reform.

The king's first object was to relieve agriculture from the heavy burdens imposed by Muhammad. He reduced taxation to a level which left an encouraging margin for the cultivator, and he abolished the annual benevolences levied by the provincial governors. On the advice of Malik Maqbul he cancelled the bonds of the agricultural loans advanced by Muhammad and which the peasants had been quite unable to repay.

Firoz gave a further impetus to the great industry of the country by extensive irrigation works and the sinking of wells, for which a ten per cent. water-rate was imposed. A number of dams and reservoirs were constructed, and five great canals were dug to distribute the waters of the Jhelum and the Sutlej, while engineers were appointed to look after the banks in flood-time. One of these canals, which still exists as the " Old Jhelum Canal," ran for more than 150 miles to irrigate the desert country up to the city which Firoz founded under the name of Hisar-i-Firoza.

The cultivated area of the kingdom increased enormously. Around Delhi alone there grew up 1200 fruit gardens and vineyards, while the revenue from the Doab, which Muhammad had laid waste and almost depopulated, rose to eight million tangas, approximately £670,000. According to Shams-i-Siraj Afif, whose *Tarikh-i-Firoz Shahi* gives a most laudatory account of the reign, the revenue of the kingdom was equivalent to about £6,850,000. About the year 1375, four years after the death of Malik Maqbul, Firoz abolished the heavy octroi duties which seriously hampered trade, although this involved a loss of about £250,000 to the revenue.

Where the religion of the great majority of his subjects, the Hindus, was not concerned, Firoz was a benevolent ruler. He abolished torture and mutilation throughout the kingdom, founded a hospital and introduced such measures as an employment bureau for clerical workers and an efficient marriage agency for Muhammadans of the middle class and the families of government servants. But while his kindliness amounted to culpable leniency when extended towards corrupt practices in his thirty-six Departments of State, his attitude in regard to Moslem heretics and Hindus was relentless, and Firoz repressed the Shia sect as sternly as he dealt with the licentious Hindu Saktas. He did not destroy existing Hindu temples but he forbade the erection of new ones, an offence punishable with death. Firoz raised a storm of unavailing protest by the Brahmans which went so far as the threat to commit *dharna* by burning themselves alive when he extended the *jizya* (poll tax on Hindus) to include them. Brahmans had previously been exempt, and they now became assessed at the lowest scale of 10 tangas (approximately 10 rupees) a year, the other grades being 20 and 40 tangas respectively.

Treatment of Hindus.

Only once in his reign of thirty-seven years did Firoz descend to the level of his predecessor in an act of vengeance. In 1379 Sayyid Muhammad, Governor of Budaun, and his two brothers, when visiting the Raja of Katehr, were murdered by their host. A year later Firoz marched into the country, massacred many thousands of its Hindu inhabitants, captured 23,000 as slaves, and instituted, for the following five years, an annual slaughter and devastation throughout Katehr.

Firoz devoutly believed that he was serving God by looking upon the public practice of the Hindu religion held by the vast majority of his subjects as a capital crime, and it is recorded that he burnt a Brahman alive for this act. He accordingly made efforts to convert the people from Hinduism to Islam. To quote his own words: " I proclaimed that everyone who repeated the creed and became a Musalman should be exempt from the *jizya* . . . and a great number of Hindus were admitted to . . . Islam . . . and were favoured with presents and honours." In this way a part of the existing Muhammadan population of India originated.

A feature of the reign was the slave-raiding which the king
Slave-Raiding. systematically encouraged through his fief-holders on their campaigns. Siya-ud-din Barani records that there were about 180,000 slaves in the kingdom. These all became Muhammadans and appear to have been well treated during the lifetime of Firoz, although most of his personal attendants were murdered by his grandson Abu Bakr.

Firoz made no effort to reconquer the Deccan, an enterprise
Campaigns. which the incomparably more able and energetic soldier Muhammad had not attempted. Firoz had no military ambition and was in fact an irresolute and incapable commander. But in November 1353 he was stirred into taking the field with a force of 70,000 cavalry when Shams-ud-din Ilyas Shah, the independent ruler of Bengal, made an incursion into Tirhut. Ilyas was driven back, but Firoz failed in his attempt to conquer Bengal. It was on his return from this campaign that he founded a new capital, Firozbad, and connected it with Delhi, ten miles distant, by means of a regular transport service with fixed rates for the hire of vehicles. After a second and equally abortive invasion of Bengal in 1359 Firoz, who was the most indefatigable builder in Indian history and an enthusiastic restorer of ancient monuments, founded the palace city of Jaunpur.

In the cold weather of 1360 Orissa was successfully invaded. But the army lost its way on the return march and strayed through the jungles and hill country of Chota Nagpur for about six months, while Maqbul the acting regent had considerable difficulty in dealing with the unrest which broke out in Delhi.

A similar incident occurred during the retreat of Firoz after the disastrous campaign of 1362 in Sind, when no news reached Delhi for months and Maqbul was obliged in the interests of good order to publish a fictitious despatch from the field army. In the following year the Jam Mali of Sind was forced to sue for peace, which was granted on the easy condition of an annual tribute. The repression of a rising in Etawah in 1377 was another military operation in which Firoz was successful, and then in 1380 he began his terrible vengeance on Katehr.

The king was now seventy-five and his intellect began to weaken.

Death of Firoz. Khanjahan, the son of Maqbul Khan, took up the reins of government, but the regent abused his position and soon fell, to be followed first by a son and then by a grandson of the failing king. Firoz died in September 1388. He had held the kingdom together by the popularity of his measures to improve the lot of his subjects and he had irreparably weakened the power of the crown by his systematic decentralization of authority. After Firoz came the deluge.

NOTE.—The account in this chapter of the death of Sultan Tughlak is the one given by Ibn Batutah. The story, however, is not supported by Ziya-ud-din Barani, the Indian historian of the reigns of Balban and the Khalji and Tughlak dynasties, who wrote the *Ta'rikh-i-Firuz Shahi* (Trans. Asiatic Society of Bengal, Biblio. Ind. Series, Calcutta, 1862). But Barani cannot be considered, either from the character of his work or from the fact that Muhammad Shah was his royal patron and intimate, to be as good evidence as Ibn Batutah. Firishta (*History of the Rise of Mahomedan Power in India*, Vol. I. pp. 407–408) gives all the conflicting accounts, from elephants pushing the building over to " the most entertaining surmise " of magical art, but his own view is patricide.

CHRONOLOGY

711.	Arab invasion of Sind by Muhammad Qasim.
c. 750.	Ghopala founded Pala dynasty in Bengal.
c. 750.	Rashtrakuta dynasty in the Deccan.
c. 840–890.	Reign of Mihira Parihar (Bhoja) of Kanauj; Rajput ascendency in Western India.
973.	Tailapa II Chalukya in power in the Deccan as ruler of Kalyani.
977.	Sabuktigin ascended throne of Ghazni.
985.	Accession of Rajaraja-deva the Great.
998–1030.	Mahmud of Ghazni.
1001.	Invasion of India and defeat of Jaipal I at Peshawar.
1018–1019.	Capture of Kanauj.
1021.	Mahmud conquered the Punjab.
1024.	Sack of Somnath.
1030–1040.	Mas'ud Ghaznavid.

1042–1049. Maudud Ghaznavid; followed by Ma'sud II and Ab-dur-Raschid (1052); Tughril (1053); Farrukhzad (1053–1059).

1059–1099. Ibrahim Ghaznavid.

1076–1126. Vikramaditya King of Kalyana; regained Chalukya suzerainty over Mysore.

1079. Ibrahim captured Gujerat.

1099. Mas'ud III Ghaznavid; 1115 Shirzad; 1116 Arsalan Shah; 1118 Bahram Shah; 1152 Khusru Shah.

1160. Accession of Khusru Malik, last of the Ghaznavids.

1170–1192. Prithiviraja Chauhan of Rajputana; united Ajmer and Delhi kingdoms; took Chandela 1182.

1173. Ghiyas-ud-din Ghori took Ghazni.
Rise of Hoysala power.

1175. Muhammad Ghori began conquest of Northern India.

1192. Second Battle of Taraori.

1193–1206. Qutb-ud-din Aibak Viceroy of Northern India.

c. 1202. Conquest of Bengal by Ikhtiyar-ud-din.

1206. Death of Muhammad Ghuri. Aibak became King of Delhi.

1210. Death of Aibak.

1211–1236. Reign of Iltutmish (Slave Dynasty of Delhi).

1221–1222. Invasion of Chingiz Khan.

1236–1240. Raziyya Queen of Delhi.

1240–1246. Rule of "The Forty" with nominal kings of Delhi.

1246–1266. Nasir-ud-din King of Delhi with Balban chief minister.

1266–1287. Balban King of Delhi.

1290–1296. Firuz Shah III founder of Khalji dynasty of Delhi.

1296–1316. Ala-ud-din Khalji.

1297–1308. Mongol invasions.

1297–1311. Ala-ud-din's conquests in Central and Southern India.

1316–1320. Khalji dynasty ends in anarchy.

1320–1325. Tughlak Khan founder of Tughlak dynasty.

1325–1351. Muhammad Shah Tughlak.

1327–1347. Disintegration of Delhi Empire.

1351–1388. Firoz Shah Tughlak.

BIBLIOGRAPHY

Cambridge History of India, Vol. III.

Firishta's *History of the Rise of Mahomedan Power in India*, tr. Colonel J. Briggs (London), 1829.

(Firishta states that he consulted thirty-five original MSS., and twenty additional authorities are quoted in the body of his *History*.)

Al-Badaoni's *History of India*, tr. Rankin and Lowe (Calcutta), 1898.

A reliable and vivid account of Muhammad Tughluq based on personal knowledge is given by Ibn Batutah in his *Tuhfat-un-Nazzar fi Ghara ib-i-il Amsar*. Incomplete English translations are to be found in *Cathay and the Way Thither* (Hakluyt Society, 1916) and in the comprehensive *History of India as told by its own Historians* (Elliot and Dowson, 1867–77). Ibn Batutah was an African traveller who was in India as an official at the court of Muhammad Tughlak between 1333 and 1342. He then left on an embassy to China, was again in India after shipwreck off Calicut in 1347 and did not return to his native Fez until 1349.

CHAPTER V

Pre-Mogul India

ALA-UD-DIN KHALJI had given the throne of Delhi a brief supremacy over almost the whole of India. After the death of Firoz, Delhi practically ceased to exist as a sovereign State, and the story of Indian history is taken up for a time by the kingdoms, once provinces of that empire, which rebelled against the tyranny of Muhammad Tughlak and by the great Hindu kingdom which arose in the south. None of these States was affected by the terrible invasion of Timurlane at the end of the fourteenth century, and their fortunes up to the momentous events of the early part of the sixteenth century are described in this chapter.

The fitful and uncertain suzerainty which Delhi, even at the height of its imperial power, had been able to exercise over the two eastern provinces virtually ended in 1339 when Muhammad Tughlak was staggering under the disaster of his Tibetan campaign and the terrible famine then ravaging Northern India. But it was not until 1356 that his cousin Firoz formally recognized Shams-ud-din Ilyas Shah as the independent sovereign of the united kingdom of Eastern and Western Bengal.

Bengal.

Ilyas died in 1357 and his line continued to rule for about fifty years, although towards the end of this period the country was actually being governed by Raja Ganesh of Dinajpur, who had defeated Hamza the ruling king in 1404. If the most detailed account is reliable Ganesh was a religious bigot who took advantage of an opportunity unusual in Indian history and persecuted the Muhammadans of Bengal until his death in 1414. His actual reign only lasted a year and he was succeeded by his son Jatmal, or Jadu, a convert to Islam, who took the title of Jalal-ud-din Muhammad.

125

Generally speaking, the Muhammadan rulers of Bengal were tolerant towards the religion of their Hindu subjects, but Jalal-ud-din was an exception. He had been made a convert, as a matter of policy, when his father's kingdom was invaded by the Moslem ruler of Jaunpur, and when he refused to revert to Hinduism he was imprisoned for his obstinacy. His zeal for his new religion and the strong resentment engendered by his treatment led him to persecute the members of his former faith with considerable energy during the seventeen years of his reign, and the existing numerical superiority of the Muhammadans in Bengal [1] may be attributed to his proselytizing efforts.

The Dinajpur line came to an end with the murder of Shams-ud-din Ahmad in 1442, when one of the chief ministers, Nasir Khan, a descendant of Ilyas, ascended the throne. His son Rukn-ud-din Barbak paved the way for the orgy of regicide which followed his death in 1474 by raising African slaves, of whom he had about eight thousand, to high positions in the government. Three African slave rulers and one youthful member of the house of Ilyas sat on the throne between 1486 and 1493, when Sayyid Ala-ud-din Hussein, whose family had come from Tirmiz on the Oxus and who had shown great ability as a minister, was elected king by the nobles.

Hussein proved an admirable choice. His first acts were to destroy the dangerous power of the Hindu household troops, whom he replaced by Muhammadans, and to expel all Africans from the kingdom. This measure put an end to all chance of a negro ruling caste arising in Bengal, a state of affairs which had been threatened by the accession of three African kings in seventeen years.

After re-establishing his government in those provinces which had fallen away from their allegiance during the six preceding reigns, Hussein turned to foreign conquest and invaded Assam in 1498. The Ahom capital was taken, but the bad climate and the im-

---

[1] About 55 per cent. (1941 Census) on a rising proportion in relation to Hindus. In the half century 1881 to 1931 the percentage of Hindus in all India fell steadily from 74·3 to 68·2.

possibility of sending up reinforcements in the rainy season brought about the failure of the expedition. Hussein made no other attempt at invasion, devoting himself instead to holding his frontiers and to building mosques and endowing alms-houses until his death in 1518. He was succeeded by his eldest son Nasir-ud-din Nusrat Shah, who lived to see the Mogul conquest of North-Western India and the appearance of the Portuguese in his own kingdom of Bengal. A strong ruler at the beginning of his reign, he sank into debauchery and was assassinated in a palace conspiracy in 1533.

Ala-ud-din Hasan had freed the Deccan from the appalling *The Deccan.* tyranny of Muhammad Tughlak in 1347 and was elected king of the country under the title of Ala-ud-din Bahman Shah. He claimed descent from the half-mythical hero Bahman, son of Isfandiyar,[1] from whom the dynasty which he founded is named. His reign of eleven years falls into three periods. Bahman had first of all to consolidate his kingdom by compelling the petty Hindu rajas of the Deccan to acknowledge his supremacy and by suppressing the revolts of some of his Moslem officers; measures which were accompanied by a politic leniency and rewarded by peace from rebellion for the rest of his reign.

Bahman had made the city of Gulbarga (renamed Ahsanabad) his capital, and as soon as his authority had been firmly established he organized the government of the kingdom in four provinces: Gulbarga, Daulatabad, Berar, and Muhammadan Telingana.

He then entered upon the third phase of his rule and extended his dominions by conquest westward to Goa and Dabhol and eastward into Hindu Telingana. During his invasion of Gujerat in 1357 he fell ill of a surfeit of wine and venison and returned to his capital to die in 1358.

Bahman was succeeded by his eldest son Muhammad I, a king *Muhammad I.* whose administrative ability was as outstanding as the unmeasured ferocity with which he waged almost incessant war against his powerful Hindu neighbours.

[1] *Camb. Hist. India,* Vol. III. p. 170 and footnote, and pp. 372, 373.

The institutions which he organized lasted throughout the reigns of his successors and were adopted by the rulers of the five States into which the Deccan eventually became broken. Muhammad ruled his kingdom with the assistance of eight Ministers of State: the Lieutenant of the Kingdom, the Prime Minister, Minister of Finance, Minister of Foreign Affairs, the Assistant Minister of Finance, the Peshwa (who ultimately absorbed the office of Lieutenant of the Kingdom), the Kotwal (Chief of Police and City Magistrate of the capital), and the Chief Justice who acted as Minister of Religion and Endowments.

The four provincial governors collected the revenue, raised and controlled the fighting forces, and made all the civil and military appointments in their provinces. The king maintained his authority by the annual royal progresses instituted by Muhammad and continued by his successors. But this autocratic form of dominion status depended entirely upon the personal factor, the character of the king himself and the loyalty of the governors; and this decentralization led finally to the dismemberment of the kingdom. Provincial rebellions eventually became frequent, and in Muhammad's own lifetime the Governor of the Daulatabad province raised a revolt which was put down with difficulty. Highway robbery, which at one time threatened to become a serious problem, was suppressed by indiscriminate massacre.

Muhammad's reign marked the beginning of the almost continuous warfare waged between the Bahmani kings and the rajas of Vijayanagar.

A purely domestic financial measure taken by Muhammad was the original cause of the earliest hostilities which led directly to the slaughter of 400,000 Hindus of both sexes. Bahman had issued hardly any gold coinage, and Muhammad for religious and political reasons substituted gold from his own mint for the Hindu currency which had previously been used throughout the Deccan. Bukka I of Vijayanagar and Kanhayya of Warangal resented this measure, and in the face of repeated warnings incited the Hindu bankers of the Deccan to melt down the new gold and hoard it. Muhammad met this by decreeing the execution, on a given day in the summer

PLATE XVII.

(a) JAMI MASJID, AHMADABAD
By permission of the Secretary of State for India in Council

(b) AHMAD'S TOMB, AHMADABAD
By permisson of the Secretary of State for India in Council

PLATE XVIII.

MURAL CARVING, TEMPLE TO VISHNU AT VIJAYANAGAR
Early sixteenth century

of 1360, of every Hindu banker and money-changer in the kingdom. Bukka and Kanhayya then declared war.

Apart from the sickening horrors of the general massacres which followed Muhammad's victories in Vijayanagar in 1366–67, these campaigns are memorable for the first mention in Indian history of the use of artillery, when the King of the Deccan took the guns from his forts and turned them into elephant batteries, manned by European and Ottoman Turkish artillerymen.[1]

Atrocities were met by reprisals, and finally a convention was made between Muhammad and Bukka that non-combatants should in future be spared. Though sometimes violated, this agreement went a long way to mitigate the horrors of war until it was broken by the Hindus more than fifty years later.

In 1367 Muhammad completed the great mosque of Gulbarga which possesses the only roofed-in courtyard to a mosque to be found in India. But the outstanding feature of Bahmani architecture is the fortification of their strongholds,[2] for the kingdom was surrounded by powerful enemies, the rajas of Vijayanagar, Telingana and Orissa, the Gonds, and the Sultans of Khandesh, Malwa and Gujerat. Nothing in Northern India is to be compared with the immense strength and ingenuity of the fortifications of Daulatabad, a fortress with an outer wall $2\frac{3}{4}$ miles in circumference, and whose only entrance, a rock-hewn tunnel, was defended by charcoal fumes. In their general appearance the Deccan forts resemble the military architecture of medieval Europe and may perhaps have been planned by Turkish and other foreign mercenaries who served in the armies of the Deccan kings.

Muhammad I died in 1377 and was succeeded by his son Mujahid, who continued hostilities against Vijayanagar until his murder a year later. Muhammad II, a grandson of Bahman Shah, who followed him on the throne, was a lover of peace and of literature and the friend of the great Persian poet Hafiz. There were no foreign wars during his nineteen years' reign,

Muhammad II.

---

[1] *Camb. Hist. India*, Vol. III. p. 381 and footnote.
[2] For detailed descriptions of Deccan military engineering of the period see *Camb. Hist. India*, Vol. III. Ch. XXIII. pp. 631–633, by Sir John Marshall.

and the peace of the kingdom was broken only by the unsuccessful revolt of the Governor of the Sagar Province.

Between 1387 and 1395 a severe famine visited the Deccan and Muhammad took prompt and able relief measures. Transport arrangements were made for the distribution of grain from Malwa and Gujerat, which was sold at low rates but only to Muhammadans, and the king established free schools for orphans at a number of centres, where the children were taught, housed and fed at the cost of the State. The day after Muhammad's death in 1397, Saif-ud-din Ghori, the faithful minister of the founder of the Bahmani dynasty and of his successors, followed his master to the grave at the age of over a hundred.

Six months of the year 1397 saw two successive kings of a dis-
Firoz Shah. ordered country before Firoz Shah, a cousin of Muhammad II, ascended the throne in November. As a young man Firoz was endowed with a splendid constitution and a fine intellect, but these he undermined by hard drinking and the pleasures of the harem. Kindly and generous by nature he brought his Brahman subjects into high government posts, but his bigoted zeal to stamp out "infidelity" abroad plunged him into incessant and impolitic warfare with his Hindu neighbours. The historian Firishta states that the Bahmani kingdom reached the height of its power during his reign. But Firoz, worn out by his debaucheries by the time he was forty, let the affairs of the kingdom fall into the hands of two freed Turki slaves. At the age of fifty-two, overwhelmed by his final and disastrous campaign against Vijayanagar in 1422, he abdicated in favour of his younger brother Ahmad, and met an instant and violent end.

Ahmad Shah had proved his skill as a commander at Ellichpur
Ahmad Shah. against the Gonds in 1399 and during the disastrous Pangul campaign just before his accession. He soon made the Raja of Vijayanagar and his unfortunate subjects bitterly repent of their breach of the humane convention of 1367. Infuriated by the Hindu atrocities he had then witnessed he marched through the Hindu kingdom slaughtering men by the 20,000 and enslaving women and children wholesale. Two of the humiliating conditions

of peace which Raja Vira Vijaya was forced to accept were the payment of an enormous sum as tribute, which the raja's son, " with every appearance of delight," had to bring on the royal elephants to Ahmad's camp; and the retention by the Moslems of an immense number of Hindu captives.

Among these prisoners were two Brahmans who became Muhammadans and subsequently rose to high positions. One of them, Fathullah, became Governor of Berar and founded the independent dynasty of that State when the Deccan kingdom broke up. The other, known as Hassan, intrigued his way to the lieutenancy of the kingdom and left a son Ahmad, who founded about the year 1490 the Nizam Shahi dynasty of Ahmadnagar, one of the five kingdoms of the Deccan; a State which kept its independence for just over a hundred years.

Ahmad Shah's foreign policy was invariably aggressive and generally ill-advised. In 1424 he annexed Telingana and created a source of continuous trouble. His disastrous attempts to conquer Gujerat four years later only led to a humiliating peace.

An outstanding domestic event of the reign was the removal of the capital from Gulbarga to Bidar, then the seat of a provincial government. The ancient capital of Vidarbha, now renamed Ahmadabad Bidar, stood on a tableland 2500 feet above sea-level, the most beautiful and the healthiest site in the Deccan. By 1432 the new citadel was completed, and before the Bahmani dynasty came to an end many impressive buildings had sprung up in the city. One of these was Ahmad's own tomb, with its Persian painting and its inscriptions in gold on deep blue and vermilion.

But the most important feature of Ahmad's home policy was his lavish employment of alien troops. The Indian climate is highly injurious to settlers from colder countries, and the mixed marriages which are bound to follow accentuate this deterioration in the race. The constant stream of immigration from Central Asia kept up the standard of the conquerors in the north. But the Deccan was isolated, and the domiciled ruling race had perpetually to bring in fresh blood to furnish their best soldiers and administrators. Bahman's chief ministers were an Afghan and a Persian, but Ahmad Shah was the first Deccan king to enlist foreign recruits for his army in large numbers, and this started the long and bitter feud between Deccanis and foreigners.

Ahmad's powers had been failing for some time, and he died about 1435 at the age of sixty-four. He was succeeded by his son Ala-ud-din Ahmad.

Ala-ud-din Ahmad.

Ala-ud-din's reign which lasted twenty-two years witnessed the usual hostilities against Vijayanagar, while the Deccan government was shaken by the growing feuds between the Deccani Muhammadans and the Abyssinian settlers, who were chiefly Sunnis, and the foreign element, Arabs, Turks, Persians and Moguls, who were mostly Shias. In the course of what amounted to civil war the Deccanis killed by an act of treachery 1200 Sayyids, 1000 other foreigners, five or six thousand children and seized the wives, daughters and goods of their victims. But in the end the foreigners triumphed, for the king, emerging from a drunken seclusion in his harem, dismissed his Deccani officials.

The war with Vijayanagar in 1443 was far from being a one-sided campaign although it ended in favour of the Deccani kingdom. Devaraya II had reorganized the rabble of 200,000 mounted men and 800,000 foot which represented the army of Vijayanagar by recruiting a large number of Moslems and creating a force of 10,000 mounted foreign archers, 60,000 Hindu cavalry and 300,000 comparatively well-trained infantry.

Humayun.

Ala-ud-din died in 1458 and was succeeded by his eldest son Humayun, one of the most bestial fiends who ever sat on a throne. Of the sickening tale of the tortures Humayun delighted to inflict on innocent and guilty alike one example is enough. While Humayun was away in Telingana suppressing a Hindu revolt a rising took place in Ahmadabad, which the Kotwal did his best to put down, and the king returned to his capital by forced marches to restore order. He put to death by torture the garrison of more than three thousand men whom he considered had failed him, while the Kotwal was publicly confined in an iron cage and given for food portions of his own body which were cut off daily until he died. The fate of the rebels themselves, their wives and families is better left undescribed.

Throughout Humayun's reign the " talons of his tortures " fell on Hindu and Moslem alike; women were butchered to make a royal holiday; or the wives and children of his subjects were forcibly abducted to satisfy his lust. But at length " God, the Most High, the Most Merciful and the Succour of them that seek aid answered the prayerful cries of His people " and in 1461 Humayun died, stabbed to death, so it is recorded, by an African maidservant when he was helpless with drink.

On Humayun's death the floodgates of invasion opened upon the Deccan kingdom, to which his infant son Nizam Shah had nominally succeeded. The Hindu armies of Orissa and Telingana penetrated to within twenty miles of the capital before they were driven back, only to be reinforced by an invading host from Malwa. The Deccan was saved and the invaders expelled by the prompt action of the foreigner Mahmud Gavan, the greatest statesman the Bahmani kings ever had and a remarkably able general. Nizam Shah died suddenly in 1463 and his brother aged nine ascended the throne as Muhammad III.

The queen-mother acted as regent until her son was sixteen, with *Muhammad III.* Mahmud Gavan as chief minister; and although the foreign party predominated Mahmud pursued a generous policy towards the Deccanis, and the great offices of State were fairly divided.

In 1469 Mahmud determined to suppress the pirate fleets which infested the Malabar coast [1] and seriously interfered with Moslem trade and pilgrim ships. He annexed the territories of the Konkan rajas concerned and by a combined naval and military operation took Goa, then one of the chief ports in the kingdom of Vijayanagar. He

---

[1] Athanasius Nikitin, a Russian merchant who came to India by sea from Ormuz about this time, mentions this scourge, which persisted from the days of the Roman sea trade until it was finally dealt with by the East India Company. For Nikitin's Diary see *India in the Fifteenth Century*.

did not return in triumph to the capital till 1472. In the same year Belgaum was annexed.

A year later the Deccan was devastated by a terrible famine in which large numbers of people died of hunger and cholera, and the kingdom was further depopulated by wholesale emigrations to Gujerat and Malwa.

A rising in Telingana at the end of 1477 which Muhammad dealt with in person led to an exploit as remarkable for sheer audacity as the capture of Nadiya by Ikhtiyar-ud-din. The king was at Kondapalli when he learnt of the immense treasure of the temple of Kanchi (Conjeveram), one of the seven sacred Hindu cities, a place no Muhammadan had ever seen. Muhammad set out to raid the place, which was ten days' journey away, with 6000 picked cavalry. On the last stage he rode so hard that he arrived at the temple gates with only forty men. But these were enough. The king killed the gigantic Hindu leader in single mounted combat, his party dealt with the Brahman guards, and the temple was plundered.

The Deccan kingdom now extended westward to the sea coast, while on the east the old provinces of Gulbarga and Daulatabad had been greatly enlarged and Telingana had considerably more than doubled in size. The provinces as organized by Bahman Shah had become unmanageable, and in 1480 Muhammad partitioned each of the original provinces. At the same time the powers of the provincial satraps were considerably curtailed, all military appointments with the exception of the command of the principal provincial fortress were resumed by the king, and a system of control and inspection was introduced. These reforms were highly unpopular amongst the older nobility, who saw the wealth and authority of the governors diminished and the opportunities for peculation greatly restricted. The eight provincial governorships were allotted fairly among the two factions, Africans being put in charge of two of them.

Whilst the dismemberment of the kingdom is to be attributed to the Bahmani system of decentralization the immediate cause was the shocking crime which sullied the end of Muhammad's reign. The king had started life under every possible advantage, with a wise mother and one of the greatest Moslem statesmen of India to guide him. But he had become a confirmed drunkard, and the Deccani party who hated the Persian leader of the foreigners awaited their opportunity when the king was intoxicated to show him a highly treasonable letter to the Raja of Orissa over Mahmud Gavan's seal. The letter was a palpable forgery, but Muhammad, without making any inquiry and refusing to listen to his minister's defence and protestations of innocence, ordered him to instant execution.

Mahmud Gavan had served the Bahmani kings with unswerving devotion for thirty-five years, and he was seventy-eight years old at the time of his murder in 1481. In the council chamber he had filled the highest office with wisdom and justice and he had shown in the field the greatest skill and courage. His private life, in which he showed himself to be a devout Sunni Moslem, had been consistently one of kindliness and generosity. When the king sent for the dead minister's treasurer he found that, with all his opportunities, Mahmud Gavan had left no fortune. His great income as he received it had all been spent in charity.

Among his many endowments was the splendid college in the Persian style which he built at Bidar nine years before his death, with its great mosque and library, lecture halls, professors' quarters, and students' cubicles ranged round an open courtyard, all planned for convenience and comfort and amply provided with light and air.[1]

Retribution fell swiftly upon the king. The foreigners and the more respectable members of the Deccani party would have no more to do with him and, overwhelmed with remorse and grief, he drank himself to death within a year. He was just twenty-eight.

Muhammad Shah was succeeded in 1482 by his son the boy King Mahmud, who grew up a pleasure-seeking debauchee.

End of Bahmani Dynasty. The government was in the hands of Qasim Barid-ul-Mamalik, a Turk who had joined the Deccani faction; the State was rent by the plots of the opposing parties; and the provincial governors one after another asserted their independence. The kingdom had departed from the Bahmani house and when Mahmud died in 1518, worn out with his excesses, all that remained

---

[1] *Camb. Hist. India*, Vol. III. pp. 635–636. Sir John Marshall discusses the Deccan architecture in detail, pp. 629–636.

was the country around the capital. Kalimullah, the last of a dynasty which had dwindled into a succession of puppet kings, fled; Amir Abi Barid set himself upon the throne of Bidar; and the history of the five turbulent, ambitious and treacherous kingdoms of the Deccan began.

Bijapur, the most important of the five kingdoms of the Deccan,

Bijapur. was founded by Adil Shah. If Firishta is to be believed he was the son of Sultan Murad II of Turkey, saved from a general massacre of the royal children and smuggled out of the country.[1] He was certainly sold as a slave to Khvaja Mahmud Gavan, the great Deccan minister, and afterwards rose to a provincial governorship. In 1490 he joined with the Governors of Ahmadnagar and Berar, when they asserted the independence of their respective provinces in those words of the Koran which describe so much of Indian history: " The sword for him who can wield it, and dominion to him who conquers."

Acting upon this principle Adil Shah engaged in frequent warfare with his Moslem and Hindu neighbours until his death from dropsy at the age of seventy-five in 1510. The only notable domestic event of the reign, and it almost cost him his throne, was the attempt to impose the Shia form of religion on his Sunni subjects. Early in his rule the king married the daughter of a Maratha chief, and he freely appointed Hindus to high government offices. Adil Shah appears to have been a man of considerable attainments, a skilful musician and devoted to literature; in character he was wise, just and conscientious. But towards the end of his life the control of affairs passed into the hands of his treacherous minister Kamal Khan Deccani, while the country was invaded by the Portuguese, who seized his newly-won port of Goa in February 1510. The place changed hands three times during the year, but Adil Shah was dead before de Albuquerque finally took it in November and, exasperated by his losses, massacred the Moslem inhabitants.

Alliances in the Deccan were made as rapidly as they were afterwards broken. In 1515 and again in 1520 Adil Shah's son

[1] *Mahomedan Power in India*, Vol. III. Section II. Ch. III. pp. 4–8, where the story with its " strong corroborating facts " is given in detail.

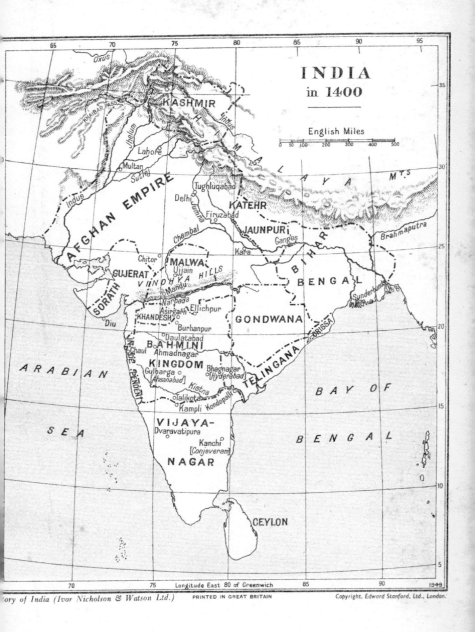

INDIA
in 1400

English Miles
0 50 100 200 300 400 500

Oxus

KHYBAR PASS

KASHMIR

Indus

Jhelum

Lahore

Multan

Sutlej

Indus

AFGHAN EMPIRE

Tughluqabad

Delhi

Jumna

Firuzabad

KATEHR

Chambal

JAUNPUR

Ganges

Kara

BIHAR

Brahmaputra

Chitor

MALWA

Ujjain

VINDHYA HILLS

GUJERAT

Mandu

BENGAL

Narbada

Asirgarh   Ellichpur

Sunderbunds

SORATH

KHANDESH

Diu

Burhanpur

GONDWANA

Daulatabad

BAHMINI

Chaul   Ahmadnagar

KINGDOM

Gulbarga

Bhagnagar

[Ahsanabad]

[Hyderabad]

TELINGANA

ORISSA

Kistna

Talikota

Kampli   Kondapalli

VIJAYA-

Dvaravatipura

BAY   OF

Kanchi

ARABIAN

[Conjeveram]

NAGAR

BENGAL

SEA

MALAYA   MTS.

CEYLON

ory of India (Ivor Nicholson & Watson Ltd.)   PRINTED IN GREAT BRITAIN   Copyright, Edward Stanford, Ltd., London.

Isma'il attacked the Portuguese, being badly defeated in the first campaign, but winning back the mainland of Goa, though not the island, in the second. But between these operations when Bijapur was invaded by Krishna of Vijayanagar Portuguese troops fought on the Moslem side. The Hindus were victorious and took 400 guns, 100 elephants and 4000 horses. Isma'il Adil Shah's reign, which began with the Portuguese war and an abortive plot against the throne by the regent Kamal Khan, ran what was then the normal course of incessant fighting. He died at the age of thirty-seven in 1534.

Mallu, the licentious son of Isma'il, was deposed and blinded by his outraged nobles after a reign of six months, and *Bijapur and* in 1535 his brother Ibrahim Adil Shah I became king. *Vijayanagar.* His chief adviser was Khusru Lari, a Turkish foreigner of outstanding ability who was given the title of Asad Khan and the great fief of Belgaum. One of the first acts of the reign, however, was to expel almost all the foreigners and replace them in the government and in the army by Deccanis and Abyssinians. A state visit to Vijayanagar in 1535, and wars with that kingdom and his Deccan neighbours, sums up Ibrahim's foreign policy. He died in 1557 [1] as the direct result of hard drinking and debauchery.

His son Ali, unlike his father, was a Shia and an intolerant bigot. But he made an alliance with the Hindu kingdom of Vijayanagar against his Moslem neighbour Ahmadnagar in 1558, when the two armies devastated that country and " left no cruelty unpractised." Six years later the four Deccan kingdoms of Bijapur, Ahmadnagar, Bidar and Golconda combined to break the formidable Hindu power which dominated the south. Talikota, one of the decisive battles of India, was fought on 23rd January 1565, the splendid city of Vijayanagar met the fate of Carthage, and with the overthrow of the great Hindu kingdom Muhammadan supremacy in the Deccan was assured.

In 1570 Ali made an alliance with Murtaza Nizam, Shah of Ahmadnagar and the Hindu Zamorin of Calicut, to expel the Portuguese from India. But the attempt was frustrated by the splendid courage and tenacity of the Viceroy Dom Luiz de Atayde, helped by

[1] Authority: Firishta. *Camb. Hist. India*, Vol. III. p. 444, gives 1558.

the dissensions of his enemies. Chaul with its garrison of 3000 was besieged for nine months by an army of 150,000 men. Goa was invested in even greater force, but its defenders who at first numbered 1600 and were only later increased to 4000 eventually forced the invaders to raise the siege with a loss of 12,000 men and 300 elephants. Not only did Dom Luiz during the crisis send reinforcements to outlying places which were being attacked, but he despatched the annual fleet of merchantmen to Portugal, and finally carried the war successfully into the enemy's country. Ali Adil Shah was killed in 1579 at a moment of disgusting debauchery. Bijapur was finally absorbed in the Mogul empire in 1686.

The Adil Shahi dynasty left its mark in India by the creation of the magnificent monuments at Bijapur in which the native art of the Deccan, as evolved by Indian artists and craftsmen, rises above the Persian influence evident in the buildings of the Bahmani rulers.[1]

Ahmadnagar, which became one of the Deccan kingdoms in 1490
Ahmadnagar. under Ahmad Nizam-ul-Malik, the son of a Vija-
yanagar Brahman, was ruled from 1508 until 1553 by Burhan Nizam Shah I, who ascended the throne at the age of seven. The government during the minority was carried on by the able minister Muhammad Khan Deccani. In 1521 Burhan gave the Portuguese permission to build a factory at Chaul, and six years later entered into an alliance with them against the State of Gujerat. In the course of this campaign the Gujerat fleet was completely destroyed. The by no means invariably successful wars waged by Burhan Nizam Shah and his successors, and the far from edifying deaths of the majority of the earlier kings, can be found in the pages of Firishta. Ahmadnagar did not become part of the Mogul Empire until 1637 during the reign of Shahjahan.

About 1490 Berar broke away from the Bahmani kingdom under its
Berar. provincial governor Fathullah Imad-ul-Mulk Deccani,
a convert from Hinduism; Imad Shahi kings ruled the country until it was annexed by Ahmadnagar in 1574.

[1] *Camb. Hist. India*, Vol. III. p. 637.

The province of Golconda which threw off its allegiance to the Bah-
manis between 1512 and 1518, was the old Telingana
Golconda. kingdom ruled until the beginning of the fourteenth
century by the Hindu kings of the Narupati dynasty. It had been
brought under the suzerainty of Delhi by Ala-ud-din Khalji in 1346,
and once more came under Moslem suzerainty ten years later, after
the invasion of Muhammad I of the Deccan in 1365. As an independent kingdom under the Qutb Shahi dynasty, it enjoyed considerable
prosperity. The old Hindu irrigation works had been kept in repair,
the country was fertile and Hindus were able to rise to high office in
the government. The administration was in general good, from the
days of its first independent ruler, Quli Qutb Shah, to its eighth and
last, Abu'l Hassan, who came to the throne in 1672. Long before
this time, however, the Deccan kingdoms, utterly incapable through
mutual jealousy of showing a united front, had begun to fall one by
one before the steady advance of the Mogul Empire, and Golconda
itself was annexed by Aurangzeb in 1687. During the reign of
Ibrahim (1550–80), the court, which had been moved from
Warangal to Golconda by Quli Qutb, was established at Bhagnagar,
renamed Hyderabad and is now, as the capital of the Nizam's
dominions with a population of 728,000 in 1941, the fourth largest
city in India.

Besides the kingdoms of the Deccan there were other independent
States stretching across the middle of India from east to west to which
reference must be made.

On the Bay of Bengal lay the State of Orissa, a Hindu outpost
against the Moslem Governors of Bengal. It had
Orissa. been invaded by Firuz Tughluq in 1360 and made
to pay tribute to Delhi. Orissa kept its independence in spite of
formidable Moslem incursions, and in 1435 the enterprising and
ambitious ruler Kapilesvaradeva ascended the throne. He extended
his sway southwards along the coast, and even menaced Vijayanagar,
which was preoccupied with its incessant hostilities against the
Deccan kingdom. It was not until 1516 that Krishna, the greatest
of the Vijayanagar kings, succeeded in winning back the territory

which had been lost, and established the Kistna River as the boundary between the two kingdoms. Orissa kept its independence until it was taken by Akbar in 1592.

The forest region between Orissa and Berar inhabited by the

Gondwana.

primitive tribes of Gonds was then known as Gondwana and divided into four kingdoms. The richest was the most northern, Garha-Mandla, which towards the end of the fifteenth century was greatly enlarged at the expense of its neighbours in the Narbada Valley. Deogarh and Khula were the most aggressive, and from the latter had come Narsingh who united many of the tribes and invaded Berar in 1398; the original cause of subsequent Muhammadan expeditions. The greatest and most wisely ruled Gond kingdom was Chanda in the south, with a long line of rulers whose policy was to avoid war. Gondwana was conquered, plundered and annexed by Asaf Khan, Akbar's Governor of Kara, when the famous and stout-hearted Queen Rani Durgavati was ruling the Garha country.

Malwa had formed the most southern portion of Harsha's

Malwa.

dominions, and in the first half of the eleventh century was ruled by the celebrated King Bhoja Paramara. In 1234 Iltutmish invaded the country, sacked Ujjain and demolished the famous Hindu temple of Mahakali. Other Moslem incursions followed, but Malwa was not annexed until 1305 when Ain-ul-Mulk subdued it for his master Ala-ud-din.

After the invasion of Timur Lang had shattered the central government, Dilavar Khan Ghori the Afghan Governor of Malwa shook off his allegiance to Delhi. The Ghori and Khalji dynasties ruled the country for about a hundred and thirty years, and then, in 1531, Bahadur of Gujerat defeated Mahmud II the last Khalji and took possession of Malwa, a circumstance entirely due to Mahmud himself, whose tortuous and aggressive policy severed the old friendship between the two countries.

Hushang Shah Ghori (1405–35) and Mahmud I Khalji raised the splendid Jami Masjid and the massive Darbar Hall [1] in Mandu, the ancient capital, with its twenty-five miles of grey embattled walls crowning the steep edge of a spur of the Vindhya hills. But within

[1] See *Camb. Hist. India*, Vol. III. pp. 617-622.

the walls there is now a choking forest of pipal, banyan, baobul and teak, amidst which rise the great mosques and palaces and tombs of sandstone and marble—all that remain of what is still the most striking fortress city of India.

The independence of Gujerat, as a State under Moslem rule, was established by Zafar Khan (Muzaffar I), the son of a Rajput convert who was sent by Muhammad Tughlak to suppress a rebellion in the province in 1391 and set himself up as king in 1396. The subsequent rise of the kingdom was due to Muzaffar's grandson Ahmad Shah (1411–42), a determined and energetic ruler who engaged in frequent and successful war with his neighbours. He built Ahmadabad, still the chief city of Gujerat, soon after his accession. But the greatest king of the dynasty was Mahmud I Begarha,[1] who showed the strength of his character by his personal courage and decision in stamping out a formidable conspiracy when he came to the throne as a boy of thirteen in 1458. Mahmud is one of the great masters of war in Indian history, and the victories which extended his dominions included campaigns in Cutch and Kathiawar and the conquest of the Hindu State of Champaner.

Gujerat.

Gujerat with its long-established and flourishing trade and its many harbours, had made itself strong at sea, and with the arrival of the Portuguese upon the coast a collision between the two powers was inevitable. After the allied Moslem fleet had been destroyed off Diu in 1509 by Almeida, Mahmud made peace with the Portuguese. He died in 1511. Mahmud was in every way a born ruler. Tall and of striking appearance with a beard to his waist, he never allowed himself to be swayed by the whisperings of the harem, and his word was law with his ministers.

Muzaffar II succeeded and reigned until 1526, dying on 7th April, thirteen days before Babur won the battle of Panipat. With his fleet he was able to resist the attempts of the Portuguese to capture Diu, while he led his armies, amongst other campaigns, to the help

---

[1] The derivation of the nickname Begarha is *be garh*, meaning " two forts," and refers to his capture of the two great Hindu strongholds of Girnar and Champaner (*Camb. Hist. India*, Vol. III. p. 316).

of Mahmud II of Malwa when his government had fallen into the hands of Rajput officers. Mandu was stormed in 1518, its Rajput defenders immolated themselves in the rite of *jauhar*, and the surviving Rajput inhabitants of the city to the number of nineteen thousand were butchered.

On Muzaffar's death the nobles split into three factions supporting the respective claims of the late king's elder sons, Sikandar, Bahadur, and Latif Khan.

Sikandar, the first-born and his father's nominated heir, was feeble and incompetent. He was promptly assassinated and Mahmud, an infant son of Muzaffar's, was proclaimed the nominal king on 12th April 1526. But Bahadur, who is said [1] to have been present as a spectator at Panipat, returned to Gujerat and assumed the kingship on 11th July. His infant brother was secretly murdered within the year, a revolt by Latif Khan ended in the death of that claimant, and Bahadur had made himself the unquestioned King of Gujerat.

In the almost ceaseless wars of the reign, Bahadur met with considerable success. Malwa was annexed in 1531, and in 1534 he stormed the Rajput stronghold of Chitor. The place had been gallantly defended by the queen mother Jawahir Bai, who was killed when leading a sortie; the infant heir Udai Singh was taken to a place of safety; and the surviving Rajputs committed *jauhar*. Thirteen thousand women, according to the legend, perished in the flames while their men, led by Baghji, Prince of Deola, rushed down the great breach to die sword in hand.

The taking of Chitor marks the turning-point in Bahadur's fortunes. Humayun had succeeded Babur at Delhi in 1530, and for a time relations were friendly between the two Moslem kingdoms. But a quarrel over a Timurid fugitive to Gujerat led to the invasion of that country by Humayun in 1535. Bahadur deserted his army and fled, finally escaping by taking ship to Diu. In the meanwhile a rebellion had broken out in Bengal, Humayun was obliged to retire and Bahadur regained his kingdom.

In 1534, before the invasion of his country, Bahadur had ceded the

---

[1] By Abu Turab, a contemporary writer (*Camb. Hist. India*, Vol. III. p. 322). Firishta only says that " Bahadur Khan was near Delhi."

island of Bassein to the Portuguese, and during the crisis he offered a factory site in Diu in exchange for the services of 500 European troops. The contingent was not forthcoming and Bahadur began to negotiate with the Viceroy Nino da Cunha for the Portuguese withdrawal from Diu. He eventually consented to visit da Cunha on his flagship, and the one certain fact which emerges from two conflicting stories is that Bahadur was drowned in Diu harbour on the 13th February 1537.

The utter confusion both as regards the succession of the later rulers of Gujerat and the disorder of the kingdom may be read in the pages of Firishta. The country was taken over by Akbar in 1572 during the chaotic reign of Muzaffar Shah III.

The architecture of the great Moslem buildings of Gujerat was founded upon the highest traditions of the Khalji school as it existed when the province broke off from Delhi. This is to be seen in such buildings as the Jami Masjid at Ahmadabad, which Sir John Marshall has described [1] "as one of the most superb, as it is also one of the most imposing structures of its class in the world." During the reign of Mahmud Begarha the architecture of Gujerat entered upon its most magnificent stage. Mahmud founded three new cities and enriched his capital of Ahmadabad with many splendid buildings.

The small kingdom of Khandesh in the Tapti Valley owed its *Khandesh.* importance to the strength of its fortress Asirgarh. Khandesh won its independence through the resistance of Malik Ahmad Khan to the Bahmani power of the Deccan about the year 1380. He founded the Faruqi dynasty, and the name Khandesh is derived from the title of Khan, which these rulers assumed. The capital of the country was Burhanpur. Sometime a dependency of its powerful neighbour Gujerat, the State remained in existence until Akbar took Asirgarh in 1601.

To the south of all these States and occupying the whole of the *Vijayanagar.* lower extremity of the peninsula, a Hindu power, the greatest since the days of Harsha, held its own from the middle of the fourteenth century for more than two hundred years.

---

[1] *Camb. Hist. India,* Vol. III. Ch. XXIII, where the architecture of the kingdom is discussed (pp. 608–616).

Muhammad Tughlak had been a menace to the very existence of Hindu religion and civilization in the south until his blind policy of aggression was checked by the successful rebellion of 1334 in Madura, which converted that province into a disordered kingdom. The third king to fight his way to the throne of Madura in 1340 was Ghiyas-ud-din Damaghani, or Damaghan Shah, who had served as a trooper in the Delhi army. Damaghan Shah, a brutal tyrant who delighted in the wholesale massacre and torture of Hindu captives—men, women and children—continued the war against Vira Ballala III, the last great Hoysala king and the one existing bulwark against the Muhammadan conquest of Southern India.

Origin of the Kingdom.

Vira Ballala was defeated at the battle of Trichinopoly in 1342, and the old man of eighty was taken prisoner and strangled by the victor, who hung the stuffed skin of the raja, in the best Delhi manner, on the ramparts of Madura. Vira Ballala's son appears also to have died in battle, but the spirit of the old king lived on in five brothers, the sons of Sangama of Anagundi, who were officers on the Hindu northern frontier. The Hindu people of Southern India groaning under alien rule and religious persecution found their leaders in Sangama's sons; the movement was inspired by the Brahman sage Vidyaranya and the kingdom of Vijayanagar was founded.

Less than ten years after the establishment of the Bahmani dynasty in the Deccan, which took place in 1347, a Hindu power had arisen in the south so formidable that Bahman Shah's trusty minister Saif-ud-din Ghuri dissuaded his master from attacking it.

When Bahman Shah died in 1358 Bukka alone survived of Sangama's sons, and the mantle of the Hoysalas descended on him. Vijayanagar, his capital, was the fortress city on the heights above the Tungabhadra, built by Vira Ballala III; and its sevenfold walls defied every invading army for two hundred years. Ab-dur-Razzaq,[1] who went to the city on a mission from Samarkand in 1442, has

---

[1] Kamal-ud-din Ab-dur-Razzaq as quoted in *India in the Fifteenth Century*, Hakluyt Society (London), 1857.

PLATE XIX.

IN THE RICE FIELDS

From "Les Hindous," French early nineteenth-century work

By permission of the Secretary of State for India in Council

PLATE XX.

INDIAN SHIPPING : "HIGH VESSELS OF THE PERSIAN GULF," PEARL FISHERS' GRABS AND CATAMARANS

From "Les Hindous," French early nineteenth-century work

By permission of the Secretary of State for India in Council

left a description in which the magnificence of the court, with its dancers, courtesans, jugglers and the performing elephants in particular, might easily be taken for a tale from the *Arabian Nights*. The royal palaces were built under Islamic influence, but the temples with their high gates and many-pillared pavilions were purely Dravidian in their architecture.[1]

Wars with the Deccan.

The sanguinary struggle between the Hindu and Muhammadan powers, which lasted as long as the kingdom of Vijayanagar was in being, began when Firoz Shah Tughlak announced his policy of non-interference in the affairs of the south, and this danger to both States no longer existed. The history of Vijayanagar consists almost entirely of the wars with the Deccan, but in 1371 Bukka I defeated and swept away the Moslem dynasty of Madura. He died seven years later and was succeeded by Harihara II,[2] the first of the line to assume the royal title. Two kings, both named Devaraya, followed, and at the accession of Devaraya II (1421–48) the kingdom was at the height of the prosperity which it reached under the first dynasty.

Nicolo Conti, a Venetian of noble family who travelled in India a little before 1440, gives the following impressions of his visit to Vijayanagar, which he calls Bizenegalia[3] : " The circumference of the city is sixty miles; its walls are carried up to the mountains and enclose the valleys at their foot. . . . In this city there are estimated to be ninety thousand men fit to bear arms. The inhabitants of this region marry as many wives as they please, who are burnt with their dead husbands. Their king is more powerful than all the other kings of India. He takes to himself twelve thousand wives, of whom four thousand follow him on foot . . . and are employed in the kitchen. A like number . . . ride on horseback, the remainder carried by men in litters of whom two or three thousand are selected as his wives on condition they should voluntarily burn themselves with him, which

---

[1] *History of Fine Art in India and Ceylon*, Smith, revised Codrington.
[2] Harihara I had been one of the wardens of the marches before his brother Bukka came to power.
[3] *India in the Fifteenth Century*, Part II.

is considered to be a great honour for them." The wholesale sacrifice of *sati* reached its climax in India at the obsequies of the Telugu rulers of the kingdom.

Devaraya II was followed by Mallikarjuna who repelled a combined attack by the Deccan kingdom and the Hindu State of Orissa. But the next king, his brother Virupaksha, was so hopelessly incompetent that Vijayanagar was in danger of breaking up, and Saluva Narasimha, with the help of his general Narasa, deposed him in 1487 and took over the government. This is known as the First Usurpation, and Narasimha in his six years' reign succeeded in winning back most of the rebellious provinces.

A second usurpation about the year 1505 brought chaos, but from this emerged Krishnadevaraya, son of Narasa and the greatest king of Vijayanagar, who ascended the throne in 1509. His own country was unsettled and a powerful vassal in open rebellion. Off the coast of Bijapur the guns of the Portuguese and Muhammadan fleets were in action, and the first of the European powers in India was raising the earliest Indian regiment to fight against their own countrymen. Away in the north the Lodi dynasty of Delhi, for all the energy and determination of its greatest king Sikandar, was not far from its end at the hands of the conquering army of Babur.

A Portuguese mission sent to Vijayanagar by de Albuquerque to conclude a commercial treaty and an alliance against the Zamorin of Calicut soon after Krishna's accession was the only contact between the two powers during the king's reign. Krishna's foreign policy was mainly to recover the provinces which had been lost to Orissa, and in this he had partly succeeded by 1516. Four years later, profiting by the dissensions between the Five Kingdoms of the Deccan, he annexed the Raichur Doab which had been the cause of heavy fighting with the Deccan kingdom since the days of Muhammad I, a hundred and sixty years before.

Krishna was an able general; in the course of his campaigns he temporarily occupied Bijapur and he destroyed the great fortress of Gulbarga, the original capital of the Bahmani kingdom. But in vivid contrast to so many of the successful soldiers of medieval India, he was merciful towards the vanquished. A zealous Hindu with strong leanings towards Vaishnavism, Krishna made most generous endowments to temples and Brahmans.

It must be remembered, however, that in those medieval times the subjects of a kingdom were held to exist solely for the benefit of their rulers, Moslem or Hindu, and the Indian peasants habitually lived in a state of misery and neglect. The usual government practice in the south was to leave the cultivator half his crop.

Athanasius Nikitin,[1] a merchant of Tver who visited parts of India including Bidar and Vijayanagar about the year 1470, noted in his diary: "The land is overstocked with people; but those in the country are very miserable, while the nobles are extremely opulent and delight in luxury. They are wont to be carried on their silver beds, preceded by some twenty chargers caparisoned in gold and followed by 300 men on horseback and 500 on foot, and by hornmen, ten torch-bearers and ten musicians."

The terrible ferocity of the punishments for offences against property were designed to protect the rich against the poor, and it is recorded that there were very few thieves in the country. The ruler of Vijayanagar was an absolute autocrat with an immense army under his immediate orders; and the provincial governors, apart from the obligation to remit to the royal exchequer one-half of their gross revenue, were supreme within their provinces.

Prostitution was rife; the courtesans were sometimes extremely rich and the State drew a considerable revenue from the brothels. Duelling was prevalent amongst the upper classes and eventually was taken up, to Firishta's horror, by the Muhammadans of the Deccan.[2]

Towards the end of his reign Krishna's health began to fail, and rebellion broke out in parts of the kingdom, which had to be suppressed. He died in 1530. Neither his brother Achyuta nor his nephew Sadashivaraya were strong rulers, and during the reign of the second of these kings Vijayanagar came to an end as a kingdom in 1565.

---

[1] *India in the Fifteenth Century*, Part III.
[2] Firishta, Vol. III. pp. 208–209.

The forces of the kingdoms of Bijapur, Ahmadnagar, Golconda and Bidar, bent on the destruction of the formidable Hindu power, concentrated at Talikota, a small frontier town in Bijapur. The allied army was commanded by Hussain Nizam Shah I, whose kingdom of Ahmadnagar had been subjected to every kind of atrocity by the Hindus during the recent invasions of his country by Bijapur and Vijayanagar. The strength of the Muhammadan forces lay in their infinitely better training and discipline, in the efficiency of their cavalry and mounted archers and in the overwhelming superiority of their 600 guns commanded by the able and experienced Chalabi Rumi Khan, who had seen service in Europe.

Battle of Talikota.

Sadashivaraya commanded the Hindu army in person. He had under him 82,000 cavalry, 900,000 infantry, 2000 elephants and some artillery. But this huge collection of men was ill-armed and undisciplined, and if Cæsar Frederick (who visited Vijayanagar two years later) is to be believed, the issue was practically decided by the defection of 140,000 Muhammadan mercenaries serving in the Hindu army.

The Kistna flowed between the opposing forces. Hussain by a skilful manœuvre crossed it without loss, and on 5th January 1565, with the river behind him, fought what is known as the battle of Talikota.

The tactics on both sides were simple.[1] Chalabi Khan had disposed his artillery in three lines according to calibre, and covered them with 2000 foreign archers who had orders to fall back when the enemy approached. The Hindus opened with matchlocks and rockets and then advanced upon the guns. They were repulsed but they came on again, and Chalabi Khan met the second attack by loading his heavy pieces with bags of copper coins, which in the Deccan were lumps of metal and equal to modern shrapnel. The effect at point-blank range was decisive and the Bijapur cavalry, supported by elephants, charged the shattered columns through the gaps between the guns. As the Hindus fell back Sadashivaraya was taken prisoner

---

[1] For further details of the battle see Firishta, Vol. III. pp. 126–130 and pp. 246–249.

and instantly beheaded, and at the sight of their leader's head on a Moslem pike the huge army completely gave way.

A hundred thousand Hindus were killed in the battle and the rout which followed. The booty taken by the men of the victorious army was enormous, the city of Vijayanagar was completely destroyed, and the country plundered for the next six months. The great Hindu power of the south was broken into a number of petty Hindu States, of which the most important was that of the Nayaks of Madura.

Conquest through the gateways of the north-west had been frequent in Indian history. While Persians and Greeks, Scythians, Kushanas and Huns had swept into the plains to become absorbed in the country, two invasions, or series of invasions, had permanently impressed their character upon India.

Results of Invasion.

Through the colour bar which developed the caste system the Aryans kept themselves from being submerged in the great mass of the Dravidian population. Dravidian culture and ideas steadfastly survived in the southern portion of the peninsula, and the proportion of true Aryan blood is small throughout India today and hardly exists at all in some provinces. But the Aryans succeeded in absorbing the Dravidians in the lower castes of Hinduism, including what are now called the scheduled (depressed) classes, the "untouchables" who comprise almost a fifth of the total Hindu population of all India, and either follow degrading occupations or represent the aboriginal tribes.

The uncompromising faith of Islam thrust its way through the warring States of India like a sword. The Muhammadans trampled under foot the images of the hated religion they were unable to destroy, and as time went on the Moslems greatly increased in numbers. On the heels of the original invaders came an unending stream of subsequent immigrants; there were countless conversions, either forced or due to the missions of great Muhammadan saints and teachers; and there was the steady increase caused by the inter-marriage of the old and new Muhammadans. But the Hindus had built up an unscalable wall in the caste system which so utterly denies the theory of human equality as taught (if not invariably applied) by Islam as well as by Christianity.

While Moslem India today partly descends from these invaders, the majority are by blood natives of the soil, from high-born Rajputs to untouchables, who have adopted, in the brotherhood of Islam, the civilization of Arabia and Persia, and so remain a distinct people proud of their political ascendancy and culture.

These were the results of invasion through the north-western passes. Thirty centuries had seen no conquest from the sea, but twenty-seven years before Babur led his army down the Khyber a new era of European intrusion and eventual supremacy broke upon the western shores of India.

Inspired by the resolve to end the Venetian monopoly of the Indian trade reaching Europe by the Levant, a *The Portuguese.* Portuguese seaman, Bartholemeu Diaz de Novaes, rounded the Cape of Good Hope in 1487; and on 17th May 1498 Vasco da Gama with his three ships, none of more than 150 tons burden, sighted Calicut, where he was hospitably received by the zamorin. In the search for an all-sea route to the Indies, America had been discovered, and the wealth from the exploitation of these new fields revolutionized western civilization. The economic transformation brought about by a different concentration of capital and a new commercialism shattered the universal attitude of Europe towards the Holy See. This was an important factor in the religious upheaval of the sixteenth century. The lure of India, with the economic results following these discoveries, had an effect upon Europe which can hardly be too strongly emphasized.[1] One result was to make Portugal during the sixteenth century the most prosperous country in Europe.

On the 13th September 1500 Pedro Alvarez Cabral appeared with his fleet off Calicut. He had sailed from Lisbon on the 9th of March, soon after da Gama's return, and on his way to India had incidentally discovered Brazil and Zanzibar. Cabral

---

[1] See *Religion and the Rise of Capitalism*, R. H. Tawney, 1926.

soon became embroiled with the zamorin in his efforts to found a settlement, but before the Portuguese commander sailed back to Lisbon he found a better harbour than Calicut in Cochin, where the Hindu raja, an enemy of the zamorin, was to prove a valuable ally.

By 1507 the Portuguese had fortified Cochin and established themselves on the island of Socotra. The Indian trade with the west was now tapped at its source, and the wealth of merchandise began to go to Europe in Portuguese ships by way of the Cape.

Direct intercourse between India and the western world had ended in the seventh century with the Arab conquest of Egypt and Persia, which had obliged all exports from India to pass through the hands of the Muhammadan rulers of the Levant, who literally held the East in fee. But this diversion of trade from the ancient route, from Moslem factories in Calicut through the Red Sea merchants of Jidda and so by Suez, Cairo and Alexandria to Europe, while it ruined the merchants of Venice and Genoa, was a heavy blow to the Mameluke Sultan of Egypt, who lost the large revenue drawn from the customs dues levied in transit. By his ingenious manipulation of the pepper trade the Sultan secured one-third of the profits on every voyage and, in addition to this, import and export duties aggregating 20 per cent. *ad valorem* were imposed in Egypt. Added to this the Portuguese ceaselessly harried the Moslem trading vessels plying between the ports of Gujerat and Jidda, and showed a hostility towards the Muhammadan people which might possibly have been justified by previous European history had it not been accompanied by horrible and most unchristian atrocities. Pilgrim ships were mercilessly sunk, and even though women and children might be among the passengers they were left to drown.

Within ten years of their arrival the Portuguese had consequently aroused the violent hostility of every Muhammadan State on the Arabian littoral. Moslem supremacy of the eastern seas was at stake and a coalition was formed by the Sultan of Egypt and Mahmud I of Gujerat, with whom the Hindu zamorin of Calicut joined forces to meet the challenge.

The allied fleet, commanded by Amir Husain, the Kurdish governor of Jedda, attacked a Portuguese squadron in the harbour of Chaul in January 1508 and overwhelmed it. But a year later the Portuguese Viceroy Francesco de Almeida sailed up the coast to Diu with his whole fleet and won a decisive naval victory in February 1509. The Moslem fleet was practically annihilated and the command of the Arabian Sea passed into the hands of the Portuguese. It was upon sea-power that the Portuguese wealth and ascendancy was founded. They never attempted to establish an empire in India, and they consolidated their naval position by building a chain of fortified posts along the coast line from the Cape of Good Hope to China. No ship could sail those seas without a Portuguese passport, and the whole of the trade with the Indies and with China was assured for nearly a century.

In November 1510 the Portuguese established themselves at Goa, the first territory in India to be directly governed by Europeans since the days of Alexander's generals; and there they have remained to this day. Alfonso de Albuquerque had become Viceroy in 1509, and he appointed Portuguese district officers with a Hindu clerical staff, while he maintained the Indian system of village local government. Muhammadans were excluded from the government service. Hindu regiments with their own officers were raised, and the earliest European-trained Indian troops first saw service against the Muhammadans at Dabpol and the Hindus at Calicut. Another of de Albuquerque's measures was to abolish *sati*, the sacrifice of the Hindu widow on the funeral pyre, which was so often only voluntary in theory. *Sati* was prohibited from time to time by rulers of various Hindu States. It was made illegal in the East India Company's territory in 1829.

But in one respect the Viceroy embarked on a policy which largely contributed to the decline of Portuguese power in India. He foresaw the drain which the demands of the eastern possessions must entail on the man-power of so small a kingdom as Portugal, and he sought to counteract it by the encouragement of mixed marriages. It may here be remarked that the English East India Company, seventy years after the foundation of their first factory at

Surat, pursued a similar policy.[1]   In the early days of the English
East India Company children of mixed marriages were frequently
educated in England and returned to hold good positions in India.
In the British case this policy had no disastrous results, but it has
led up to the present economic Anglo-Indian problem.

In 1514 de Albuquerque was recalled, but died at Goa before he
could sail. The great Portuguese Viceroy, brave, resolute and clear-
sighted, with his cruelty towards Muhammadans as the one stain
on his character, had perceived that the three keys to the eastern
trade were Malacca, Ormuz and Aden. The first two of these he
won, but with his 20 ships, 1700 Portuguese and 800 Indian troops
he failed to take the last. In his farewell letter to King Manoel he
said: " I leave the chief place in India in your Majesty's power, the
only thing left to be done being the closing of the gates of the Straits."
The majority of the governors and viceroys who followed did
little to reflect credit on themselves or upon their country. His
successor, Lopo Soares, threw away a golden opportunity to occupy
Aden unopposed, and according to the Portuguese historian Faria y
Sousa, who was there at the time, began the downfall of Portuguese
power in India by allowing his European officers to trade, a concession which ultimately led to the incomes of station commanders
being estimated on the basis of their illicit gains.

With the exception of *sati*, de Albuquerque had not interfered
with the customs of the people of Goa, but in 1540 the King of
Portugal ordered all the Hindu temples in the island to be destroyed;
and the local application of a religious intolerance then regrettably
universal in the Christian world is generally held by historians [2]
to be one of the reasons for the decline of Portuguese power in
India. The forcible union of Portugal with Spain after the battle
of Alcantara in 1580 undoubtedly hastened this decline, even though
the eastern trade was specifically retained by Portuguese merchants

---

[1] As in Surat General Letter from the Governor and Directors in London
dated 14th July 1686 (India Office MS. Records).
[2] See *Camb. Hist. India*, Vol. IV. Ch. I., by Sir E. Denison Ross, pp. 17, 18.
The work of the Catholic missionaries of the seventeenth and eighteenth centuries
in India is referred to in very different terms in the following chapter by Professor
Geyl.

and Portuguese ships. But the dominating factor which brought the Portuguese control of the Indian trade to an end was the loss of their supremacy in the eastern seas, an event which was precipitated by the Armada disaster in which the fleet of Portugal was involved. That supremacy had been established by force, the only right then recognized in practice throughout India, and it had been acknowledged in virtue of the Papal mandate by Latin Christendom, a view which was not shared by the Dutch and the English, who appeared at the beginning of the seventeenth century.

Affonsa da Sousa, in himself a worthless governor, is, however, to be credited with bringing out to Goa in 1542 the Jesuit, Francis Xavier, one of the first members of the Society. After ten years of devoted and self-sacrificing missionary work in India and the Far East, this great saint died off the coast of China in 1552 and was buried in Goa under a magnificent shrine. The relics of St. Francis Xavier are exposed still for veneration at stated periods, and are visited by crowds of Hindus as well as Christians.

The viceroyalty of da Sousa is also marked by the arrival in India in 1553 of the most famous figure in Portuguese literature, Luis Vaz de Camoens, author of *The Lusiads*. Camoens, who was of the same stock as Vasco da Gama, had been banished to India as a soldier in the ranks for wounding an officer of the court, and is said to have played a conspicuous part in the conquest of the Alagada islands.

In the middle of the sixteenth century the Indian viceroyalty extended over Mozambique, Ormuz, Muscat, Ceylon and Malacca each under a governor. The headquarters of the Viceroy were at Goa and he exercised supreme control over the civil, naval and military administrations, assisted by the Council of State and the Council of the Three Estates.

After the death of King John III of Portugal in 1557, the Portuguese power in Europe and in the East began to weaken. But Portuguese prestige in India was restored for a time by Dom Luiz de Atayde, who was Viceroy from 1568 to 1571. By his splendid courage, his unswerving devotion to duty and his skill as a commander he crushed the formidable confederacy which the kings of Ahmadnagar and Bijapur and the zamorin of Calicut had made to overwhelm the Portuguese settlements by land. But the destruction of Vijayanagar in 1565 and the consequent extinction of a flourishing trade connection was a blow to the prosperity of Goa from which the Portuguese could not possibly recover. This carries the history of the Portuguese in India to 1573, when friendly negotiations were begun between the Viceroy and the Emperor Akbar.

The history of the kingdoms then existing in India has now been brought, with one notable exception, up to their contact with the descendants of Babur, known as the Timurid dynasty. That exception is the kingdom of Delhi.

After the death of Firoz the provincial governors threw off their allegiance to Delhi. The Hindu population ceased *Kingdom of Delhi.* paying the *jizya* and began to rise against Muhammadan rule, and rebellion was rampant by 1394 in Koil, Etawah and Kanauj. The eunuch Malik Sarvar restored order, occupied Jaunpur and then declared his independence as King of the East.

Within ten years five kings, the grandsons and the youngest son of Firoz, followed one another on the throne of Delhi like transient and embarrassed phantoms.

The state of the country was an open invitation to an invader. *Invasion of Timur.* In the days of Firoz a united kingdom and a formidable army had warded off the threatened Mongol inroad of 1379. But when Pir Muhammad, grandson of Timur the Conqueror, led the advance guard of the coming invasion across the Indus at the end of 1397, all possible hope of external defence had vanished with all expectation of internal security. The fief-holders of the north-west, dissipating their forces by fighting amongst themselves, offered little resistance, and in May 1398 Pir Muhammad occupied Multan.

The kingdom of Delhi was equally powerless under its puppet King Nasir-ud-din Mahmud, grandson of Firoz, and his mayor of the palace Mallu. Four years earlier Mahmud's dominion had been bounded by the walls of his capital while his cousin the usurper

Nusrat Shah (by this time a refugee in the Doab) ruled at Firozabad over the surrounding country at the bidding of his ministers.

Timur, whose conquests were almost as unbounded as his appalling ferocity, left Samarkand in April 1398 with a force of about 90,000 cavalry, passed through Kabul in the middle of August and crossed the Indus towards the end of September. The pretext for the invasion of India had been the toleration of its Moslem rulers towards Hinduism, for Timur was a Barlas Turk and an ardent upholder of Islam. The stimulus had been the negation of government amounting to the disarmament of the kingdom following upon the death of Firoz. But the real object of the expedition was plunder.

Desolation and ruin and the piled-up corpses of unnumbered thousands of Hindus marked the advance of the conqueror, and on 7th December Timur's army encamped close to the famous Ridge overlooking Delhi. Three days later Mallu made an ineffective sortie from the city and Timur responded by massacring 100,000 adult male Hindu prisoners of war.

On the 17th of December Timur crossed the Jumna and, under the walls of Delhi, met the forces which Mahmud and Mallu had with difficulty collected. The King of Delhi's army, consisting of 10,000 cavalry, 120 armour-plated elephants carrying grenadiers and archers, and 40,000 infantry, was heavily outnumbered. Timur's dispositions to deal with the elephants were a screened trench, a line of hobbled buffaloes and the use of calthrops, and these proved entirely effective. The issue was never in doubt. The Indian attack upon the invaders' right wing was outflanked and repulsed, while Timur's advance on the opposite flank was completely successful and Mahmud's army was routed.

The defeated king found a humiliating refuge in Gujerat with Zafar Khan, the son of a Rajput convert to Islam who had renounced his allegiance to Mahmud two years earlier. The conqueror entered Delhi and after an illusory amnesty won by the entreaties of the *mullahs* the capital was given up to wholesale sack and a general massacre which lasted five days. Only the quarter occupied by the chief representatives of the Moslem religion was spared, and the spoils of precious stones, gold and silver were enormous.

Meerut was stormed early in January 1399, and by the end of February the fury of destruction and orgy of slaughter had swept over Hardwar, Kangra and Jammu. Timur recrossed the Indus on the 19th of March, and retired up the Tochi Valley from the country which he had plunged into the most fearful depths of misery, desolation, famine and pestilence. He has been described by a master hand as "an old white-haired cripple from the Far East, an intellectual specialist in chess, theology and conquests, and perhaps the greatest artist in destruction known in the savage annals of mankind." [1]

The rightful King Mahmud was still a fugitive and Nusrat Shah, emerging from his hiding-place in the Doab, set himself up in Delhi, that city of the dead where for two whole months "not a bird moved wing." But Nusrat's reign was shortlived. Mallu raised an army among the Hindus of the Doab and by the spring of 1401 had expelled the usurper from Delhi and forced the turbulent Hindus of Etawah to submit and pay tribute. He then persuaded Mahmud Shah who was living in Malwa to return and take up his position as nominal head of what remained of the kingdom of Delhi.

For the next four years Mallu, the real ruler of the kingdom, made attempts to recover complete authority over *End of the Tughlak Dynasty.* Kanauj, Gwalior and Etawah, but without conspicuous success. In November 1405 he was killed in action against Khizr Khan, known as the Sayyid,[2] whom Timur had made his viceroy over the Punjab and Upper Sind. Mahmud lived until February 1413, while the government was carried on by a group of nobles headed by Daulat Khan Lodi. The last of the Tughlaks had reigned in name for twenty years while the kingdom had shrunk to the confines of Rohtak, Sambhal and the Doab, and Northern India had suffered one of the most terrible invasions known in history. Daulat Khan ruled on until the end of May 1414, when Khizr Khan ended a victorious campaign in the Doab by seizing

[1] H. A. L. Fisher, *A History of Europe*—published in 1935.
[2] Sayyids are descendants of the Prophet; and it is extremely doubtful if Khizr Khan had a claim to the title by which he and his descendants are generally known. Al-Badaoni's " proofs " are exceedingly flimsy and Firishta thought very little of " his pretensions."

the capital and setting up Sayyid rule in Delhi nominally at the outset as Timur's viceroy.

Khizr Khan and his three descendants kept their hold on the kingdom for thirty-seven years. The founder of the Sayyid line was a man of energy and decision, and his son Mubarak Shah who succeeded him in 1421 could rouse himself to vigorous action in a crisis. But the last kings of the dynasty were feeble and vacillating. Khizr Khan Murbarak had been obliged to make frequent expeditions to recover arrears of tribute from the Hindu States of Katehr and Gwalior and from Mewat,[1] which was under Moslem government. But the reign of Murbarak's worthless nephew, Muhammad Shah, saw Gwalior and the Doab renounce the authority of Delhi; the army of Jaunpur annex parts of the kingdom, and the Mewati tribesmen raid almost to the city walls; while coming events were foreshadowed by the growing power throughout the Punjab of the Governor of Sirhind, Malik Buhlul Lodi, who ceased to remit the revenue due to the royal treasury.

In 1451, seven years after his succession, the contemptible and self-indulgent Alam Shah abdicated in favour of Buhlul; and the Sayyid line ended with a pleasure-seeking pensioner living in retirement at Budaun.

The Lodi family were Khaljis of Turkish origin who had long *Buhlul Lodi.* been settled in Afghanistan, and Buhlul, when he came with his bluff Afghan kinsmen to the effete court of Delhi, founded the line of Pathan (or Afghan) kings. Under the feeble government of the last of the Sayyids the kingdom had dwindled to no more than the city and its surrounding villages, and the Afghan soldier, shrewd, resolute and energetic, was the very man to re-establish the almost forgotten authority of Delhi.

The most pressing danger was the aggressive state of Jaunpur, and the new king at once took measures to retrieve the critical situation which faced him at his accession. He detached the fiefholders of the Doab and the State of Etawah from their allegiance to Hussain, King of Jaunpur; and then engaged in an intermittent

[1] An ill-defined tract south of Delhi.

war with his rival which went on for a quarter of a century with varied fortune until 1479, when Hussain was decisively defeated and Jaunpur was taken.

Jaunpur had been ruled for eighty-five years by its Sharqi kings, a line which was probably of negro blood.[1] Founded *Conquest of* in 1394 by Kvaja Jahan, minister of Nasir-ud-din *Jaunpur.* Mahmud of Delhi, the succession was continued by his adopted family. The outstanding features of Sharqi rule were an aggressive foreign policy which although at first successful ultimately led to the downfall of the State, and the magnificent buildings with which they enriched their kingdom. Ibrahim, the third of the line and a great patron of art and learning, by completing the Atala Devi mosque at Jaunpur in 1408 raised a fabric whose immense façade rivals the great propylons of an Egyptian temple. His two successors continued to build splendid mosques which stand to this day, but the beautiful palaces which had been built at Jaunpur were destroyed by Barbak, Buhlul's son, when he was made king of the conquered state in 1486.

After the conquest of Jaunpur Buhlul exacted the submission of the Raja of Dholpur, the Moslem Governor of Bari, and the Raja of Gwalior, and then suddenly falling ill died in July 1489. He was succeeded by his son Sikandar Shah, Barbak's younger brother.

Sikandar was a resolute and able ruler. When he came to the throne he reorganized the administration of the *Sikandar Shah.* provinces and, while instantly repressing rebellion whenever it arose, dealt leniently with the defeated rebels, who included his elder brother Barbak. But Jaunpur continued to be a thorn in his side. The Hindu landholders revolted and raised an army of 100,000 men, Barbak once more proved seditious and intrigued both with the rebels and with the deposed Sharqi King Hussain; and Sikandar was obliged to expel his brother from Jaunpur and annex the State to the kingdom of Delhi.

The king never let slip an opportunity to add to his dominions either by skilful diplomacy or by force of arms, and his kingdom grew until it extended over the Punjab, the Doab, Jaunpur, Oudh,

[1] *Camb. Hist. India,* Vol. III. p. 259.

Bihar, Tirhut and the country between the Sutlej and Bundelkhand. But Sikandar's power was more apparent than real. His hold over the feudatory States, provinces and fiefs was in practice ineffective, and the almost independent local rulers were far from being knit up in one consolidated kingdom.

Buhlul and Sikandar both by inclination and force of circumstances appointed their kinsmen and fellow-countrymen to the chief offices, and the most important posts were in the hands of Afghans, a race that has always been proud, unruly and impatient of authority.

Like his father before him Sikandar never dared to risk his precarious hold on the Punjab by drawing on its resources; had that been possible Hindustan would have been reduced far more quickly than it was. The Lodi kings contented themselves with such revenue as the province chose to remit to Delhi.

Sikandar died in November 1517. He was the greatest of the Lodi kings, and the one great blot on the character of a strong and otherwise kindly ruler was the fierce bigotry which led to the wholesale destruction of Hindu temples during his reign. Nor was the period one in which Moslem architecture flourished. Neither the Sayyid nor the Lodi kings had the resources of a great kingdom to enable them to build striking monuments to rival the palace citadel of Firozabad. But while as an innovator Firoz had been the first to incorporate machicolation in Indian fortifications, Sayyid architecture, by the introduction of blue-enamelled tiling and coloured plaster-work, was greatly to influence future decorative art.

After Sikandar's death the Lodi nobles elected his eldest son Ibrahim as king. The succession was disputed but the new king acted with energy, crushed the opposition and in 1518 carried out his father's design and took Gwalior. But his successes in the field were more than outweighed by his insensate acts of capricious tyranny, and this victory was followed by a revolt of the Afghan nobles under Jalal Khan Lodi. The insurrection was suppressed but the general discontent grew stronger and stronger, and Bahadur Khan headed a rising and proclaimed himself King in Bihar.

This was serious enough but events of still greater moment were shaping themselves in the north-west. Daulat Khan Lodi,

PLATE XXI.

(a) ATALA DEVI MOSQUE, JAUNPUR
By permission of the Secretary of State for India in Council

(b) TIMUR
By permission of the Secretary of State for India in Council

PLATE XXII.

THE COURT OF THE EMPEROR BABUR

By permission of the Secretary of State for India in Council

the powerful Governor of Lahore, warned by Ibrahim's tyrannical policy, became convinced that a royal victory over the rebels in Hindustan and Bihar would be followed by a campaign against himself. To meet this danger he not only strengthened his position in the Punjab to the point of virtual independence but he invited Babur, King of Kabul, to come to his help, and so took the first step towards the foundation of the Mogul Empire.

NOTE.—At this point between the incursions of what have been referred to as the Mongols and the establishment of the Mogul Empire an explanation of these two names is necessary. The *Oxford History of India* (1928 impression), footnote to p. 225, gives the following definition : " It is convenient to confine the term Mongol to the heathen followers of Chingiz, who were mostly ' narrow-eyed ' people, reserving the term Mogul in its various spellings for the more civilized tribes, largely of Turki blood, who became Muhammadans in the fourteenth century and from whom sprang the Chagatai . . . section of Turks to which Babur and his successors in India belonged. The Turki races ordinarily resemble Europeans in features and have not the Mongolian ' narrow eyes ' strongly marked, but Turks and Mongols intermarried freely and the Mongol blood often asserted itself. It shows in the portraits of Akbar."

CHRONOLOGY

1336. Vijayanagar city built by Vira Ballala III Hoysala.
1342. Death of Vira Ballala III.
1347. Bahman Shah established Bahmani kingdom of the Deccan.
1356. Bengal recognized as independent by Delhi sultanate.
1358. Bukha I, ruler of Vijayanagar kingdom.
1358–1377. Muhammad I, King of Deccan.
1360. Wars between Deccan and Vijayanagar began.
1387–1395. Deccan famine.
1394. Disintegration of Delhi kingdom of Firoz Shah Tughlak.
1398–1399. Timur (Tamurlane) invaded Northern India.
1414. Commencement of Sayyid dynasty of Delhi.
1451. Lodi dynasty of Delhi founded by Buhlul.
1463–1481. Mahmud Gavan, chief minister of Deccan.
1481–1518. Break-up of Bahmani kingdom into the five kingdoms of the Deccan.
1489–1517. Sikandar Shah Lodi, extended Delhi sovereignty over Northern India.
1498. Vasco da Gama landed at Calicut.
1510. Portuguese established at Goa.
1517–1526. Ibrahim Lodi, King of Delhi.
[1565. The Moslem States of the Deccan crushed Vijayanagar at Talikota.]

L 161

BIBLIOGRAPHY

Mahomedan Power in India, Muhammad Qasim Firishta, tr. Colonel J. Briggs (London), 1829.

History of India as told by its own Historians, Elliot and Dowson, 1867–77.

Cambridge History of India, Vol. III.

India in the Fifteenth Century, Hakluyt Society (London), 1857.

A Forgotten Empire (Vijayanagar), Sewell, 1904.

Marco Polo's Travels (tr. Sir Henry Yule). Vol. II gives the Venetian traveller's references to India.

(Marco Polo sailed to India from Java about the year 1292 and coasted round the peninsula, touching at the principal ports between Mumpali and Somnath.)

NOTE.—Muhammad Qasim Firishta was born at Astrabad on the Caspian about the year 1570. He came as a boy to Ahmadnagar and went on to the court of Ibrahim Adil Shah II of Bijapur in 1589. There he wrote the great work from which the more modern histories of the period have been compiled, on the growth of Muhammadan power in India up to the year 1612. The history may be said to have been begun in the field when the author, serving with the Bijapur army, was wounded in the 1589 campaign against a usurper of the Ahmadnagar throne. It was first published in its present form under even more difficult conditions, for the original English translation of Firishta, made from the Persian by Lieut.-Colonel John Briggs of the Madras Army, was destroyed when the Peshwa Baji Rao burnt the British Residency in Poona in November 1817. This misfortune adds interest to a footnote in the translation Colonel Briggs eventually published. In comparing the great diamond which fell to Babur after Panipat with other well-known stones, he mentions at the end of the list " the Nassuck diamond which was discovered among the Peshwa's treasures, dug up by the translator of this work, only weighs 89 carats."

CHAPTER VI

Mogul India

INDIA at the time of the Mogul invasion was a country divided against itself. The Khalji empire which the tyrannical folly of Muhammad Tughlak had broken into a number of lesser kingdoms had split up into even smaller States. In the north the Afghan sultanate of Delhi barely cast its shadow beyond the city walls. In Rajputana there was about as much unity as in the Highlands of Scotland at the same period. Far to the south the Hindu king of Vijayanagar was paramount beyond the Kistna River, and a menace to his disunited neighbours of the Deccan.

But while the political state of the country was an open invitation
Hindu Religious Movements. to so daring a soldier of fortune as Babur, there were stirring beneath the surface forces which were to prove in the end too strong for the empire of the Great Moguls. The fires of adversity had brought into greater prominence than ever before the doctrine of the essential unity of God; a doctrine which involves the belief[1] that " every god accepted by Hinduism is elevated and ultimately identified with the central Reality which is one with the deeper self of man. The addition of new gods to the Hindu pantheon does not endanger it." From this doctrine the religious revival known as the *Bhakti* movement was born a century before the coming of Babur. Without such a movement it is highly improbable that either the Marathas or the Sikhs would have formed themselves into the powerful combinations which they afterwards became.[2]

Throughout the ages the leaders of Hindu religious thought

[1] Sir S. Radhakrishnan of Calcutta University (Upton Lectures, Oxford, 1926) in *The Hindu View of Life* (London, 1927), p. 46.
[2] *Mughal Rule in India*, Edwardes and Garrett, p. 2.

and practice have always experimented with new forms as conditions altered. Hinduism has been described as a movement not a position, a process not a result; although its essential ideas have remained unchanged since the time of the Vedas.[1] Contact with the civilized Dravidians of the south transformed Vedism into a theistic religion. The stimulus given by Islam resulted in the new conceptions of the Deity as preached in the fifteenth century to all who would listen through Northern India by Ramananda and his strangely assorted disciples, who included a Rajput, a currier, a barber and the Moslem weaver poet Kabir.[2] Western ideas, which became familiar to the higher castes with the close British connection beginning in the nineteenth century, resulted in a fresh impulse; and this has found expression partly in religious reform and a broader social outlook but more conspicuously in political aspirations.

Babur. Zahir-ud-din Muhammad, surnamed Babur (The Tiger), was born in Ferghana, his father's khanate in the Valley of the Jaxartes now called Khokand, on 14th February 1483. He represented both the Turki and the Mongol races of Tartars and numbered two great conquerors among his ancestors. On his father's side he was in the direct line of Timur, while through his mother he descended from Chingiz Khan.

Almost from the day when Babur succeeded his father in his twelfth year his life was crowded with adventure. He was driven out of Ferghana, tried several times in vain to regain the lost ancestral kingdom of Samarkand and finally, in 1504, when he was twenty-one, he took Kabul and established himself there as king. Fifteen years later he made his first appearance in India and penetrated as far as the River Jhelum. In virtue of the conquest of Hindustan by Timur, Babur looked upon the people of the country as his subjects, exacted tribute, and forbade any ill-treatment and plundering of the

---

[1] For a detailed exposition of this, the Hindu, standpoint see *The Hindu View of Life.*

[2] His works have been translated by Rabindranath Tagore : *One Hundred Poems of Kabir,* Macmillan, 1921.

inhabitants by his soldiers, in striking contrast to the behaviour of his ancestor.

He noted in his diary for 1519 [1] that " the people of Hindustan and particularly the Afghans are a strangely foolish and senseless race, possessed of little reflection and less foresight. They can neither persist in and manfully support a war, nor can they continue in a state of amity and friendship." In a later criticism of the country and its people Babur comments on the absence of ice and baths, and considered the " gang of dirty fellows " with small oil lamps a poor substitute for candles and candlesticks.

Three more incursions into India followed the first, and negotiations were opened with Daulat Khan, Governor of Lahore, who proved as treacherous to Babur as he was to his rightful suzerain, Ibrahim Lodi the King of Delhi. Then on 17th November 1525, " The sun being in the sign of the Archer," Babur led his army of 10,000 cavalry [2] down the Jellalabad road towards Hindustan. When he reached Sialkot he learnt that Daulat Khan, at the head of an army of malcontents, had been defeated by Ibrahim Lodi; and with a well-founded distrust of his so-called ally, Babur secured the Lahore Governor's submission before coming to grips with the King of Delhi. Then Babur "placed his foot in the stirrup of resolution and his hand on the reins of confidence-in-God and marched against Sultan Ibrahim."

On 12th April 1526 Babur's ten thousand faced the hundred thousand men and the hundred elephants of the
Panipat. Afghan army on the plain of Panipat.[3] The enormous disparity in numbers was to an appreciable extent balanced by the Mogul strength in artillery, but Babur's greatest asset may be described in his own words [4] : "Ibrahim was a young man of no experience. He was negligent in all his movements; he marched without order; retired or halted without plan and engaged in battle

[1] *Memoirs of Babur*, written by himself in Turki, 2 vols., tr. Leyden and Erskine.
[2] Firishta, Vol. II. p. 41. Babur gives 12,000 as the total, including merchants and followers (*Memoirs*, Vol. II. p. 194).
[3] Firishta, Vol. II. p. 44.
[4] *Memoirs of Babur*, Vol. II. pp. 181–188, describing the battle.

without foresight; . . . and was too miserly to raise additional forces, or even to pay his troops in the field."

Babur's tactics were those of the Ottoman Turks, then the leading military power; a strong holding position—which he had been given ample time to prepare—coupled with turning movements in force. His right rested on the town of Panipat, his left flank was defended by ditches and abattis. Wagons and fascine breastworks extended along the whole front, with occasional gaps through which a cavalry squadron could charge. At dawn on 21st April Ibrahim's forces advanced in mass to the attack. Met by volleys of arrows, heavy musketry and well-directed artillery fire they wavered, and Babur sent his cavalry reserves round the flanks to take the enemy in rear, while his whole line was ordered to advance. "The sun had mounted spear-high when the onset of battle began, and the combat lasted till midday, when the enemy was completely broken and routed. By the grace and mercy of Almighty God this mighty army in the space of half a day was laid in the dust." Sixteen thousand of the Afghan army were killed in action according to Firishta, and five thousand men lay dead round Ibrahim Lodi. By launching his cavalry in instant pursuit, Babur gave the beaten army no opportunity to rally.

Babur followed up his victory by the immediate despatch of a flying column to occupy Agra, while he settled the civil and military administration of Delhi and took over the treasury. Before he entered Agra, which was to be the new capital, in triumph early in May he spent a few quiet days visiting the tombs, palaces and gardens in and around Delhi.

With the great cities of Delhi and Agra in the victor's hands the Afghan dynasty was at an end, but Mogul rule in Northern India was still far from secure, and Babur was confronted with a danger from within which threatened the utter ruin of his whole enterprise. The fierce heat of an Indian May was taking heavy toll among the ranks of an army drawn from the uplands of the north, and while the generals made outspoken protests to their leader, the men began openly to prepare to go back to Kabul. It was the first chapter of Alexander's retreat over again, but the story had a different ending. Babur viewed the crisis as flat mutiny, but the address he made to his officers restored the lost morale of his army, while those who still wished to return home were allowed to go and were treated by the king with great generosity.

It was now possible to deal with the external problems. The great Afghan fief-holders were naturally hostile to the prospect of Mogul rule, but Babur gradually induced the majority to make their submission by a characteristic display of clemency and tact.

An even greater danger threatened from the Hindu confederacy, *The Hindu Challenge.* headed by the gallant veteran Rana Sangrama Singh of Mewar, one of the greatest of the princes of Chitor, the conqueror of Mahmud II of Malwa, and a far more formidable opponent than Ibrahim Lodi. Sangrama, in his bid to restore Hindu rule in Northern India and win an empire for himself, took the field with seven great rajas, a hundred and thirteen lesser chiefs, 80,000 horse and 500 war elephants.[1] Early in February 1527 Babur marched to meet him with his heavily outnumbered force. The odds against them greatly disheartened the Mogul troops, but Babur rose to the emergency with his unfailing courage. After pledging himself to renounce the wine " to which he had been formerly much addicted," he made so stirring an appeal to his army that they all took oath after him on the Koran " that none will even think of turning his face from this warfare nor desert from the battle, till his soul is separated from his body."

The armies met at Khanua, near Sikri, on 16th March 1527,[2] and once more the fate of Northern India hung in the balance. The battle was won by the devastating effect of the Mogul guns, and the Rajput confederacy was completely routed. Sangrama got back to his own country, bent on raising another army, to be poisoned by his own ministers. The military power of the Rajputs was broken and Babur, advancing into the country, took the stronghold

[1] *Annals and Antiquities of Rajasthan*, Lieut.-Colonel James Tod (Oxford), ed. 1920, I. 348.
[2] *Memoirs of Babur*, Vol. II. p. 204.

of Chandari in spite of its obstinate defence. The next two years were spent in securing the eastern border by operations against the Afghan rulers of Bihar and Bengal.

Babur had established an empire stretching from the Oxus to the Bengal frontier and from the foot of the Himalaya to Gwalior. But he did not live to conquer Bengal, Gujerat or the Deccan.

Babur died on 24th December [1] 1530. He was not quite forty-seven, but his hard life and the Indian climate had sapped the constitution of the man of tireless energy who insisted on swimming every river he saw.

The story of his death, as told by his daughter Gul-badan Begam —Princess Rose-body—is well known.[2] His son Humayun was dangerously ill, and Babur decided to save him by the Eastern rite of " circumambulation," which is still used in Persia. The efficacy of the rite depends upon the offering of the most treasured possession, and Babur swept aside the suggestion that he should sacrifice the great diamond which Nadir Shah first called the Koh-i-noor, the " mountain of light." Walking round his son's sick-bed he prayed : " O God! If a life may be exchanged for a life, I who am Babur give my life and my being for Humayun." His prayer was answered. Humayun at once recovered, and three months later all that was mortal of Zahir-ud-din Muhammad Babur was carried to Kabul to be buried in the garden he loved.

Babur from a homeless wanderer rose to be the ruler of an empire entirely by the force of his personality, his *Babur's Character.* dauntless courage and the cheerfulness with which he shared the hardships of his men. He never commanded a great army in the field, but his campaigns invariably showed sound tactics and inspiring leadership.

In the wide range of his interests he was an unusual type of soldier. In Persian he was an accomplished poet, in his native

[1] Firishta, Vol. II. p. 64. *The History of Humayun* gives 26th December as the day of Babur's death, but the authoress was seven at the time and wrote her history in the reign of Akbar.

[2] *The History of Humayun,* tr. by Annette Beveridge.

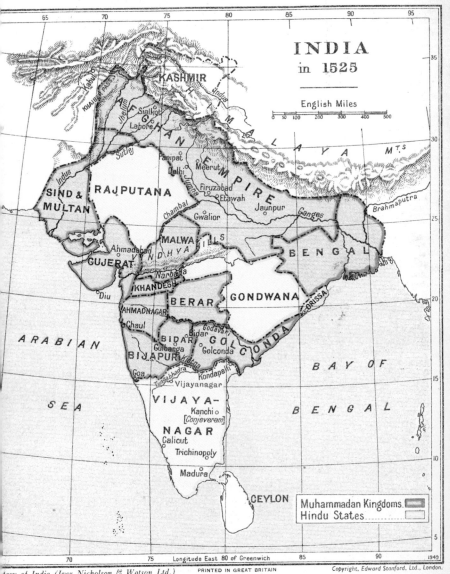

INDIA
in 1525

English Miles

0 50 100   200   300   400   500

KASHMIR

KHYBER PASS

Kabul

AFGHAN

Sialkot
Jhelum
Lahore

HIMALAYA MTS.

Indus

Sutlej

Panipat
Delhi
Meerut
Firuzabad
Etawah
Jumna
Jaunpur

E M P I R E

SIND &
MULTAN

RAJPUTANA

Chambal

Gwalior

Ganges

Brahmaputra

MALWA

HILLS

BENGAL

Ahmadabad

VINDHYA

GUJERAT

Narbada

Diu

KHANDESH

BERAR

GONDWANA

AHMADNAGAR

Chaul

Godavari

ORISSA

BIDAR

Bidar

GOLC

Gulbarga

Golconda

BIJAPUR

Kistna

O N D A

A R A B I A N

Goa

Tungabhadra

Kondapali

Vijayanagar

B A Y   O F

VIJAYA-

Kanchi
[Conjeveram]

Calicut

S E A

Trichinopoly

B E N G A L

NAGAR

Madura

CEYLON

Muhammadan Kingdoms
Hindu States

35

30

25

20

15

10

5

65   70   75   80   85   90   95

70   75   Longitude East 80 of Greenwich   85   90

1949

tory of India (Ivor Nicholson & Watson Ltd.)   PRINTED IN GREAT BRITAIN   Copyright, Edward Stanford, Ltd., London.

Turki he was master of an admirable style, and he was an excellent musician; as an athlete he could take a man under each arm and leap along the ramparts from one pointed pinnacle to another; he was a keen big-game hunter and he excelled as a swordsman and with the bow; his *Memoirs* show him equally happy securing a new plant for his garden, or composing a set of verses in the stress of a campaign, for he wrote his elegies himself. Before Khanua he renounced wine and he kept his pledge; but in earlier days, "when he was inclined to make merry, he used to fill a garden reservoir with wine, upon which was inscribed the well-known verse:

> " Give me but wine and blooming maids,
>   All other joys I freely spurn:
> Enjoy them, Babur, while you may—
>   For youth once past will ne'er return."

But as he grew older the opium habit, which he had acquired under the stress of his early hardships, became stronger; and before his death its enervating effect was beginning to tell upon him.

Judged by the standard of the times in which he lived, Babur was not cruel, and his children were devoted to him. Unless a place refused to surrender and stood the assault, he neither put the garrison to the sword nor sacked the town and enslaved the inhabitants; and if he inflicted a terrible punishment on those convicted in the plot to poison him, it is well to remember the atrocities in the name of justice then prevalent in Europe. On the other hand he pardoned ingratitude and treason again and again, and he carried his liberality to such an excess in his everyday life that it bordered on prodigality. Babur was an ardent Moslem, he looked upon fighting the Hindus as a " holy war," and he never omitted his daily prayers.

Firishta describes Babur as " handsome in his person, his address engaging and unaffected, his countenance pleasing and his disposition affable." The miniature in the British Museum gives an irresistible impression of bubbling wit and great good humour. His own *Memoirs* are full of character-sketches of his acquaintances, such as the description " an extremely witty and jocose man, but fearless in debauchery," while Babur reveals himself in his own pages as a Prince Hal who could turn in a moment from his boon companions to the affairs of the kingdom which he governed with wisdom, justice and mercy.

With the coming of Babur, India stood in the dawn of a new era. The Maurya government of Asoka had been guided by religious principles. The rule of the Sultans of Delhi had been definitely influenced by the religious leaders of Islam, who came first in the precedence of the court. In Europe the first half of the sixteenth century saw the break-up of the unity of Christendom in the Protestant Reformation and the great political reactions which followed. In India there arose the frankly secular rule of the Moguls. The new empire was of course Moslem, and on friendly terms with the Islamic rulers of Persia and Ottoman Turkey. But it was truly Indian as well, and during the reigns of Babur's earlier successors Muhammadans and Rajputs and other Hindu elements were drawn more closely together as a result of the sympathetic study of the learning, history and tradition of Hinduism.[1]

Babur left four sons. The eldest, Kamran, was Governor of Kabul and Kandahar, while the second son Humayun, in accordance with his father's wishes, became Emperor of the Mogul conquests in Upper India and the plains of the Ganges.

But Humayun's position was insecure. Bengal was unconquered; Bahadur Shah, the powerful Afghan King of Gujerat and Malwa, was actively hostile; and Humayun's brothers were openly disloyal; while the intrigues of the Portuguese, now masters of the western seaboard, created a disturbing influence.

The first of Humayun's difficulties came from Kamran, who forced the Emperor to transfer the Punjab to him, under a nominal suzerainty. This meant a serious loss, both in revenue and in men, to the imperial government, and at the same time Humayun was cut off from the Mogul recruiting grounds beyond the Indian frontier on which Babur had relied.

The reign, however, began auspiciously. Muhammad Lodi was expelled from Jaunpur, and with him the Lodi dynasty ceased to

[1] A. Yusuf Ali, *The Making of India* (London), 1925, Ch. IX.

exist as a ruling family. Bahadur Shah was thoroughly beaten at the battle of Mandsur in 1535. Mandu, the capital of Malwa, was occupied, the great fortress of Champaner was taken by escalade, in which Humayun greatly distinguished himself, and Gujerat was in the Emperor's hands.

These successes were, however, counterbalanced by the serious situation which had in the meantime arisen elsewhere. Humayun's younger brother Askari, at the head of part of the army, had raised a rebellion, Bahadur Shah was collecting fresh forces and, most dangerous of all, Sher Khan Sur,[1] the Afghan ruler of Bihar, was a formidable and threatening neighbour.

Humayun now betrayed the weakness and indecision of the opium addict,[2] which was to lead to disaster. After long hesitation he moved out from Gujerat and defeated the rebels near Lucknow. But he had still to reckon with Sher Khan. Hostilities broke out almost immediately and a series of indecisive operations followed. In 1538 Humayun invaded Bengal, recovered the province of Gaur which Sher Khan had occupied, and then relapsed into disastrous inactivity. His forces were dwindling from sickness and desertion and, as Firishta points out, the Emperor should have forced an action with Sher Khan at all hazards. But he allowed his enemy to reconquer the country and finally, with supplies running out and the rising floods of the rainy season endangering the line of communications, the Mogul army was obliged to retreat. At this juncture Humayun's younger brother Mirza Hindal raised a rebellion at Agra and proclaimed himself emperor, to be crushed immediately by Kamran, who, however, refused to send any reinforcements to the hard-pressed Humayun.

Assailed by flagrant disloyalty at home, by treachery and desertion in the field and with an active enemy pressing upon his retirement, Humayun opened negotiations with Sher Khan. According to Firishta, terms of peace, giving Sher Khan Bengal and Bihar on

[1] " Lion Lord " (of the) Sur (family) ; a title of honour conferred on Farid Sur, when an official in Bihar, for killing a tiger with one stroke of his sword in the presence of his master Muhammad Shah, and whose son he ousted from the throne (Firishta, Vol. II. pp. 98–109).

[2] Firishta, Vol. II. p. 83.

payment of a nominal tribute, had already been signed when the Afghan army, in the early morning of a day in June 1539, attacked Humayun's forces at Chausa. Taken completely by surprise and with the Ganges behind them, the Mogul troops were cut to pieces. Humayun, with the utmost difficulty, escaped to Agra, where he tried in vain to enlist the active help of his brothers in the face of a common danger, and raised fresh forces which were more a rabble than an army.

Sher Khan proclaimed himself emperor, and formed an alliance with Gujerat and Malwa to enforce his title. Humayun, abandoned by Kamran, marched with 100,000 mounted levies to meet the pretender's army of 50,000 men. His troops deserted in thousands, he was out-generalled by Sher Khan, who once more made his opponent fight with the Ganges behind him, and on 17th May 1540, near Kanauj, Humayun was completely defeated. This time the result was decisive. For the next fifteen years Humayun was a wanderer and an exile, flying from Sind to Marwar, from Marwar to Persia, before he established himself in Afghanistan, while Sher Shah, as he was now known, reigned in his stead.

From 1540 until 1545 Sher Shah ruled the empire. After the *Sher Shah.* decisive defeat of the imperial army and the pursuit of Humayun towards the Indus, Sher Shah secured the submission of the Punjab. Next he strengthened his hold on Bengal by reorganizing the fiefs and by the judicious appointment of Qazi Fazilat as Governor in the place of Khizr Khan, who had made an unsuccessful attempt to assert his independence.

Sher Shah then decided to subdue the Rajput chiefs, and invaded *Campaigns.* Malwa in 1542, the year in which his forces took Multan and reduced the surrounding districts. The Rajput war was a hard-fought struggle, in which Sher Shah met with only partial success, while he disgraced his arms by the treacherous massacre of the garrison of Raisin. In the end, however, Chitor surrendered and Sher Shah laid siege to Kalanjur, where he was fatally injured by the explosion of a field magazine, and died on 22nd May 1545.

Sher Shah was more than a successful soldier; he was a statesman
who introduced a number of admirable reforms.
Sher Shah's Reforms. Exclusive of Bengal, the realm was divided into
forty-seven [1] administrative units of manageable
size, and the principles of land survey and revenue then laid down
were elaborated during the reign of Akbar. Sher Shah also fixed
the standard of the rupee at 178 grains, a standard which was maintained by the Mogul emperors who followed him and which approxi-
mates to the present British India rupee of 180 grains.[2] A further
reform was in the judicial system, and Firishta records [3] : " Such
was the public security during his reign that travellers and merchants,
depositing their property on the roadside, lay down to sleep without
apprehension of robbery."

Considering the shortness of his reign, Sher Shah's record in the
construction of public works is remarkable. From Bengal to the
Indus, along two thousand miles of road, rest-houses were built
every mile and a half, a succession of wells were dug and lines
of fruit trees planted by the roadside. Horse posts were established to quicken the government postal service and for the use
of merchants and others. Similar arrangements were made from
Agra, the capital, to Manda. Sher Shah also built a number of
mosques.

According to Abu-l-Fazl, the far from impartial author of the
Akbar-nama, Sher Shah " surpassed even his father in wickedness "
and was " a tyrannical mischief-maker." Hasan Khan was certainly
anything but a good husband or parent, and Farid (as he then was
known) left his home to enlist as a private soldier in the service of
the Governor of Jaunpur. Here he educated himself, especially in
history and poetry, and learnt the entire works of the poet Sa'di by
heart. But he ruled the family fief, when it was entrusted to him,
by doing justice to the poor, by seeing that the strong did not
infringe the laws with impunity, and greatly increased the prosperity
of the people.

On his record Sher Shah was a wise and just ruler, lenient to

[1] *Akbar-nama*, Vol. I. p. 399.
[2] *The Making of India*, p. 103.
[3] Vol. II. p. 125.

his enemies, and one of the few occasions on which he showed the savage cruelty of his race was at Raisin. Firishta tells a story which may be taken to illustrate his ideals. " On being told that his beard grew white," Sher Shah replied: " It was true that he obtained the throne in the evening of life; a circumstance he always regretted, as it left him so short a time to be of use to his country and to promote the welfare of his people."

Sher Shah was followed by his second son Islam (Salim) Shah, a weak and unworthy successor. He died in 1553 and was succeeded by his young son Firoz, who was assassinated after a reign of three days. His murderer, Mubariz Khan, who was his cousin, and uncle by marriage, then seized the throne, assuming the title of Muhammad Adil Shah. The new king was completely illiterate, wantonly extravagant and an offence to the Afghan nobility; and the country under the misgovernment of his Hindu minister Hemu rapidly lapsed into anarchy. Muhammad Shah with his highly unpopular minister soon fled to Chunar. Sikandar Sur, a grandson of Sher Shah, rising to power in the midst of civil war, persuaded the Afghan nobles to elect him as king. But his reign was brief. The chiefs quarrelled violently over the distribution of honours, the state of the country became even more chaotic, and Humayun seized the opportunity to regain his lost empire.

End of the Sur Dynasty.

Humayun's wanderings had begun with an attempt to take Bakar and the terrible hardships in the Sind desert which followed his repulse. Most of his men deserted him but he was rejoined by the Turkoman Bairam Khan, who lived to play a prominent part in Humayun's restoration and was tutor to his great successor. For a time Humayun took refuge with the Raja of Umarkot, and here, in the cold weather of 1542,[1] his Queen Hamidabanu gave birth to Akbar. Afghanistan with the treacherous Kamran on the throne proved too dangerous,

Humayun's Exile.

---

[1] Firishta gives 14th October, the date recorded by Gul-badan Begam in the *Humayun-nama* ; Abu-l-Fazl, a contemporary, gives 15th October in his *Akbar-nama*.

and the fugitive at last found sanctuary at the hospitable court of Tahmasp, Shah of Persia.

This was the turning-point in Humayun's fortunes. In 1544 Tahmasp gave the exiled Emperor an army to invade Afghanistan and Humayun captured Kandahar and Kabul, where he found Hamida and his little son whom his brother had taken from him. At the end of protracted fighting Kamran and Askari, the two brothers who had shown him persistent hostility, were sent to Mecca, Kamran, the main cause of his troubles, being blinded before he went, and Humayun ruled in Kabul.

In December 1554 Humayun with 15,000 cavalry and Bairam Khan as his principal general left Kabul to invade India. Lahore and the Sirhind district were occupied without opposition. Continuing the advance Bairam Khan surprised the Punjab army of 30,000 men under Tatar Khan in a night attack on the Sutlej and routed it. Sikandar Khan advanced to meet the invaders with 80,000 cavalry, great strength in artillery and a number of elephants. Humayun came down from Lahore, joined forces with Bairam Khan and on the 18th June 1555 completely defeated the Afghan army at Macchiwari. Sikandar escaped to the Punjab, where he could raise new forces; and Humayun entered Delhi as Emperor.

Akbar was made nominal Governor of the Punjab with Bairam Khan as his adviser, and active operations were begun against Sikandar. But before these could be brought to a successful conclusion Humayun fatally injured himself by falling on the steps of the Sher Mandal palace, and died in January [1] 1556, at the age of fifty-one.

---

[1] The day of the month is uncertain. According to the *Tabakat-i-Akbar* of Nizam-ud-din Ahmad the date is 17th January, the *Akbar-nama* gives the 24th, and the *Badshah-nama* of Abdul Hamid 26th January. Concealing the king's death for purposes of policy, which appears to have been done, had a precedent in the case of Babur.

CHRONOLOGY

1519. Babur's first incursion into India.

1526. 21st April. Babur defeated Ibrahim Lodi at Panipat; Delhi and Agra occupied: Mogul dynasty founded.

1527. 16th March. Babur defeated Sangrama Singh at Khanua. Moslem supremacy assured.

1528–1530. Babur's sovereignty extended from Oxus to Bengal frontier, and from the Himalaya to Gwalior.

1530. December. Death of Babur, accession of Humayun.

1535. Humayun's conquests of Jaunpur, Malwa and Gujerat.

1540. 17th May. Decisive defeat of Humayun near Kanauj by Sher Shah of Bihar.

Humayun an exile.

Sher Shah ruler of Northern India.

1545. Death of Sher Shah; succession of weak Sur kings.

1555. Humayun by his victory at Machhiwari (18th June) over Sikandar Sur regained his kingdom.

1556. January. Death of Humayun.

BIBLIOGRAPHY

Rise of Mahomedan Power in India, Firishta, tr. Colonel J. Briggs (London), 1829, Vol. II.

Mughal Rule in India, Edwardes and Garrett, 1930.

Memoirs of Babur, written by himself, tr. Leyden and Erskine (Oxford University Press), 1921.

History of Humayun, by Princess Gul-badan, tr. Annette Beveridge (Royal Asiatic Society's Oriental Trans. Fund), 1902.

History of India as told by its own Historians, Elliot and Dowson, 8 vols. (1867–1877). A valuable source of reference, especially for the Mogul Period.

PLATE XXIII.

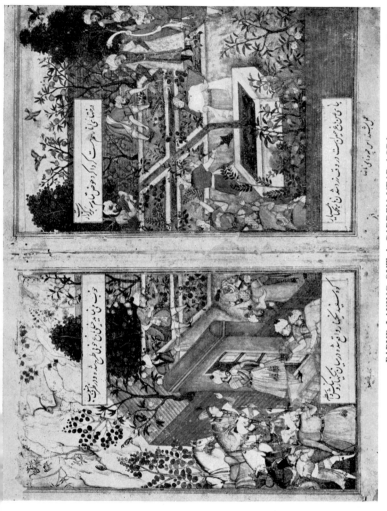

BABUR LAYING OUT A GARDEN NEAR AGRA
Painted by Bishandas and Nanda
By courtesy of Indian Museum, South Kensington

PLATE XXIV.

ILLUSTRATION FROM A MS. BOOK
Mogul School of Humayun, sixteenth century
By courtesy of Indian Museum, South Kensington

CHAPTER VII

Akbar

THE news of Humayun's death reached Akbar at Kalanaur in the midst of the campaign against Sikandar, and Bairam Khan lost no time in having the new emperor proclaimed at Delhi and formally enthroned at Kalanaur on the 14th or 15th February [1] 1556. Akbar was then three months short of fourteen years of age.

His reign consists of three periods. The first, from his accession to the fall of the Regent Bairam Khan in 1560; the second, the short phase of harem government and unscrupulous ministers; and the final stage, from 1562 onwards, when he established himself as the first truly national ruler of India since the days of Asoka, and one of the greatest sovereigns in history.

The entire civil and military power was vested in Bairam Khan *Situation at* and his position was an unenviable one. On all *Akbar's* sides the situation seemed pregnant with disaster. *Accession.* Sikandar, still powerful in the Punjab, only awaited an opportunity to regain his throne; nor was he the only member of the Sur dynasty in the field. Muhammad Adil Shah ruled in Chunar, and his Hindu minister Hemu was at the head of a huge force that had been raised to oppose Humayun, and in a career of victory had already defeated his master's rival and cousin Ibrahim Sur. The Moguls were in the midst of a hostile population and in a country ravaged with famine. Akbar's natural refuge in the event of defeat was Afghanistan, which was, however, practically independent, and where the regent to the Emperor's younger brother Hakim Mirza was struggling with open rebellion.

[1] Abu-l-Fazl explains why the 15th and not 14th should be the date (*Akbarnama*, Vol. II. p. 5, and see footnote). But most authorities give the 14th.

The Mogul army in the Punjab succeeded in defeating Sikandar Sur, who was driven into the hills, Nagarkot was subdued, and friendly relations were established with Dharmchand, the local raja.

Hemu now assumed the offensive, Agra was taken and Delhi was lost to Akbar by the cowardly incompetence of its Governor Tardi Beg Khan, who was subsequently executed by the regent's orders as a salutary example to others. Hemu, the Marwari merchant-minister, confident of victory and resolving to win the empire for himself as Maharaja Vikramaditya, advanced with 100,000 men to crush the Moguls. Akbar's forces barely numbered 20,000 and his nobles urged a retreat to Kabul. But the young Emperor vigorously supported Bairam Khan in his determination not to abandon India without a struggle, and the little Mogul army marched down from Jullundur to give battle.

At the first contact Hemu lost all his artillery in an advance-guard action, and on the 5th November 1556 the main bodies of the two armies met on the field of Panipat. The weight of numbers told heavily, the Mogul right and left wings were thrown into confusion, and Hemu led his elephants in a charge upon the centre. But with victory apparently within his grasp an arrow struck the Hindu commander in the eye and made him temporarily unconscious. The Afghan army, believing their leader to be dead, broke and fled in all directions hotly pursued by the Mogul troops. Hemu was captured and, on Bairam's advice, killed by Akbar; fifteen hundred elephants and an immense treasure were taken; Delhi was entered in triumph the following day and Agra was soon afterwards occupied. The victory was decisive and it only remained to deal with the less formidable rivals to the throne.

Panipat.

The Mogul army returned to the Punjab and Sikandar was besieged in the fortress of Mankot, which surrendered in July 1557 after holding out for six months. Sikandar was allowed to retire to Bengal, where he lived quietly upon his *jagirs* until his death two years later; Ibrahim Sur resigned himself to the inevitable situation and took refuge with the Raja of Jagannath; while Adil was killed fighting in Bengal.

Akbar had already conferred upon Bairam Khan the title of Khan Khanan (noble of nobles), which carried with it precedence immmediately below princes of the blood, and the regent, now married to the Emperor's niece Salima Sultan Begam, was by far the most powerful man in the kingdom. The court was established at Agra, and Bairam Khan applied himself to the tasks of administration and the education of his ward. He was more successful in the first of these duties. Between the years 1558 and 1560 the expansion of the empire went on with only one check, the failure to take the Rajput stronghold of Ranthambhor. The occupation of Gwalior established a strong point in Central India, Ajmer in the heart of Rajputana was taken, and the annexation of the province of Jaunpur secured the eastern frontier. The empire of Babur had been largely regained.

Expansion of the Empire.

Meanwhile Akbar continued to be the despair of his tutors. He preferred athletics and the exercise of his remarkable gift of controlling the wild animals he loved to lessons, and he grew up to become a magnificent shot and first-class polo player while apparently unable even to identify the letters of the alphabet. But he was an omnivorous listener and his prodigious memory enabled him to master the immense number of books read aloud to him. At his death he had in his library 24,000 MS. volumes but no printed books.[1]

Akbar's Education.

As a boy his only scholarly interests lay in poetry and art, an amazing side to a youth with a passion for outdoor sport and a strong natural bent for mechanics. One of his tutors (his father tried four in turn) introduced Akbar to the works of the Sufi poets, and he learnt by ear long passages of Hafiz and Jalal-ud-din Rumi. The strain of mysticism and the leaning towards free-thinking which these instilled are the key to a character over which authorities have completely differed, from the contemporary al-Badaoni and Abu-l-Fazl to Vincent Smith and Laurence Binyon.

Akbar, his early life spent amidst the intrigues of an oriental court and its bitter disillusionments, was " eternally seeking for the signs

[1] He refused Jesuit offers. *Jesu. Compendio Spiritual da Vida Christão* (Goa 1561) is the first known book printed in India.

and steps of a God," and he had from boyhood mystical experiences which seemed to be direct communion with the Divine Presence. A close student of Muhammadan history and theology he later acquired a wide knowledge of the philosophy and literature of Hinduism, Jainism and Zoroastrianism. Foreigner though he was by descent and early upbringing, Akbar identified himself completely with the Indian Empire which had come to him by force of arms. The rigid Moslem historian al-Badaoni had no sympathy with this deep understanding, and when ordered in 1591 to collaborate in the translation of the *Mahabharata* into Persian he records his intense dislike of the undertaking, and his contempt for the great Hindu epic. Akbar's search for a religion which would satisfy him led him at the risk of his own assassination to invite Jesuit missionaries to explain the doctrines of Christianity.

Akbar took up art with enthusiasm. Humayun had decided that both he and his son should learn drawing and study painting, and in 1550 two rising Persian artists, Mir Sayyid Ali and Abdus Samad, came from Kabul and gave Akbar the knowledge and appreciation which afterwards led to the foundation of the Indo-Persian school of art.

He taught himself music, studying Hindu vocalization, and was the patron of the great singer Tansen of Gwalior. He could play various instruments, his favourite being the kettle-drum, and he kept seven private orchestras.

But with all this he was intensely practical, a master of detail and uncommonly useful with his hands. One of his hobbies was to found cannon in his own arsenal; and his active brain was continually busy with inventions ranging from batteries which could be fired in salvos of seventeen guns with one match to useful devices in elephant gear and novel forms of travelling carriages.[1]

He mapped out for himself a most remarkable method of education. For an illiterate man whose only known writing is the laborious and childish signature reverently attested by Jahangir on the fly-leaf of a *Life of Timur*,[2] Akbar's attainments may justly be termed unparalleled.

[1] *Ain-i-Akbari*, Vol. I. pp. 112–115, 127, 128, 275.
[2] *Akbar*, Binyon, p. 11.

At the beginning of the Regency, Bairam Khan, a Persian Shia, had aroused considerable hostility by the fact that Tardi Beg, whom he had executed for the loss of Delhi, was a Sunni, the dominant sect in India; and the Protector's strong and arrogant rule added to the number of his enemies. Plots against Bairam Khan multiplied. To al-Badaoni "mountains were made of mole hills," but Abu-l-Fazl took a contrary view. It is clear, however, that while the Regent lived in state the Emperor was kept extremely short of money; and by the time he was eighteen Akbar had grown strongly to resent the restrictions put upon him.

The ladies of the court headed by the Emperor's foster-mother, Maham Anaga, persuaded Akbar to inform Bairam Khan that the Regency was at an end, and while the Emperor took the government into his own hands his minister was ordered to make the pilgrimage to Mecca. The circumstances of his disgrace stung Bairam Khan into rebellion. He was defeated by the imperial troops, taken prisoner and then pardoned by Akbar, who once more ordered the fallen minister to go on his pilgrimage. Bairam Khan, furnished with the means suitable to his position and former services, set out for Gujerat. But he was not destined to see Mecca. He was murdered at Patan by an Afghan, and Akbar took his little son Abdurrahim under his protection, and when the boy grew up made him a general and khan khanan as his father had been before him.

During the next two years Akbar found that he had exchanged the Regent's leading-rein for the petticoat government of the court. Whatever half-formed ambitions may have passed through the mind of Bairam Khan, Maham Anaga's one object was to advance her reprobate son Adham Khan to power. She also brought into prominence Pir Muhammad Khan, a successful soldier, but a man of violent brutality.

With these counsellors Akbar entered upon his policy of aggression. The first blow fell on Malwa, which was overrun in 1560 by the troops of Adham Khan and Pir Muhammad. Droves of prisoners were killed, and Rupmati, the beautiful consort of the defeated ruler Baz Bahadur, poisoned herself rather than fall into the hands of the conqueror.

Malwa Campaign.

Adham Khan began to make his own arrangements for the government of Malwa; while he sent no more than a few elephants to the Emperor, retaining the treasure, royal ensigns and all the captured women, royal ladies and dancing girls alike. But Akbar, although he allowed himself to be guided by his foster-mother, was no longer prepared to overlook infringements on his prerogatives, much less acts of sedition. Travelling faster than a warning message could be sent from Agra he suddenly appeared at Adham Khan's camp and accepted without comment the spoils of war which his unfaithful servant presented to him with the excuse that he had intended to offer them in person.

The Governor of Jaunpur, Ali Quli Khan Uzbeg, now proved equally seditious, and Akbar, in the heat of July, hurried to that province and exacted a similar submission.

Adham Khan had been recalled from Malwa, and Pir Muhammad, in a position of absolute power in that State,[1] began a campaign through Khandesh and across the Narbada, " practising to the utmost the code of Chengiz Khan, massacring or making prisoners of all the inhabitants, and swept everything clean and clear . . . he robbed the crown from the pulpit, the turban from the preacher, the cupola from the mosque, the lamp from the minaret." [2] But retribution came swiftly. While retiring before the army of Baz Bahadur, Pir Muhammad was drowned when crossing the Narbada.

Akbar as he grew into full manhood began to realize his position and its responsibilities. To get to know his people he mingled in disguise among the crowds at night, on one occasion barely escaping recognition by a trick[3]; and early in 1562 by marrying the daughter of Raja Bihari Mal, the Rajput ruler of Jaipur, he proclaimed his determination to be a really Indian ruler and to found a truly Indian dynasty. Akbar's sympathy with his Hindu subjects and their religion dates from this marriage, which was followed eight years later by alliances with Rajput brides from Bikanir and Jaisalmir.

[1] Al-Badaoni, Vol. II. p. 46.   [2] *Ibid.*, Vol. II. pp. 46, 47.
[3] *Akbar-nama*, Vol. II. Ch. XXXVI.: " The strange story and wonderful adventure which happened to His Majesty the Shahinshah."

A precedent with far-reaching consequences was created when Raja Bihari Mal and his son were enrolled among the nobles of the imperial court.[1] The Rajput nobility had in the past been the solid bulwark of Hinduism as opposed to Islam. Akbar by his policy of securing them in their ancient privileges and at the same time throwing open to them military service and an official career under the crown, took the first step in the transformation of the Rajput chiefs from stubborn foes into the stoutest defenders of the empire.

As a preliminary towards ridding himself of the influence of Maham Anaga, whose powers amounted to those of a prime minister, Akbar appointed as his vizier Muhammad Khan Atka,[2] a loyal servant since before the second Panipat. In May 1562 Adham Khan made a desperate attempt to restore the family influence. He entered the palace with some followers and had murdered the minister, whom he found at his devotions, when Akbar met him, felled him to the ground with his fist and then had him thrown from the palace terrace. Maham Anaga died broken-hearted shortly afterwards, and the Emperor's foster-mother and her worthless son lie buried in a magnificent tomb erected by Akbar near the Kutb Minar.

End of Court Influence.

The supreme control of affairs was now in Akbar's own hands. In the next two years he introduced two reforms. The first was the removal of the tax levied on pilgrims. The second, the abolition of the *jizya*, was in pursuance of the Emperor's policy of gaining the loyalty and support of his Hindu subjects. In finance, Akbar had given the eunuch Khwaja Malik I'timad Khan control over the revenues which, in Abu-l-Fazl's words, "were in the hands of embezzlers," and were now put on a sound basis by this able minister. I'timad Khan was succeeded by Raja Todar Mal, whose system of land revenue administration following the policy of Sher Shah still forms, though remotely, the basis of modern scientific methods.[3]

[1] Firishta, Vol. II. p. 208.
[2] Shamsu-d-din Muhammad Khan Atka.
[3] *Indian Statutory Commission Report*, Vol. I. p. 338.

Throughout his reign the Emperor pursued a systematic policy of aggression, the only alternative, in the state of India at that time, to a series of defensive wars to preserve his own throne from destruction. He built up his great empire by the sword, and consolidated his conquests by the subsequent exercise of tact, common sense and impartial justice. His ambition to enlarge his empire was, however, the sole reason for his unprovoked attack upon Gondwana in 1563. This country, which was admirably ruled by the able and beautiful Rani Durgavati, was invaded by an army under Asaf Khan. The Rani died in battle, and Chauragarh the capital was taken, together with immense booty, of which very little found its way to the Emperor.

Conquest of Gondwana.

The Uzbeg nobles had done their full share to secure the throne for Akbar. But the Emperor's policy of concentrating all authority in his central and personal government violated their ideas of semi-independent fiefs. The discontented faction, headed by Khan Zaman Ali Quli Khan Uzbeg, Governor of Jaunpur, who had greatly distinguished himself under Bairam Khan at Panipat, resolved to depose Akbar and make Kamran's son, Mirza Abu-l-Qasim, Emperor. The struggle between the crown and the feudal aristocracy came to a head when the Emperor summarily defeated the plot by having his nephew secretly executed in 1565, and the Uzbeg nobles came out in open rebellion. The civil war went on until Akbar finally broke the power of the nobles at the battle of Manikpur in June 1567, and Ali Quli Khan was killed.

The Uzbeg Revolt.

Early in the same year Akbar's brother Muhammad Hakim Mirza was driven out of Kabul by Suliman, the ruler of Badakshan, before the Emperor's troops, which he had asked for, could come to his help. On reaching India, Hakim was persuaded to put himself at the head of these reinforcements and seize the Punjab while Akbar was still fighting the Uzbeg nobles in the eastern provinces. The Emperor, who looked upon the north-west frontier as a greater source of danger than the rebels in the east, came up by forced marches towards Lahore, and his brother, with the cavalry he had with him, beat a

The Afghan Invasion.

PLATE XXV.

AKBAR HUNTING
Mogul School, showing European influence in its perspective
By courtesy of Indian Museum, South Kensington

PLATE XXVI.

RAJPUT PALACE AT DATIA (EARLY SEVENTEENTH CENTURY)

By permission of the Secretary of State for India in Council

hasty retreat. Returning to Kabul, Hakim surprised Suliman's forces and regained possession of the city.

Akbar's next objective, when he had crushed the Uzbeg revolt, was the Rajput State of Mewar and the famous
The Rajput War. stronghold of Chitor. Eight miles of fortifications crowned the high rock rising from the plain, and the place, which had only been taken by Ala-ud-din Khalji after a six months' siege, was looked upon as practically impregnable. The Rana of Mewar had given sanctuary to Baz Bahadur, the fugitive ruler of Malwa, and on his refusal to give him up the Emperor declared war in 1567. The Rana, Udai Singh, unworthy of the name of Rajput, fled at the approach of the Mogul army, and "the brave and chivalrous Jaimal " [1] took command at Chitor.

The Moguls began their siege operations by mining, digging zigzag trenches, and driving galleries. But the explosion of the mines was not at first successful, the garrison built up the breaches in the walls as soon as they were made, and the besiegers in spite of their heavy guns could make no headway against the storm of musketry and artillery fire. At the end of six months, however, in the midst of an assault, Akbar shot down a Rajput leader who seemed to be directing the defence. An hour later the garrison had deserted the walls, and fire broke out at several places in the fort. It was the *jauhar*.[2] The dead leader was Jaimal, and in spite of the heroism of Fath Singh of Kailwa, a boy of sixteen, resistance was abandoned, and 8000 Rajputs came out to die to a man rather than surrender.

Akbar afterwards set up at Delhi statues of Jaimal and of Fath Singh mounted on elephants, but he sullied his victory by the massacre of 30,000 countrymen who had taken part in the defence. Enlightened far in advance of his age in his peace administration though he was, Akbar conducted war according to the time-honoured methods of his predecessors. Chitor was deserted, and the beautiful city of Udaipur became the new capital.

In 1569 Ranthambor, which was held by Rao Sujan the Hara chief of Bundi, a vassal of the princes of Mewar, surrendered after a

---

[1] Al-Badaoni, Vol. II. p. 105.
[2] *Akbar-nama*, Vol. II. p. 472.

stout resistance, and Akbar conceded honourable terms in exchange for a recognition of Mogul suzerainty.[1] Kalanjar opened its gates and the possession of these three great fortresses secured Akbar's position in Northern India. But Rana Partap Singh, who had succeeded Udai Singh, though frequently hard pressed by the Mogul forces, never submitted.

The hopeless disorder in Gujerat decided Akbar to take over the country, and in 1572 he marched to Ahmadabad and received the submission of its nominal ruler Muzaffar Shah. A cousin of the Emperor's, Ibrahim Hussain Mirza, remained, however, in the field. He was defeated at Sarnal in December of that year, and Surat fell two months later. During the siege of Surat the Emperor met Europeans for the first time in the small Portuguese force which had come to help in the defence. Instead of fighting, the Portuguese made a treaty with Akbar by which they agreed to facilitate the pilgrimages to Mecca. Ibrahim Hussain was not finally defeated until September 1573. In the height of the rainy season Akbar set out with 3000 men, covered about 600 miles in eleven days and completely surprised Ibrahim Hussain, "whose spies had seen Akbar in Agra fourteen days before."[2] The greatly superior forces of Ibrahim Hussain were routed and their leader taken prisoner.

Annexation of Gujerat.

Gujerat, in spite of periods of considerable unrest, remained under the government of the Moguls for nearly two hundred years, and the possession of so rich a province on the sea coast, and the great port of Surat, were of the highest value to the empire.

Sulaiman Kararani, the Afghan King of Bengal, had preserved his practical independence by formally acknowledging Mogul suzerainty. But his son Da'ud bin Sulaiman invited inevitable defeat by declaring war on the Emperor. The campaigns of 1574 and 1575 were each followed by peace negotiations and a renewal of hostilities by Da'ud, but in July

Conquest of Bengal.

---

[1] The interesting peace treaty upholding Rajput honour, to be found in Tod's *Annals and Antiquities of Rajasthan*, Vol. III. p. 1482, can be read in the more accessible *Mughal Rule in India*, pp. 35, 36.

[2] Firishta, Vol. II. pp. 241, 242.

1576 the King of Bengal was killed at the battle of Rajmahal and the country became part of the Mogul Empire.

On the night before Panipat, Akbar's kingdom lay within the encampment of his army. In twenty years, largely by the rapidity of his movements and the boldness of his leadership, he made himself master of India from Cutch to the Sunderbands and from the Himalaya south to the Narbada. During the latter part of the reign the steady extension of the empire was as a rule brought about by his generals and rarely by Akbar in person. The religious rebellion of 1580 in Bengal and the Afghan campaign will be referred to later.

Later Conquests. Kashmir, in its isolation, has never played a part in the great movements of Indian history. Its quiet valleys had fallen under the authority of the Maurya Empire and of the nomadic conquerors from Central Asia. Hindu rule ended and the country became chiefly Muhammadan when the Prime Minister Mirza Shah, an adventurer from Swat, seized the throne and founded a Moslem dynasty in the first half of the fourteenth century. When the line came to an end the confusion and dissensions which followed greatly contributed[1] to the success of the Mogul invasion in 1587. In 1591 Akbar himself finally reduced the country to order.

Orissa had been added to the empire in 1590, Sind was subdued by the combined land and river war of 1592, while the highly unsatisfactory situation in Afghanistan was settled in 1594 by the capture of Kandahar, which followed the annexation of Baluchistan and Mekran.

The Deccan. In the closing years of his reign Akbar resolved to annex the Deccan, and when his embassies returned from the south in 1593 with the news that the Deccan kingdoms with the exception of Khandesh refused to acknowledge Mogul paramountcy, the Emperor determined on war. The imperial forces, led by the Emperor's son Prince Murad and Abdurrahim the Khan Khanan, invaded Ahmadnagar, then in the throes of two rival claimants to the throne. The capital was obstinately defended by

[1] Firishta, Vol. II. p. 260.

the Princess Chand Bibi, but the peace made in 1596 ceded Berar to the Emperor.

In the meanwhile the violent jealousy of Murad towards the Khan Khanan had weakened the Mogul leadership, and when the imperial army met the forces of Ahmadnagar, Bijapur and Golconda, the result was a drawn battle. Akbar recalled Abdurrahim and appointed the minister and historian Abu-l-Fazl in his place. In May 1599, when Murad died of delirium tremens, the situation was at a deadlock, and at this juncture Miran Bahadur Shah of Khandesh joined the Deccani allies.

Akbar sent the Khan Khanan to the Deccan with a large force and came south himself, leaving the central government under the charge of the Prince Royal Muhammad Salim. The Khan Khanan, with Prince Daniyal, was ordered to take Ahmadnagar, and Akbar himself, after entering Burhanpur, the capital of Khandesh, went on and besieged Asirgarh.[1] The fortress was of immense strength, heavily armed and well provisioned, and the Mogul forces were unable to carry it by assault. In the midst of the siege, news reached Akbar that Salim had rebelled and set himself up as Emperor at Allahabad. But Akbar was determined to take Asirgarh, and succeeded by bribery where force had failed, the fortress surrendering in January 1601. Ahmadnagar, with the heroic Chand Bibi murdered, had fallen in August 1600. Akbar organized the country into three provinces under Prince Daniyal, and in May 1602 he returned to Agra as the proclaimed Emperor of the Deccan. Ahmadnagar had not, however, been properly subdued and soon reasserted its independence.

Salim asked his father's forgiveness and was made Governor of Bengal, but there was no real reconciliation between them until after the death of Daniyal in 1604, when Salim became the only son left to Akbar.

The conquest of the northern part of the Deccan was the last of Akbar's military operations. He did not live to carry his invasions further south, and Bijapur, Golconda and the small Hindu States which had survived the collapse of Vijayanagar, did not come within his empire.

[1] Firishta, Vol. II. pp. 276–278.

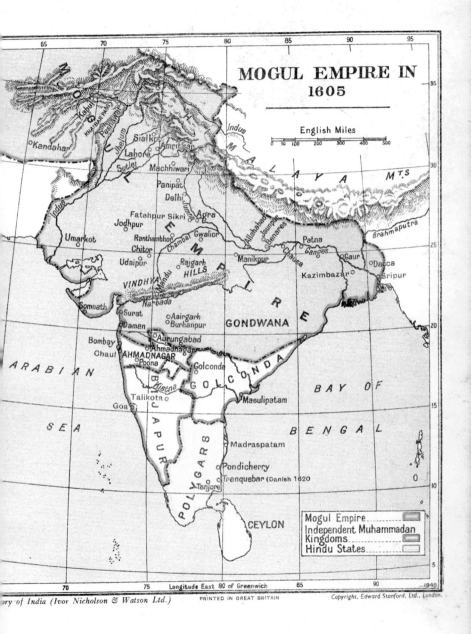

MOGUL EMPIRE IN 1605

English Miles

0 50 100 200 300 400 500

MOGUL
Kabul
KHABAR PASS
Peshawar
Kandahar
Sialkot
Jhelum
Lahore
Amritsar
Sutlej
Machhiwari
Panipat
Delhi
Fatehpur Sikri
Jodhpur
Agra
Umarkot
Ranthambhor
Chitor
Chambal Gwalior
Udaipur
Rajgarh
Manikpur
Allahabad
Jaunpur
Benares
VINDHYA
HILLS
Mandu
Somnath
Narbada
Surat
Asirgarh
Damen
Burhanpur
Bombay
Aurungabad
Chaul
Ahmadnagar
AHMADNAGAR
Poona
Golconda
Krishna
GOLCONDA
Talikota
Goa
Masulipatam
BIJAPUR
POLYGARS
Madraspatam
Pondicherry
Tranquebar (Danish 1620)
Tanjore
CEYLON

Indus
HIMALAYA MTS
Indus
Brahmaputra
Ganges
Patna
Chausa
Gaur
Kazimbazar
Dacca
Sripur
GONDWANA
BAY OF BENGAL
ARABIAN SEA

35
30
25
20
15
10
5

Mogul Empire
Independent Muhammadan Kingdoms
Hindu States

ory of India (Ivor Nicholson & Watson Ltd.)   PRINTED IN GREAT BRITAIN   Copyright, Edward Stanford, Ltd., London.

After the disappearance of the Sur dynasty, Akbar's wars were chiefly to extend his empire and were not waged in a struggle for existence. But the greatest crisis in his reign after Panipat was directly due to his unorthodox and intensely unpopular attitude towards Islam. This brought Bengal into open rebellion which threatened his throne, while the more veiled hostility of many of those surrounding him menaced him with assassination.

Strong Sufi influence came into his boyhood, but until he was thirty-three the Emperor was a practising Sunni,
Akbar's Religion. regular in his devotions, a builder of mosques and a pious pilgrim whose favourite shrine was that of the saint Miyan-ud-din Chisthti at Ajmer. But Akbar's restless intellect in its quest of absolute truth in religion was not satisfied. The differences between the sects of Islam were disturbing, and in 1575, the year before the great mosque at his new capital Fathepur-Sikri was finished, he built the Ibadat Khana. Here he summoned doctors of the Sunni and Shia, Hanifi and Sharifi sects to expound their doctrines, and where, as al-Badaoni records, feeling ran high, amidst shouts of " fool and heretic." From 1575 to 1578 he listened to the contending theologians with increasing doubt of Islam as the one true faith rising above his insatiable love of argument.

At this point another factor came into play. In the words of Laurence Binyon [1]: " Akbar, who to all things brought the test of conduct and experience, judged of religions far less by their abstract tenets than by their fruits in the life of those professing them. And only a year after the House of Worship had risen in its bright newness, a certain piece of news was brought to the capital which greatly impressed him. The first two Christian missionaries had arrived in Bengal. Their converts had defrauded the imperial revenue; the priests thereon refused them absolution. What was this creed which set its face against dishonesty even to a foreign government? "

Akbar was determined to find out, and after a visit to the court by Father Pereira, "a man of more virtue than learning," an imperial

[1] *Akbar*, pp. 91, 92.

message was sent to Goa for " two learned priests with the Law and the Gospel." The Emperor promised to welcome them and guaranteed his protection. Three Jesuit fathers were sent, Rudolf Aquaviva, Anthony Monserrate, and Francis Henriquez. Aquaviva, the leader of the party, son of the Duke of Atri, was only thirty years of age, and he greatly impressed the Emperor by his sanctity, his gentleness and the austerity of his life. Henriquez, a Persian convert from Islam, was the interpreter, and Monserrate, a Spaniard of Catalonia, became the historian of the mission. The Jesuits arrived at Fathpur-Sikri at the end of February 1580.[1]

Since the visit of Father Pereira two years earlier, Akbar had made considerable progress in his religious inquiries. " Crowds of learned men from all nations and sages of various religions and sects came to the court and were honoured with private conversations." [2] The faith of his own people had been left behind, and in 1579 Akbar took a step which may in some ways be compared with the action of Henry VIII forty-four years earlier in separating England from the Holy See. Henry was declared head of the Church in England but he showed in the Six Articles, and by burning persons expressing heretical opinions on the eucharist, that the Mass still mattered. Akbar, through Shaikh Mubarak, introduced in the Ibadat Khana the doctrine that a king should not be merely the temporal but also the spiritual guide of his subjects. This struck at the supremacy of the Koran as the one authority in Islam; and as the Act of Supremacy paved the way for the change of religion effected in England during the reigns of Edward VI and Elizabeth, so the road was opened for the introduction of the Emperor's short-lived Din Ilahi.

Modern writers[3] whose opinions must be treated with respect, maintain that " Akbar in his reforms kept in view the Prophet's own sayings and the pronouncements of the most enlightened earlier doctors of the Islamic law." But al-Badaoni, whose pages blaze with indignation and invective, charges Abu-l-Fazl (who was a son of

---

[1] *The Jesuits and the Great Mogul*, Sir E. Maclagan, pp. 23–26.
[2] Al-Badaoni, Vol. II. p. 263.
[3] *E.g.* The Rt. Hon. Syed Ameer Ali, *Islamic Culture*, Quarterly Review, October 1927.

Mubarak) and Hakim Abu-l-Fath with having " successfully turned the Emperor from Islam and led him to reject inspiration, prophet-ship, the miracles of the prophets and of the saints and even the whole law."

A document was drawn up [1] which was to some extent a compro-mise, and this was signed by a representative group of Moslems, including the Mufti of the Empire and the learned Khan of Badakshan. Akbar was given the title of Iman-i-Adil (just leader), and it was laid down that in cases of conflicting opinions by the religious authorities the Emperor's decision should be binding. As al-Badaoni observes, the intellect of the iman became law, and opposition was impossible.

Religious toleration was established, but in such a form that the regulations issued by Akbar after 1579 pressed heavily upon orthodox Moslems. It is difficult to sustain the argument that the Emperor's object was to clean Islam of corrupt practices.[2] But the accusation of religious persecution may be weighed by comparing Akbar's methods, such as the prohibition of new mosques and the removal of orthodox Moslems from the judicial bench, with the position of Protestants in England during the reign of Mary Tudor, of Catholics in England under Edward VI and Elizabeth, and the penal laws as enforced in Ireland " where the law did not presume a Papist to exist " until 1793.

On the other hand, while adopting various Hindu customs, Akbar would not permit what he judged to be inhuman or unjust practices of Hinduism. He enacted that the custom of *sati* should not be carried out by force and he legalized the remarriage of widows, which was contrary to a strictly political policy of conciliating the Hindus.

His attitude towards the Jesuit missionaries was one of great and friendly interest. But as Akbar within a month of their arrival began publicly to perform the Parsee rites of sun-worship, and found in Christianity an intolerance of other faiths which was contrary to his instinctive feelings, while reports must have reached him of the

---

[1] Given *verbatim* by al-Badaoni, Vol. II. pp. 279, 280.
[2] But see article " The personality of Akbar " in *Islamic Culture* for July 1927, by P. K. Menon, a Hindu writer.

Inquisition at Goa, it is not surprising that the conversations and the public discussions led to nothing.

The Emperor's religious experiments and his obvious prejudice against Islam aroused a storm of anger in the court and through the country. Bengal rose in rebellion in 1580 and the Qazi of Jaunpur, Mullah Muhammad Yazdi, issued a proclamation insisting on the duty of rebelling against the Emperor.[1] He and other leaders of the revolt were executed as traitors when captured, but the rising took several years to suppress. It was made yet more serious by the aim of the rebels to replace Akbar by his half-brother Muhammad Hakim of Kabul, who supported the insurrection by an invasion of the Punjab.

Rebellion in Bengal.

Akbar decided that the more critical situation lay on the north-west frontier. He left the campaign in the eastern province to Raja Todar Mal and Khan-i-Azam Mirza Aziz while he undertook the operations against Muhammad Hakim in person. Muhammad had penetrated as far as Lahore with 15,000 cavalry, but when he found that the great fief-holders showed no intention of joining him his courage failed him and he beat a retreat.

Invasion of Afghanistan.

Akbar in this campaign left nothing to chance. He had collected an army of about 50,000 men and 28 guns; and took with him Muhammad Qasim Khan, the architect of Agra Fort and the best engineer in the empire, to make roads across the border. The Emperor sent forward heralds to announce his peaceful intentions towards the inhabitants, and he arranged for the payment of all supplies required for the army. Akbar left Fathpur Sikri in February 1581 and he entered Kabul, after trifling opposition, in August.[2] He allowed Muhammad Hakim to remain as ruler in Afghanistan until his death from drink four years later, when the country was absorbed in the empire.

Early in the campaign Akbar hanged his finance minister, who

[1] Al-Badaoni, Vol. II. p. 284.
[2] See *Monserrate's Commentary*, pp. 72 *et seq.* The Jesuit Father accompanied Akbar on the campaign and wrote a detailed account.

PLATE XXVII.

AKBAR DIRECTING THE ASSAULT ON RANTHAMBOR, 1568

By courtesy of Indian Museum, South Kensington

PLATE XXVIII.

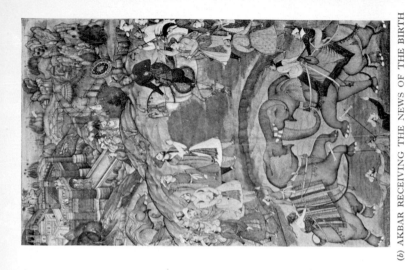

(b) AKBAR RECEIVING THE NEWS OF THE BIRTH OF PRINCE MURAD WHILE WATCHING AN ELEPHANT FIGHT

From the "Ain-i-Akbari." *Artists*: Farrukh Beg and Basawan

By courtesy of I. I. i. e. M. em. Sanct V. min. inc

(a) REJOICINGS AT THE BIRTH OF PRINCE SALIM

From the "Ain-i-Akbari." *Artists*: Kisir the elder and Dham Das

By courtesy of Indian Museum, South Kensington

was now known as Khwaja Shah Mansur, for high treason. Opinions differ as to his guilt; it is maintained by Abu-l-Fazl and Monserrate, but al-Badaoni considered that " his numerous oppressions formed the halter round his neck," and is not alone in believing the vizier innocent of the charge. He had, however, been under suspicion for some time, though it is highly probable that at least the captured correspondence for which he was executed was forged. His ability and capacity for work in realizing arrears of taxes and preparing new assessments had been remarkable, but his strictness had roused the enmity of the *jagir* holders, and he had ruined numbers of the poorer classes.

The Divine Religion.
When Akbar returned from Kabul in triumph the crisis was over, and in 1582 with his authority firmly re-established he entered upon the third stage of his religious progress. In his search for a personal religion which he could whole-heartedly follow, the Emperor had another object in view. He was determined to be a truly national ruler and, as Urdu had become a common language for his Moslem and Hindu subjects, so he wished to obliterate the antagonistic differences in religion by providing a faith which all alike could accept. None of those which he had investigated would serve his purpose.

A thousand lunar years had elapsed since the mission of the Prophet, and the Emperor, convinced that the era of Islam must be at an end,[1] proclaimed the *Din Ilahi*,[2] or Divine Religion, which was to establish uniformity of creed. Akbar declared himself to be the Vice-Regent of God on earth and the exponent of His commands; and his disciples and those whose diseases he was held to have cured prostrated themselves when he appeared.

The precepts of the new faith were simple. There was one God; and the sun, the stars or fire might be worshipped as the manifestation of the Deity. The conquest of evil passions and the practice of virtue and abstention from meat summed up a religion in which there was neither priest nor public worship. The novice was given a symbol,

---

[1] Al-Badaoni, Vol. II. pp. 310 *et seq.*
[2] See *Ain-i-Akbari*, Vol. I. pp. 162–167. " His Majesty as the Spiritual Guide of the People," and Abu-l-Fazl's preface to the volume.

possibly a likeness of the Emperor which, according to al-Badaoni, was worn on the turban.

Abu-l-Fazl was one of the strongest supporters of the *Din Ilahi*, but it made no appeal to the masses and was none too well received by the nobles of the court. One of the Emperor's closest friends, Khan-i-Azam Mirza Aziz, a son of Maham Anaga, was fearlessly outspoken in his criticism of the Divine Religion. Azam Khan was a distinguished general and an able provincial governor, but he is best remembered for his remark: " A man should marry four wives: a Persian woman to have someone to talk to; a Khurasani woman for his housework; a Hindu woman for nursing his children; and a woman from Transoxania, to have someone to whip as a warning for the other three."

The Rajput Raja Bhagwan Das, Commander of Five Thousand and Governor first of the Punjab and then of Bihar, never became a follower of the *Din Ilahi*, and his son Man Singh observed to Akbar: " If discipleship means willingness to sacrifice one's life I have already carried my life in my hand: What need is there of further proof? If, however, the term refers to Faith, I certainly am a Hindu. If you order me to do so I will become a Mussulman, but I know not of the existence of any other religion than these two."[1] The new religion died with Akbar.

Successful though he was in adding to his empire, Akbar's last years were clouded with sorrow. The Brahman wit *Akbar's Last Years.* and poet Mahesh Das, the bosom companion and disciple whom Akbar had made Raja Bir Bal, was killed in action on the north-west frontier in 1586 during a disastrous retreat.

In the same year Todar Mal died. He greatly distinguished *Todar Mal.* himself as a leader of men, but his fame rests on his revenue work, which began when he became a minister in 1583. He at once introduced his reforms, made his new assessment and issued his coinage regulations. He also substituted Persian in the place of Hindi in government accounts.

[1] Al-Badaoni, Vol. II. p. 375.

194

In 1589 Akbar lost his comrade in arms Raja Bhagwan Das, who had fought by his side at Chitor and in Gujerat.

Akbar's three sons were a bitter disappointment. Murad died of

Family Troubles and Death of Akbar. drink in 1599 and Daniyal followed him in 1604, the year in which the Emperor's mother Hamida died broken-hearted in her old age by family troubles. Salim was more than a source of endless anxiety through his open disloyalty. He had reason to hate Abu-l-Fazl and he contrived the murder of his father's most faithful friend and counsellor for thirty-five years, when he was returning from the Deccan in 1602.

In September 1605 the Emperor was taken ill with dysentery. His constitution had always been magnificent, and he was not yet sixty-four, but plots were springing up for his grandson Khusru to succeed, and the load of anxiety and uncertainty proved fatal to his chance of recovery. On 22nd October, just a month after his illness began, he saw the Jesuit fathers for the last time, and when they came back two days later they were turned away. Prince Salim, backed by the nobles to whom he had sworn to uphold the faith of Islam, came at last into the presence of his dying father. Akbar could no longer speak but he opened his eyes and motioned to his son to put on the emblems of sovereignty, the imperial turban and the sword of Humayun. Then the Emperor signed to him to go; he had chosen his heir.

The end came in the early morning of 27th October 1605, and with his closest friends around him, the creed of the Prophet in his ears and the name of God upon his lips, Akbar died.

Jalal-ud-din Muhammad Akbar Padshah Ghazi was buried according to the rites of the Sunnis, which horrified the Jesuit fathers by their severe simplicity; and the son who had carried him to his grave through the broken wall of the red-sandstone fort of Agra reigned in his stead.

While Abu-l-Fazl and al-Badaoni have recorded their violently contrasting views [1] of the commanding personality who ruled India

[1] Al-Badaoni's opinion, which made the publication of the *Muratakhab-ut-Tawarikh* impossible while Akbar was alive, is given with virulent frankness in Vol. II. pp. 348–350.

for nearly fifty years, the first Europeans to visit Upper India since the days of Asoka have given us a vivid description of the Emperor's appearance.[1]

"One could easily recognize even at the first glance that he is the King. He has broad shoulders, somewhat bandy legs *Akbar's* well-suited for horsemanship, and a light brown *Appearance.* complexion. He carries his head bent towards the right shoulder. His forehead is broad and open, his eyes so bright and flashing that they seem like a sea shimmering in the sunlight. His eyelashes are very long. His eyebrows are not strongly marked. His nose is straight and small, though not insignificant. His nostrils are widely open as though in derision. Between the left nostril and the upper lip there is a mole. He shaves his beard but wears a moustache. He limps in his left leg though he has never received any injury there. His body is exceedingly well-built and is neither too thin nor too stout. He is sturdy, hearty and robust. When he laughs his face becomes almost distorted. His expression is tranquil, serene and open, full also of dignity and when he is angry of awful majesty." He was then thirty-eight years of age. A pleasant touch is given by the remark that "he drives a two-horse chariot in which his appearance is very striking and dignified."

The Jesuit mission were deeply impressed by the Emperor's accessibility to his people, great and small—it is recorded of him that the Emperor was "great with the great and lowly with the lowly"—and above all by his simple and straightforward nature; a conclusion which was reached by intimate personal observation. This is not, however, the opinion given by Father Daniel Bartoli, S.J., who published a history of the Mission of 1580–83 in Rome in 1663. Akbar figures here as a consummate dissembler, open in appearance, inwardly subtle and deceitful and bent only on his own aggrandizement.[2]

Like all the Mogul Emperors, with the exception of the abstemious Aurangzeb, and to a lesser degree Shah Jehan, Akbar indulged in excessive wine drinking, and Monserrate records that he used to

---

[1] *Monserrate's Commentary*, pp. 196, 197, 199.
[2] Laurence Binyon's summary of Father Bartoli's judgment, *Akbar*, pp. 16–17

drink " *post* " (a mixture of diluted opium and spices) " until he sank back stupefied." He did not, however, take to tobacco.[1]

The most remarkable feature of Akbar's reign, more striking even than his conquests, his system of government, or the dream-city of Fathpur-Sikri which he abandoned fifteen years after it was built, was the overwhelming force of the Emperor's own personality. He, a foreigner, and a Moslem amidst a vast population of Hindus, had to rely entirely—until he had won over some of the Rajput chiefs—upon foreigners and Moslems like himself to support his throne. Yet these were the men, many of them fanatical, whose strongest feelings he outraged by repressive religious measures and by the open repudiation of Islam. The Emperor, who in 1577 granted to the Sikh community the site on which to build their temple at Amritsar, a few years later forbade not only the building, but even the repair of the mosques. Yet from the storm of indignation and the religious war which he brought upon himself he emerged stronger in authority than before. A born leader of men and one of the mightiest kings in history, Akbar transformed the Moguls from military adventurers into a great dynasty.

[1] Introduced about the end of 1604 by the Portuguese. By 1617 the habit of smoking was prevalent. In spite of Jahangir's efforts to stop it this was the origin of the flourishing Indian tobacco trade.

CHAPTER VIII

Akbar's System of Government

BABUR had been occupied with conquest; and Humayun had neither the ability nor the energy to reform the government of the Delhi Sultans which simply consisted in the exaction of tribute. It was left to the able usurper Sher Shah to create an administrative organization and revive, on easier terms, the land revenue methods of Ala-ud-din Khalji. Upon this foundation Akbar built up his military system of government.

The central government was the Emperor himself, and on his ability, energy and sense of impartiality the whole fabric of the Empire depended. An uncontrolled autocrat, policy and administration were the outcome of his own decisions, and he was the final judicial court of appeal.

The flaw in this system was its complete dependence upon the personal factor, and while the earlier emperors were strong and, with the exception of Aurangzeb, reasonably moderate and broad-minded, the later emperors were incompetent. The consequences have been summed up by one of the earlier administrators of the East India Company in Bengal.

" The Mogul dominion, in the best times, and under the wisest princes, was a government of discretion. The safety of the people, the security of their property and the prosperity of the country depended upon the personal character of the monarch. By this standard his delegates regulated their own demeanour: In proportion as he was wise, just, vigilant and humane the provincial viceroys discharged their respective trusts with zeal and fidelity, and as they possessed or wanted the recited qualifications the inferior agents conducted themselves with more or less diligence and honesty. A weak monarch and a corrupt minister encouraged and produced every kind of disorder: for there was no law paramount to the sovereign's will. Few of the officers of government were liberally paid; and property was left to accumulate, from breach of trust, abused patronage, perverted justice, or unrestrained oppression. . . . Long before [the Company took over the revenue administration of Bengal] the vigour of the empire had been irrevocably weakened; and its institutions, as far as they can be traced in the ordinances and practice of its best princes, had been violated." [1]

Akbar's empire consisted of twelve (eventually fifteen) *subahs* or provinces under military governors who were called *subadars*. The province was divided into *sarkars*, or divisions, and each division into a number of *parganas*, or districts, which were the working administrative units. A district was in charge of a military commander and of a revenue collector; the former, like the provincial governor, presiding over the criminal court in addition to his duties of civil administration.

The Mogul government was a well-organized system of foreign domination imposed upon India by conquest; and the problem of holding together the provinces of which the Empire was composed was solved by carefully devised safeguards. The major provinces were administered by separate establishments which acted as checks upon each other. The governor of the province had his own strictly circumscribed powers which, incidentally, did not include direct authority over the civil magistrates' courts such as they were. The chief treasury officer (*diwan*) held an independent position and was responsible solely to the imperial treasury for the entire finance of the province, revenue, customs and expenditure; and it was this official and not the governor who took possession of the larger *jagirs* in the Emperor's name when the life-interest in these fiefs fell vacant by death. The fortified strategic points and the imperial ports on the seaboard were governed by officers who were appointed by the central authority and were not under the provincial governor's orders.

The Mogul emperors at the height of their power maintained an efficient army under their direct command which could defend the frontiers and suppress rebellion. It was only after the death of

---

[1] Minute made by Sir John Shore (Lord Teignmouth) in 1790; quoted in the Fifth Report of the Select Committee, House of Commons. The Report is printed in *Early Revenue History of Bengal*, Ascoli, p. 107.

Aurangzeb, the last of the great emperors, when the governors swept the provincial safeguards away and became absolute rulers in all but name, that these imperial deputies " had nothing to fear but an army from Delhi which was always coming but never came." [1]

Yet, with all these administrative precautions, the best and strongest safeguard was the good will of the people of India, which Akbar built up by his sympathetic understanding and which Aurangzeb by his fanaticism destroyed. [2]

Government Officials.

The public service was, in theory, thrown completely open to Hindus as a career in the reign of Akbar. But the Government Lists in the *Ain-i-Akbari* [3] show that out of 415 higher officials, 51 only were Hindus and that these were almost all Rajputs, whom it was Akbar's policy to conciliate; in forty years only two Brahmans appear in these upper grades. Of the rest there were very few Hindustani Mussulmans in the higher ranks of the army and civil service; the majority were Persians and Afghans. The whole service was directly under the Emperor's orders, and his acute judgment of ability and character is shown in his appointments. There was no regular promotion, entrance to the imperial service was by selection, and dismissal at the Emperor's pleasure.

Appointments were graded on a military scale borrowed from Persia, rising from " Commanders of Ten " up to " Commanders of Ten Thousand," the number indicating the quota of troops (cavalry ranking as the more important) that the officials were supposed to furnish in war, in addition to carrying out their peace duties. A " Five Thousand " commandership, the highest post open to persons not of royal blood until the latter end of Akbar's reign, carried a maximum salary of Rs. 30,000 a month and was worth at least 18,000 net income, with the purchasing power of the rupee five or six times as great as it is today. [4] The third grade of the lowest rank, " Commander

---

[1] *Indian Administration to the Dawn of Responsible Government*, Professor B. K. Thakore (Bombay), 1922, pp. 15, 16.

[2] See the admirable summary made by Sivaji in his letter to Aurangzeb (Appendix to Ch. XI.).

[3] Vol. I. pp. 308-528, and note on p. 536.

[4] Stabilised in 1927 at 1s. 6d.

PLATE XXIX.

(a) A KASHMIR VALLEY
By courtesy of Indian Railways Bureau

(b) ABU-L-FAZL   (c) AKBAR
By permission of the Secretary of State for India in Council

PLATE XXX.

(b) DANCING GIRLS PERFORMING BEFORE
A GRANDEE
By permission of the Secretary of State for

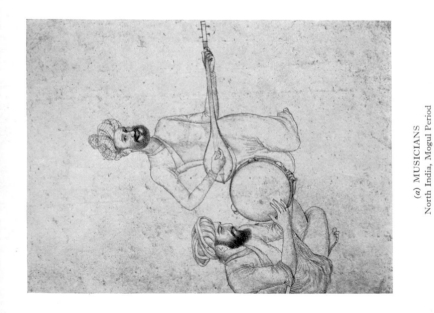

(a) MUSICIANS
North India, Mogul Period

of Ten," drew Rs. 75 a month, the cost of upkeep of his section being about 44 rupees.

In spite of Akbar's regulations to remedy matters, irregularities were rife, as al-Badaoni and Abu-l-Fazl agree, and effectives fell far short of the official quotas. Officials were paid either in cash or by the *jagir* system which Akbar tried unsuccessfully to end. The pay was enormous, but charges on salaries were heavy, and the later emperors were in the habit of withholding a varying number of months' pay during the year. Thrift was not encouraged, for the Emperor was heir to the estates of his officers; appearances had to be kept up; bribery may be said to have been essential; and *jagirs* were an uncertain source of income.

The Mogul Empire was essentially a land power. It had no
The Services. fleet to guard its own shores let alone to rival the achievements of the great navy of the Cholas, which had commanded the Bay of Bengal six hundred years earlier, and made the overseas expeditions that conquered Ceylon, Lower Burma and the Nicobars.

The army consisted of three establishments. The Emperor kept a relatively small body under his own command, and this included all the artillery, with its cadre of foreign specialists. Next in order of efficiency were the troops furnished by the " Commanders." The cavalry arm, with perhaps a quarter of a million effectives, in which Pathans and Rajputs predominated, was the one *corps d'élite*, the infantry consisting of a large and motley collection of fighting men and followers. Lastly came the territorial forces, raised when required by the landed proprietors (*zamindars*). The cavalry, whose strength is given as 343,000 in the *Ain-i-Akbari*, were serviceable troops, but the host of untrained, unpaid, pressed " foot soldiers," estimated at four million, can be left out of account.

There were no special departments such as agriculture, commerce, education, forests and police, nor the social services of health and welfare now prominent in British India and great Indian States.[1] But revenue matters, involving the submission

[1] *E.g.* Hyderabad (*Adm. Report* 1935-6, Deccan Govt. Press, 1938): Mysore (*Adm. Report* 1936-7, Bangalore Govt. Press, 1938).

of assessment statements twice a year from every village, together with appointments and payment of salaries, which were accompanied by the interminable red-tape of an Indian public office, employed huge secretariats whether at the administrative headquarters of the Mogul Empire or the lesser bureaucracy of the zamorin's government in Calicut.

The classes who depended on State employment for their livelihood, of whom the more important at least were predominantly foreigners, have been summed up by W. H. Moreland,[1] in their relationship to the governed: "The higher ranks, while comparatively few in numbers, controlled the expenditure of a large proportion of the income of the country, and on their attitude depended the welfare of the classes by whom that income was produced. The lower ranks were at least sufficiently numerous to make up in the aggregate a substantial portion of the population; and from the economic standpoint they must be regarded as parasites, feeding upon the fruits of the worker's toil and, beyond an imperfect and precarious measure of security, contributing nothing to the common stock."

The benefits without payment which the mass of the people derived from the government were almost negligible. Roads were few and bridges infrequent; there was no organized medical assistance; and there is no evidence that Akbar's educational scheme ever materialized.[2] Charitable endowments only helped special classes and localities.

The upper classes were able to live much more luxuriously than they can today, allowing for the altered facilities of civilization. The middle classes formed a small and unimportant part of the community.

Poverty and Famine. The overwhelming majority of the people of India have always been desperately poor, and the agricultural community, artisans and labourers lived even more hardly in the Mogul period than they do today. The rural population which consisted then, and still consists, chiefly of small-

---

[1] *India at the Death of Akbar*, p. 82.
[2] *Ain-i-Akbari*, Vol. I. pp. 278, 279; and cf. *India at the Death of Akbar*, note to p. 278.

holders and labourers, have always lived on the very margin of subsistence in appalling housing conditions. India's *per capita* income can only be roughly estimated, but for British India Rs. 20 in 1868 (Dr. Dadabhai Naoraji), Rs. 30 in 1897–8 (Lord Curzon) and Rs. 48–51 rural and Rs. 162–166 urban areas in 1931–2 (Dr. V. K. R. V. Rao)[1] may be quoted. Rural poverty largely explains Gandhi's campaign to bring money to the villages by their weaving and other industries.

Especially outside Bengal, the menace of famine through the failure of the rains hung over the country, nor was there any concerted relief policy in existence until the second half of the nineteenth century. Famine meant heavy mortality; and sixteenth-century accounts record the selling of children as slaves for about one rupee, and the dreadful recourse to cannibalism, as in 1555 and in 1596. On this latter occasion Akbar started famine relief measures, but it is considered that the organization then possible could hardly have done more than provide food for the starving in the towns.

Agriculture.
The provincial governors were ordered to pay special attention to irrigation works, but these efforts were not systematic and, on precedent, would have been for the convenience to townships and travellers rather than for the benefit of the cultivators. The experiment of appointing colonization officers (*karoris*) in 1574 to increase the cultivated areas failed, and this al-Badaoni attributes to the cruelty and rapacity of the officials.[2]

Reviewing the evidence as to security of tenure in the time of Akbar, Moreland comes to the conclusion that the peasant ran a real danger of having his holding taken from him by officials, a possibility which Bernier noted had the inevitable result of keeping the country badly cultivated.

The Peasants.
The predominating industry of India has always been agriculture, which still entirely occupies more than 70 per cent. of the population, as against 8 per cent. in England. India has remained throughout the ages a land of almost innumerable

---

[1] *The National Income of British India*, 1931-1932, Dr. V. K. R. V. Rao, pp. 2, 188 ; for detailed wage earnings see pp. 122-184.

[2] *India at the Death of Akbar*, pp. 266, 128-130.

villages,[1] and the conditions of a peasant's life have changed very little since Mogul times, when due allowance is made for the security which British government has given to the country. Professor Thakore [2] has described " the villager . . . his children growing up in squalor almost like cattle, his cattle sharing the same room and the same affection as his children, and the dust and the glare over all." The rural population has always lived in this way, in its mud hovels or bamboo huts.

The fields of the cultivators, ranging from about five acres in the south and east to about two and a half acres elsewhere, are scattered about the neighbourhood of the village, and are farmed by the family, helped by occasional hired labour and a pair of bullocks. In normal times this provides for their meagre standard of living. The Government of India in its modern reports on agriculture makes reiterated appeals to individual initiative, and these are seconded by the efforts of the educated classes interested in agriculture to institute up-to-date methods of farming. But the small-holders, who are the farmers of India, are slow to abandon the ways of their forefathers.

The cluster of huts forming an Indian village is today what it was in the early Indo-Aryan kingdoms, a self-contained *Village Government.* community. Originally the headman was nominated by the king; later the office became hereditary. The village is governed, now as in the days of Akbar, by its headman, with his satellites, the accountant and the watchman, who are usually hereditary office-holders.

The accountant keeps the record of the villagers' land rights and the individual accounts due for land revenue. He also reports upon the crops; and it may be said that, under modern conditions, the Indian crop forecasts which influence the world's grain markets are based on the figures of the village accountants.

The village watchman, or *chaukidar*, has been the real foundation of law and order in rural India since Indian history began. In the

---

[1] In all India, with its population of 388,800,000 (1941 Census) barely 11 per cent. are town-dwellers, the normal percentage in England being about 79.
[2] *Indian Administration to the Dawn of Responsible Government.*

PLATE XXXI.

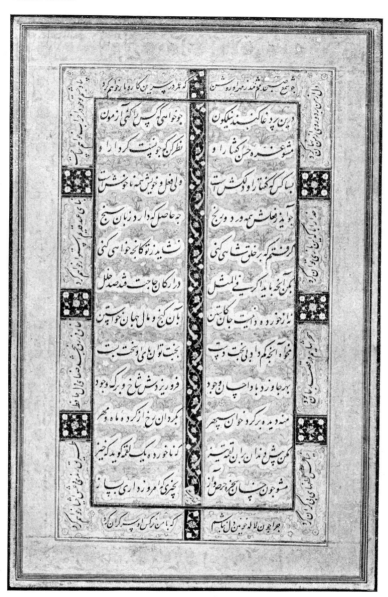

CALIGRAPHY BY MIR ALI OF HERAT

By courtesy of Indian Museum, South Kensington

PLATE XXXII

(b) THE PRINCE AT THE WELL
Rajput Painting, eighteenth century
By courtesy of Indian Museum, South Kensington

(a) GIRL IN GARDEN WITH PEACOCK
Rajput Tempera Painting, seventeenth century
By courtesy of Indian Museum, South Kensington

districts today the effectiveness of the police administration is bound up with the village watchmen. The police stations, each with its station officer and about a dozen constables, scattered through a district of modern India, cannot possibly exercise close supervision. The more remote villages in particular normally rely upon the *chaukidar*, who reports crime, arrests offenders, keeps his eye on suspicious characters, and helps the police with local information when a case is investigated in his village.

On these three functionaries, the headman, the watchman and the accountant representing law, order and the revenue system in half a million villages, the practical administration of India has always rested—however largely the march of conquerors and the magnificence of Oriental courts may figure in the pages of history.

A village has its local priest, a religious mendicant and, in all except the smallest hamlets, the carpenter and the smith, the weaver, the potter and the oil-presser are to be found carrying on their trades, much as their forebears did two thousand years ago.

Some of the villagers may have a permanent title in their lands as owners, or as tenants with hereditary rights of occupancy, and these holdings are sometimes wholly or partly sublet. Below the small-holders come the labourers, frequently of different caste from the actual cultivators; and at the bottom of the scale are the members of the depressed classes, who earn their daily bread by casual labour, working in leather, or some other menial employment.

The demand for the village produce, should there be some town in the neighbourhood, is small, and even today relatively few of the villages of India have been touched by metalled roads or railways. Nor has modern civilization in other ways greatly affected the immense agricultural population in the great stretches of country where post offices are many miles apart and telegraph offices even more distant from each other. But this is a matter of indifference to communities in which ability to write a letter is looked upon as remarkable, and enough education to read a vernacular newspaper is rarer still; and where, as often as not, some wandering pedlar brings the news from the outside world. The general outlook upon life is much the same in a twentieth-century Indian village as in the days of Akbar. Whatever changes the future may bring, the village horizon is still bounded by weather and water, crops and cattle, festivals and fairs, family ceremonies, the dread of famine which the Government of India has for some time happily lessened, and the weight of the debt owed to the local money-lender.

The assessment of Todar Mal, Akbar's finance minister, is the connecting link between the land revenue system of ancient India and the method followed by British administration of the territories under its rule. The land revenue system, by which the Indian peasant still makes direct or indirect payment to the State, is one of the oldest universal institutions in the country, and is prescribed in the sacred law of Hinduism.

The earliest references show that the payment was made in kind,[1] under the supervision of the village headman, or some other official, a reasonable proportion being considered as one-sixth of the gross produce, or even up to one-third in cases of emergency. This payment in kind of the " King's Share " is the origin of the land revenue system as it exists today. Government demands may at times have risen to half, but the Muhammadan conquests made little alteration in an arrangement which accorded with the existing institutions of Islam. Money payments of the revenue were known in the pre-Moslem period, but the use of coined money for this purpose became more general as the Muhammadan kingdoms expanded in the sixteenth century. Assessments levied uniformly for a series of years had been made in Hindu India long before the days of Sher Shah and Todar Mal. The land revenue due upon the large extent of territory left in the hands of Hindu chiefs under Moslem rule was met by the payment of a fixed tribute, and the local rulers were given a free hand in raising the money from the peasants.

Akbar's revenue system varied in different parts of the country. In Sind the original Indian practice was followed, a proportion of the produce was taken, and the risk of a bad year was equally shared by government and cultivator. But in the most productive part of the country, from Bihar up to Lahore and Multan, the standard of

[1] Rent payment in kind still exists in places in Scotland.

revenue payments was set by the regulation system of assessment. Akbar fixed his claim at one-third of the average yield over a period of ten years, a method which transferred much of the risk to the peasant and practically made him a cash-paying tenant. At the same time the heavy government claim of $33\frac{1}{3}$ per cent. left him with an exceedingly small surplus, even in a good year. The maintenance of himself and his family, occasional replacement of cattle and implements, and wages, have been calculated to amount (in Northern India) to about one-half of the gross yield in a favourable season. A very slight loss due to accidents of season would absorb the whole balance.[1] The gross income per head of the rural population has not changed by any large proportion, the difference between the peasant of Akbar's time and the present day being, in this respect, that the modern tenant-cultivator has more money to spend when seasons are bad.

In addition to the revenue derived from the land there was a tax on salt which raised the price of this necessity of life to a high figure. It was not, however, a new impost levied by the Moguls. Like the land tax it had been known in India since the days of the Mauryas, when salt was a State monopoly on which transit as well as import duties were levied; and it was a royal monopoly in the time of the Gupta dynasty. The Mogul government, certainly in Bengal,[2] taxed salt by a high transit duty and also by leasing out, for an annual sum, the monopoly to manufacture it.

Salt Tax.

Until the British supremacy, Akbar, more nearly than any ruler since Asoka, approached the idea of a united India. This dream of an imperial sway over the whole country is to be found interwoven, from the earliest times, with the religion and the political thought of its people. One of the oldest of Hindu public rites was the Rajasuiya sacrifice, which was celebrated by a king who threw out a challenge of supremacy to the world, and making good his challenge by victory over a great oppressor and the raising of the oppressed to happiness and prosperity, won the title

Ideals of Unity.

[1] *India at the Death of Akbar.*
[2] *Political and Military Transactions in India*, Prinsep, Edn. 1825, Vol. II. p. 433.

of Chakravartin.[1] The same idea of supremacy is to be found in the works of Manu, who places among the duties of the king the obligation to increase his territory.[2] Akbar's efforts to combine the opposing elements of Hinduism and Islam endangered his throne; the "universal faith" which he offered to his subjects died with him; and his successors soon forgot the principles which made Akbar a truly national ruler.

Although actually embodied in the allegiance of the Princes of India to the paramountcy of the British crown,[3] visible political unity was not manifested in name until Queen Victoria was proclaimed Empress of India in 1877.[4] Yet, as Joseph Davey Cunningham wrote in 1849,[5] "Hindustan, from Kabul to the valley of Assam and the island of Ceylon, is regarded as one country, and dominion in it is associated in the minds of the people with the predominance of one monarch or of one race." This instinct had, moreover, found expression in the aspirations of the Sikh Guru Govind eighty years after Akbar's death, and explains the attitude of Indian rulers, Moslem and Maratha alike, towards the emperors long after Mogul power had become only a name.

Absence of Dramatic Literature. One of the great forms of literary expression in Hindu India, especially during the golden age of the Guptas and Harsha, was the drama, but until the nineteenth century Moslem drama did not exist. The nearest approach is found in the varied themes of shadow plays—"the magic shadow shapes that come and go" in Fitzgerald's version of Omar's *Rubaiyat*—and the place of the Hindu theatrical company was filled at a Muhammadan entertainment by the story-teller. The well-known collection of *The Arabian Nights* was compiled in the tenth century, and there is evidence which points to an Indian origin of the stories.[6]

[1] *The Making of India*, A. Yusuf Ali, pp. 49, 50.
[2] *The Institutes of Menu*, Edn. 1825, Vol. II. Ch. VII.
[3] See *Report of the Indian States Committee*, Cmd. 3302 of 1929, para. 58.
[4] Royal Titles Act, 1876; Proclamation in India, 1st January 1877.
[5] *History of the Sikhs*, Edn. 1918, p. 275.
[6] Indian Quarterly Review *Islamic Culture*, Jan. 1927, Art. by J. Horowitz.

Religious writings, works on jurisprudence and on Arabic
grammar are important features in Moslem literature,
Historical Works. but the most celebrated literary productions in India
of the period are the works on history. Muhammad Qasim Firishta,
Abu-l-Fazl Allami and Abdu-l-Qadir Ibn-i-Mulk Shah (al-Badaoni)
all wrote in Akbar's reign.

No Hindu historian of India had appeared since Bana wrote his
history of Harsha in the seventh century; and the course of great
events when the Mogul Empire was at the height of its power and
vigour is seen from the Muhammadan standpoint, with the glimpses
afforded by the Jesuit mission to the imperial court and the accounts
of European visitors to the country. The chronicles of the old
Hindu kingdoms are nearly all of them lost, but some of those of the
Rajput States were collected more than a century ago by Colonel
James Tod and published in his *Annals and Antiquities of Rajasthan.*
In the eighteenth century a number of histories were written in
Persian (the official language) by high-caste Hindus.

In the lists of poets, with quotations from their works, given in
the *Ain-i-Akbari,* Shaikh Abu-l-Faiz-i-Faizi is as
Poetry. distinguished as his brother Abu-l-Fazl is renowned
as a historian. Faizi wrote poetry for forty years, spending his
money on charity and devoting his skill in medicine to the poor. Sur
Das, "the blind bard of Agra," is included, but not the most re-
nowned poet of the age, Tulsi Das (1532–1623). His Hindi epic
Rama-charitmanas is still a "healthful breath of autumn breeze"
in the Hindu households of Upper India. It tells of the love of a
personal God incarnate in Rama, whose spouse Sita is the ideal
of Indian womanhood.

Painting had been originally restricted in the Islamic world
to conventional designs, and portrait and other
Painting. subject-painting was introduced later in countries
under the looser Persian influence. On the other hand, Hindu
genius had long ago expressed itself in the frescoes of Ajanta and
afterwards in the early Rajput paintings. Akbar instituted weekly
exhibitions of pictures to encourage Indian artists to come to his
court. The Persian influence so clearly seen in the earlier examples of

o   209

the Mogul school founded by the emperor gave place to Hindu ideas and treatment when Hindu artists, amongst whom were Daswanth, Basawan, Kisir and Maskin, began to outnumber the Persian court painters. In the end the Indian style of art predominated. The great artist Daswanth had been a palki-bearer, whose sketches drawn upon a wall attracted Akbar's notice.[1] Laurence Binyon has recorded that Rembrandt made drawings based on Mogul paintings. In its later phases Mogul art came to borrow more from Europe than from Persia, but these borrowings were never really assimilated.

Nearly all the paintings of Akbar's reign are found in manuscripts. These are themselves examples of the beautiful and elaborate penmanship and illumination which are an orthodox form of Islamic art.

Under Akbar, Mogul architecture created a series of masterpieces.

Architecture. In the words of Abu-l-Fazl [2]: " His Majesty plans splendid edifices, and dresses the work of his mind and heart in the garment of stone and clay."

The Emperor introduced Hindu styles of architecture in many of his buildings, as in the Jahangiri Mahal in Agra fort and at Fatehpur-Sikri—with the exception of its incomparable mosque and the magnificent Buland Darwaza.

In regard to the decorative art of the period " the choicest Italian work does not surpass, if it equals, the superb carving on the white marble cenotaph of Akbar which occupies the topmost storey of his mausoleum at Sikandra." [3]

CHRONOLOGY

1556. Accession of Akbar.
       Battle of Panipat.
       Bairam Khan became Regent.
1560. Fall of Bairam Khan.
1562. Court influence ended with the death of Adham Khan.

---

[1] See *The Court Painters of the Grand Mogul*, by Laurence Binyon, with coloured and other illustrations (Oxford University Press), 1921.

[2] *Ain-i-Akbari*, Vol. I. p. 222.

[3] *History of Fine Art in India and Ceylon*, V. A. Smith, 2nd Edn. revised by K. de B. Codrington (Oxford), 1930. A full description of Mogul architecture and a series of admirable illustrations are given in this work.

1563. Conquest of Gondwana.
1567. Battle of Manikpur ended Uzbeg revolt.
1568. Fall of Chitor.
1569. Birth of Prince Salim (Jahangir).
1569–1576. Building of Fatehpur-Sikri.
1573. Conquest of Gujerat.
1576. Battle of Rajmahal and annexation of Bengal.
1578. The first Jesuit Mission.
1579. The Decree of Iman-i-Adil.
1580. The Bengal Rebellion.
1581. Kabul Expedition.
1582. Proclamation of the *Din Ilahi*.
1587. Conquest of Kashmir.
1592. Conquest of Orissa and Sind.
1593–1601. The Deccan Campaign.
1594–1595. Annexation of Baluchistan and Mekran. Capture of Kanda-
                har: Afghanistan absorbed in Mogul Empire.
1595–1598. Famine and plague.
1596. Annexation of Berar.
1599. Conquest of Khandesh.
1600. Fall of Ahmadnagar; Surrender of Asirgarh.
1601–1604. Revolt of Prince Salim.
1605. Death of Akbar.

BIBLIOGRAPHY

Akbar-nama, Abu-l-Fazl, tr. H. Beveridge (Calcutta), 1907–1912.
Ain-i-Akbari, Abu-l-Fazl, tr. Blockman and Jarrett (Calcutta), 1875–1891.
Akbar the Great Mogul, V. A. Smith, 1919.
Akbar, Laurence Binyon, 1932.
Rise of Mahomedan Power in India, Firishta, tr. Colonel J. Briggs (London),
    1829.
Muntakhab-ut-Tawarikh, al-Badaoni, tr. Lowe and Cowell (Calcutta), 1884.
Mughal Rule in India, Edwardes and Garrett, 1930.
Monserrate's Commentary, tr. Hoyland and Banerjee (Oxford University
    Press), 1922.
India at the Death of Akbar, W. H. Moreland, 1920.
Poverty and Kindred Economic Problems in India, G. Findlay Shirras
    (Government of India Publications), 3rd edn., 1935.

CHAPTER IX

The European Trading Companies

THE beginning of the seventeenth century witnessed the appearance in India of the Dutch and the English to put an end to the Portuguese monopoly, which had lasted a hundred years, and take their share in the Indian trade.

The Indian merchants with whom they had to deal were experienced business men, Muhammadans and Hindus, who controlled the wholesale trade in the different localities, subject to government intervention from time to time to create a state monopoly. Throughout the country there were recognized market prices, influenced by varying supply and demand; there were rings and combines; financial machinery for credit, exchange and insurance, including war risks and an overdue market, and the use of brokers had been developed; and although there were no bankruptcy laws the institution was generally recognized. In the Mogul Empire the standard coin was the silver rupee, approximating to that now in use. The currency of Southern India was based on a gold standard and the chief coin, equal to about $3\frac{1}{2}$ of Akbar's rupees, is known in European writings as the "pagoda."

Indian Trading Companies.

The chief agricultural produce consisted of cereals (wheat, barley and rice), millets, pulses, oil seed, sugar-cane, cotton and hemp, indigo (though hardly any in Bihar), drugs (poppy and betel), pepper and spices. Wheat was quoted at 80–85 lbs. for the rupee, inferior grades of rice were cheaper, but in times of famine wheat rose to seven times its normal price. About the end of the sixteenth century the tobacco plant was acclimatized in Gujerat, and later on the Coromandel coast. The fishing industry and the pearl trade in the south were conducted as they are today.

Raw Materials.

In Akbar's time the production of gold and silver was negligible.

PLATE XXXIII.

(*a*) PLOUGHING WITH BULLOCKS
By courtesy of Indian Railways Bureau

(*b*) THE VILLAGE POTTER
By courtesy of Indian Railways Bureau

PLATE XXXIV.

FISHERMEN
From " Les Hindous," French early nineteenth-century work
By permission of the Secretary of State for India in Council

Northern India mined copper, Southern India imported it. The whole of India relied on its own resources for iron, which could only be worked where wood for smelting was available within reach of the ore. Coal was not mined. There were two important diamond fields in the Deccan. Salt was obtained from the Sambhar lake, the Punjab mines and the water of the sea, sources of supply which have not changed with the centuries.

The milling of grain was, generally speaking, a domestic under-taking as it is today. The spinning-wheel and the hand loom were entirely village industries. Spirits and fermented liquors were common. Highly skilled craftsmen supplied the luxury market with such articles as jewellery and perfumes.

Manufactures.

Cotton weaving was by far the most extensive industry in India (agriculture excepted), though most of the people, unlike the Vedic Indians of early days who generally wore woollen garments, had nothing more than a cotton cloth about their loins. In Bengal jute to some extent took the place of cotton loin cloths. Carpet-making was introduced by Akbar at Agra and Lahore, but the output was small. Silk weaving was quite a minor industry at the beginning of the seventeenth century.

In the sixteenth century there was a steady demand in India for a limited range of foreign goods. Gold and silver being required for coinage and to an even greater amount for display, headed the imports. Horses were needed in large numbers as remounts for the army. Deficiencies in metal, copper, tin, zinc, lead and quicksilver, had to be made up. The list of luxuries was a longer one, and included precious stones, such textiles as silks, velvets and brocades, European wines, African slaves and anything rare or unusual. To pay for these imports India exported in the main textiles and pepper, and minor items such as spices, indigo and opium.

Imports and Exports.

The ports of Calcutta, Bombay and Karachi did not exist. Surat, Broach and Cambay, then the most important harbours in India, with Surat as the point of departure for Mecca, were, after 1573, under Mogul rule. The Portuguese commanded the trade route into the Gulf by their

Ports.

possession of Diu and the mainland settlement of Daman. Lower down the coast were Goa and Cochin, the former being the Portuguese centre for the overseas trade. Goa had risen to prosperity by its traffic with Vijayanagar, and the extinction of the wealthy Hindu kingdom was a contributory cause of the decay of Portuguese power in India. On the Coromandel coast Masulipatam, the port of Golconda, traded with Pegu and Malacca. Sripur on the Meghna, the eastern capital of Bengal until shortly after the death of Akbar, owed its importance to its position on a waterway which led to Agra.

Land transport conditions, bad roads, few bridges, and the absence of wheeled-traffic south of Golconda, diverted the goods traffic of India wherever possible from bullock-carts, camels and pack oxen to coasting vessels. On the western coast the constant danger of pirates enforced the use of convoys, but this was preferable to the exactions of extortionate local officials on land and the activities (not unknown in Europe at the time) of robbers on the roads.

Comparatively little trade crossed the land frontiers, and there were only two regular routes; from Lahore to Kabul, *Caravans.* which tapped the main caravan road between Western China and Europe; and from Multan to Kandahar, which connected up with Persia. These routes through the highlands across the border were only used at intervals, and by strong bodies of men, who protected themselves from the marauding tribesmen by piqueting heights, and made their way through the country by paying blackmail to fort commanders.

From the time of the Maurya emperors inland transit dues had been a regular source of revenue in India. This *Transit Dues.* greatly handicapped internal trade, and one of Jahangir's first orders was an attempt to put an end to the levy of road and river tolls within the empire.

Foreign merchants living in India were not then, as they would be now, in any way under the laws of the country. *Position of Foreign Traders.* For aliens to run a business in Asiatic countries was not a matter of course. It was only allowed by conventions made with the sovereign power through the local authorities, and the communities thus formed enjoyed extra-territorial privileges under resident governors of their own.[1]

The Portuguese ignored this arrangement. Their first experience had been at Calicut, where they were welcomed by the zamorin's subjects who were interested in the import trade, but strongly opposed by the Arab and Egyptian communities controlling the exports to the Red Sea ports. The opposition was successful and the Portuguese failed to get their concession. As representatives of the King of Portugal and not as merchants they subsequently relied on their naval power to force concessions, or to seize territory, over which they exerted the rights of sovereignty, although some later settlements, such as Hooghly,[2] were founded more in accordance with Oriental custom.

The merchants of Holland and England when they arrived in India accepted the position as they found it, and established by negotiation what amounted to self-governing colonies. The original English and Dutch plans for trading with India and the Far East had not contemplated settlement abroad, but merely voyages to sell their goods and return with eastern merchandise. Force of circumstances changed the organization from trading voyages to the local agencies known as factories; from these factories to forts; and eventually the forts expanded into territorial sovereignty.

On their first voyages the trading companies found that many *The Problem of* of the articles popular in Europe were unsaleable *Purchasing Power.* in India and that there was not a large demand for any of their goods. Cargoes were cut down to limited amounts of woollen cloth, lead, cutlery and fancy articles, and these were altogether insufficient to meet the cost of the merchandise they required from India.

The problem, as it presented itself to the English merchants,

---

[1] W. H. Moreland in Ch. VIII. of *From Akbar to Aurangzeb* (1923). In *India at the Death of Akbar* (1920), p. 247, the same author merely states that it is " probable that such agreements were the regular practice."

[2] Founded in 1537, according to Sir W. Hunter's *Imperial Gazetteer of India* (2nd Edn., 1885), Vol. V. p. 490. But reasons for putting the date perhaps as late as 1575 are to be found in A. Abdul Ali's article in *Islamic Culture*, July 1933.

was to find the purchasing power for the indigo and calico which they wished to buy in Surat, and the raw silk which came almost entirely from Persia. The simplest solution would have been to pay in gold and silver, which India would have welcomed. There was, however, a strong prejudice in England against what Sir Thomas Roe called bleeding to enrich Asia, and the export of coin was strictly limited by the government. An alternative was to borrow capital in India. But the amount available was not large, the rate of interest (about 18 per cent.) was crippling to enterprise, and this expedient could only be used in emergencies. The method adopted by the English Company and by the Dutch was to employ part of the available capital exclusively for trade in Asia, and send home the profits which were earned but not the capital itself.

The giving of presents to gain the patronage of the authorities, " particularly the Great Mogul," was the Company's equivalent to the outlay of modern firms in advertisement, a commercial necessity. In 1639 the English factors wrote that they might obtain any concession in reason from Shah Jahan in return for a present of " toys." The gifts required by the Emperor included " large looking-glasses, English mastiffs, our King's Majesty's picture, large, in Parliament robes, a pair of gloves, and a good buff coat."

The East India Company began at once to develop, on a rising *The Cotton Trade.* demand for calico, a flourishing trade in Indian plain and printed piece-goods, and to undersell the more expensive continental linen. England at that time made hardly any linen, while the Dutch were large linen manufacturers and delayed entering a trade which would have injured their home markets.

But about 1676 calico printing works were established near London. The new industry objected strongly to the cut-prices of Indian printed calicoes and joined the silk-weavers and woollen manufacturers of the country in agitation that the growing use of fabrics from a foreign country, which India then was, threatened the ruin of home industries. Opposition to the imports from India

PLATE XXXV.

(a) A GOLDSMITH
By courtesy of Indian Railways Bureau

(b) SALT PANS IN SOUTHERN INDIA
By courtesy of Indian Railways Bureau

PLATE XXXVI

STENCILLED COTTON CLOTH
From Rajputana, eighteenth century
By courtesy of Indian Museum, South Kensington

grew stronger, serious riots of the working people occurred in 1696 and 1697, and in 1700 an Act was passed [1] forbidding the wear of Asiatic silks and printed and dyed calicoes, though these could still be brought in for re-exportation.

In addition to purely protective measures, the war with France obliged Queen Anne's government to raise money for revenue purposes by indirect taxation, and duties were levied from 1703 onwards on piece-goods, spices, pepper and other articles.[2]

In 1720 violent protests from the English woollen and silk manufacturers induced Parliament to forbid the use, with certain exceptions, of calicoes dyed or printed in England. This prohibition was maintained until 1774, when the British calico printers were once more allowed to dye and print stuffs made wholly of cotton, provided that these were manufactured in Great Britain. The measures taken to protect the woollen industry were due to the fact that it was then still looked upon as the main source of the nation's wealth.

Speaking generally, English trade policy with India throughout the seventeenth and in the eighteenth centuries followed the broad principles accepted by all European countries at that time. The most important of these was trade monopoly. The second was the regulation of foreign trade for the protection of home industries, with measures to supply these industries with their raw material. The third principle was that on balance each branch of foreign trade brought into the country more wealth than it took out.[3]

In the seventeenth century, with none of the inventions which have brought the most distant places within easy reach and immediate touch of each other, affairs in the East bore at times little relation to the political situation in Europe. Holland and the government of Spain and Portugal made a twelve-year truce in 1609, with effect in

[1] *Camb. Hist. India*, Vol. V. p. 110.
[2] *Trade Relations between England and India*, C. J. Hamilton (Calcutta), 1919, pp. 107, 108.
[3] *Ibid.*, pp. 86–89.

the East from 1610; but the Dutch and the Portuguese fought in spite of its terms. Portugal and England had no quarrel in Europe, and England was at peace with Spain after 1604 ; yet a Portuguese squadron attacked Best and his two ships off Goa in 1612, to be heavily repulsed, and two years later the King of Spain ordered the Portuguese Viceroy to drive the English out of India; while in 1618 Dutch and English ships were fighting east of the Straits of Sunda, to the horror of their respective home governments when they heard of it.

The union of the Spanish and Portuguese crowns in 1580 had threatened the trade between Holland and Portugal with extinction. This, combined with the strong national spirit of the new commercial centre at Amsterdam, inspired the Dutch merchants to make a bid for the eastern markets, and the early ventures owed their success to the reports on the Portuguese position in the East, furnished by Jan van Linschoten. This remarkable man became secretary to the Portuguese Archbishop of Goa at the age of twenty and remained in India from 1583 to 1592, when he returned to Holland. His *Itinerario* is a brilliant and encyclopaedic account of every conceivable condition in the Portuguese Eastern Empire, and gives a clear appreciation of its points of strength and weakness.

The Dutch United Company.

As the expeditions to the East Indies which began under Cornelis de Houtman in 1595 started injurious competition and risked glutting the European market with spices, the States General of Holland intervened. In March 1602, fifteen months after the London East India Company was formed, the combine known as the Dutch United Company was embodied. It had a large capital and it was backed by the formidable sea-power of Holland. The Company, whose policy was guided by its seventeen directors, had the exclusive right to trade in all countries between the Cape of Good Hope and the Straits of Magellan, and within these limits was empowered to make war and peace, annex territories and build fortresses.

218

The pre-companies, as the pioneer ventures were called, had thought only of trade and how to avoid the Portuguese. But the strong fleets which were now sent out each year boldly attacked the Portuguese at Mozambique, Malacca and Goa. They failed at these strongly held places but they won a foothold in the Spice Islands; and by the effective use they made of their squadrons the Dutch gained the command of the Eastern seas. Portuguese India had been built upon naval supremacy and its loss was utter ruin.

Influence of Sea Power.

The Dutch soon found that the merchandise they brought from Europe was not saleable in the Spice Islands, where Indian cotton goods were the recognized trade medium, and to meet this difficulty they established agencies in India to provide them. In 1605 they started factories at Masulipatam and Nizampatam in Golconda, and a year later at St. Thomé and Negapatam. Trouble arose over the heavy import and export duties levied by the local authorities, but this was remedied; and the Portuguese attempt to drive the Dutch from the Coromandel coast in 1612 was successfully resisted.

Rise of the Dutch.

But no conquest or expansion in India ever tempted the Seventeen to abandon their main object, which was to gain the monopoly of the trade in spices and pepper, then the great commercial link between Asia and Western Europe. In 1609 a Governor-General and a Council of the Indies had been appointed and ten years later Jan Pietersoon Coen, the creator of Batavia, by the ruthless energy of his administration founded the Dutch Eastern Empire. From then onwards the Dutch began to export slaves from Bengal and other places, buying them regularly from Indian dealers with the permission of the authorities.

The East India Company's efforts to divide the Far Eastern trade with the Dutch at the expense of the Portuguese came to an end after the tragic occurrence at Amboyna in 1623. Frequently referred to as a " massacre," the actual facts were bad enough. Ten members of the English factory there, with a Portuguese and nine Japanese, were tortured and put to death by the Dutch authorities after an irregular trial on the charge of conspiracy to seize the local fort. After 1624 the East India Company retained only one pepper factory in the island of Sumatra. By the Treaty of Westminster in 1654 Cromwell exacted belated reparation for Amboyna, and damages were paid to the relatives of the sufferers. The sum of £85,000 was awarded to the company as indemnity in respect of its own claims, but the Commonwealth government promptly borrowed £50,000 and did not repay it.[1]

The Dutch had opened up commercial centres at Surat and Ahmadabad in 1616 and in Agra two years later; and by 1653 they had developed a prosperous trade on the Hooghly and at Patna. By heavy reinforcements of ships and men from Europe they completed the conquest of Ceylon from the Portuguese in 1660, and the Malabar coast settlements by 1663. The Portuguese, their power broken and their trade destroyed, were left with Goa, Daman and Diu.

The English Company had built up their connections through friendly negotiations with the Mogul emperors and the Portuguese; the Dutch by the consistent use of their sea-power in capturing the ships and fortified places of their Portuguese rivals. In the rivalry between the Dutch and English the East India Company's factories were secure within the Mogul dominions. But when England and Holland were at war the Dutch took a heavy toll of English ships in the east.

The United Company stood at the height of its prosperity in the middle of the seventeenth century when Holland had command of the Eastern seas and the prospects of the East India Company were at their lowest. But the heavy cost of their naval and military establishments was an ever-increasing drain on Dutch commercial profits. In spite of the great prosperity of their trade in Surat, Bengal and Ceylon, expenditure gradually grew greater than income, until towards the end of the eighteenth century the deficit became enormous. Peculation was rife, and private trading, against which the directors were powerless, was general.

The close of the eighteenth century saw the earlier position of Dutch and English in India reversed, for Great Britain now had

[1] *Court Minutes of the E.I.C.*, 1655–1659, Ethel B. Sainsbury and Sir W. Foster (1916), Vol. V. pp. iv–vii.

command of the sea; and in addition the settlements of the United Company were exposed to the attacks of the English troops. In 1824 the Dutch exchanged their holding in India for the British possessions in Sumatra, and severed their connection with the country.

In 1620 the Danish East India Company, founded four years earlier, made a settlement at Tranquebar on the east coast. But without sufficient capital the venture was never a success. Twice at the beginning of the nineteenth century when hostilities broke out between Great Britain and Denmark, Tranquebar and the later factory at Serampur were captured and given back. In 1845 the settlements were sold to the English company.

Danish East India Company.

Henri IV tried to establish an Indian trading company, and as early as 1527 [1] a Rouen merchant ship had visited Diu. But it was not until 1664 that Colbert, with the financial backing of Louis XIV, founded the *Compagnie des Indes Orientales*. The company was given the trading monopoly from the Cape of Good Hope to the South Seas, and a perpetual grant of Madagascar, but the French people did not support the venture with enthusiasm.

French Company of the East Indies.

An energetic advance agent secured a factory concession at Surat before the French fleet arrived there in 1668; and in 1673 Sher Khan Lodi, the ruler of Bijapur, gave the company the site upon which Pondicherry now stands. In 1690 Deslandes founded the settlement of Chandernagore. Pondicherry was taken by the Dutch in 1693, but the place was restored after the Treaty of Ryswick four years later.

The creator of Pondicherry, François Martin, till the day of his death at the end of 1706 made tremendous efforts to develop French trade and strengthen the position of the settlements. But the outbreak of war in Europe in 1701 meant commercial disaster to the Company.

The challenge to the English East India Company made by Dupleix in the eighteenth century was not a simple bid for the markets of India but a struggle for political supremacy.

[1] *Camb. Hist. India*, Vol. V. p. 61, quoting the Portuguese João de Barros.

Hostility to Spain made the venture popular, but the East India

Foundation of the East India Company of London.
Company came into existence because the Dutch merchants controlling the European market raised the price of pepper to an exorbitant figure. To counter this " The merchants of London . . . joined together and made a stock of seventy-two thousand pounds to be employed in ships and merchandises, for the discovery of a trade in the East India to bring into the realm spices and other commodities," and the first step was taken along the road which led to the Indian Empire under the British Sovereign and Parliament.

On the 31st December 1600 Queen Elizabeth granted the original charter conferring on the Company fifteen years' monopoly of English commerce from the Cape of Good Hope to the Straits of Magellan. James I, nine years later, made the period indefinite though subject to revocation at three years' notice.

Private enterprise had begun, after the return from India of

The First Voyages.
Ralph Fitch, with the voyage of James Lancaster to the Nicobars (1591–93). The first two voyages of the chartered Company (1601–03 and 1604–06) were made to Sumatra, Bantam in Java and the Moluccas. But the ships of the third expedition were sent to India, and anchored at the mouth of the Tapti below the port of Surat on 24th August 1608. William Hawkins, a merchant who spoke Turkish, went up-country and was well received by Jahangir at Agra, but the Portuguese persuaded the Emperor to refuse permission for the English to trade in Gujerat. The resolute action of Sir Henry Middleton, who reached India in 1611 and held the Red Sea traffic from Surat and Diu to ransom, had, however, so great an effect that early in 1613 a permanent factory was established at Surat; and an English merchant was sent to Agra with presents, to watch over the Company's interests at court.

In March 1615 the first East Indiaman sailed back to England with a cargo of indigo and cotton goods, and English trade with India had begun. As the Company found difficulty in procuring suitable ships they established a dockyard of their own at Deptford,

222

and their first vessel, *The Trade's Increase*, was described as " the goodliest and greatest ship ever framed in the kingdom." [1]

The first known Englishman in India was Father Stevens, S.J., of Winchester and New College,[2] who went to Goa in 1579. Six years later, as rector of Salsette Jesuit College, he helped Newbery and his companions Fitch the merchant, the jeweller Leedes and Story the painter when the Portuguese imprisoned them as spies. Newbery carried Queen Elizabeth's letter of 1583, proposing to " the most mighty Prince, Lord Zelabdim Echebar, King of Cambaia; Invincible Emperor . . . the mutual and friendly traffic of merchandise on both sides." John Mildenhall, hoping for trade concessions in 1603, also saw Akbar. But Sir Thomas Roe, sent by James I, was the first English Ambassador to the Great Mogul. Jahangir rejected a commercial treaty, but Roe at Agra from 1615 to 1619 greatly raised English prestige. He found " the factoryes at Surat . . . and elsewher . . . in the Mogores countrye in a desperate case; proclamations out against them to prohibit them of all trade and to depart the land." [3] When he left, the agencies at Surat, Agra, Ahmadabad and Broach were on a satisfactory footing. His stand against Portuguese power can be seen in his letter to the Viceroy at Goa, protesting against high-handed interference with English merchants, which ends " Your frend or enemye at your owne choyce. D. Tho. Roe, Ambassador of the Majestie of England." [4]

Trade Expansion.

In 1611 a factory had been established at Masulipatam. This was closed down in 1641 when Fort St. George was built near Madraspatam, on the Coromandel coast. The chief factor in charge was called the president, and from this title the name presidency came to be given to the three provinces of Bengal, Madras and Bombay.

[1] *Trade Relations between England and India*, p. 91.
[2] *The Jesuits and the Great Mogul*, p. 80.
[3] Court Minutes of the East India Company, 6th October 1619.
[4] Under date 20th October 1615, *Embassy of Sir Thomas Roe*, pp. 57, 58.

The president at Fort St. George looked after the growing trade of cheap piece goods from the Hindu state of the Carnatic, the remains of Vijayanagar, and when Mir Jumla, then commanding the Golconda army, took the surrounding district in 1647 the company remained on good terms with the conquerors.

Friendly relations had already been established with the Portuguese by the convention of Goa in 1635, which made it safe to send ships home singly, and allowed the coastwise traffic to be developed. The Malabar export trade in saltpetre, pepper and spices, which opened out, went some way to compensate for the tightening of the Dutch monopoly in the Far East. To balance Dutch commercial enterprise in Bengal settlements were planted about 1650 on the Hooghly, at Kasimbazar and at Patna.

Two years later the East India Company's fortunes were at their *Crisis in the Company's Affairs.* lowest ebb. Profits had from the beginning been steadily drained by the extensive and demoralizing private trading both in the country and by export by the Company's servants to augment their low salaries, a form of illicit compensation which went on until 1787.[1] But a more serious matter was the violation of the Company's trade monopoly by the Courteen Association of 1637, which built factories on the Malabar coast, and after the demise of that short-lived venture by the flotation of Lord Fairfax's Company in 1649. With civil war in England the protection of the Royal Charter was gone.

The situation in India became still more critical when war broke out between England and Holland, for the Dutch fleet commanded the Eastern seas. The Company had to abandon Bantam, factories in Bengal were shut down and the settlements on the Coromandel coast were reduced to Fort St. George and Masulipatam. The Company's uncertain status, added to the trade depression existing in England, made it impossible to raise fresh capital for trade

[1] In 1657 the salary of the Chief Agent at Hooghly (Bengal headquarters) was £100 a year, and the pay of the Fourth and Fifth Agents was £20 (*Factory Records*, 1655–1660, pp. 188, 189). Clive joined at Madras in 1744 as a writer on a salary of £5 a year paid quarterly (*Life of Lord Clive*, Sir G. Forrest, Edn. 1918, Vol. I. p. 20).

PLATE XXXVII.

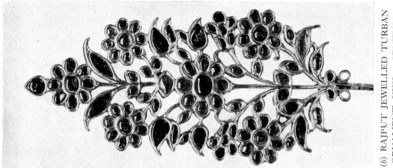

(b) RAJPUT JEWELLED TURBAN
ORNAMENT, XVIITH CENTURY
By courtesy of Indian Museum,
South Kensington

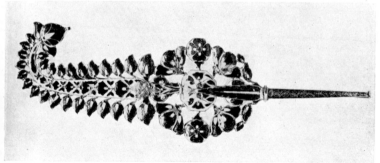

(a) MOGUL JEWELLED TURBAN
ORNAMENT, XVIITH CENTURY
By courtesy of Indian Museum,
South Kensington

PLATE XXXVIII.

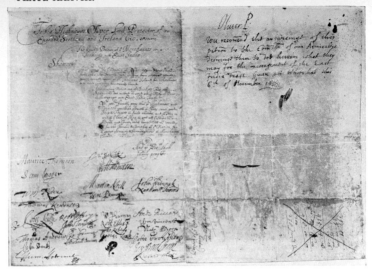

(a) LETTER FROM THE EAST INDIA COMPANY
AND CROMWELL'S ENDORSEMENT

(b) SIR THOMAS ROE

development by the customary terminable loans; and commercial activities had to be still further restricted by withdrawing from Agra and other inland stations. At the same time the position was aggravated by the arrival of numerous private merchant ships from England which caused ruinous competition.

The prospect appeared so hopeless that in February 1657 the East India Company announced their intention to dispose of all their rights and withdraw from the trade. The Protector, who had been considering the idea of the " regulated system " of independent trade followed in the Levant, quickly made his decision and gave the Company, in October, a new charter on the lines of those of Elizabeth and James I. This definition of the Company's rights made it easy to raise the money required, this time in permanent stock. Nearly £740,000 were subscribed, although only half was called up.[1]

King Charles II granted a fresh charter in 1661, by which the Company were empowered to seize and deport *Settlement Administration.* interlopers, to wage war and make peace with non-Christian princes, and to appoint governors who, with their councils, were to exercise civil and criminal jurisdiction over their settlements. Madras had ceased to have a president when the staff was reduced during the crisis, and the agent at Fort St. George was accordingly appointed governor in 1666 over the factories which reappeared along the Coromandel coast. On 27th March 1668, Bombay, a part of the dowry of Catherine of Braganza, was transferred by King Charles to the Company and the Surat president was made Governor of Bombay island.

For nearly twenty years Surat remained the commercial centre and the seat of the presidency. But its position *Rise of Bombay.* was insecure, and the Maratha chief Sivaji sacked the place in 1664, and again six years later. Gerald Aungier, who had become governor in 1669, saw the possibilities of Bombay and by his measures set her on the road to prosperity. He established law courts, settled the local revenue, and gave every inducement to merchants and craftsmen to settle on the island. A suitable

---

[1] *Camb. Hist. India*, Vol. V. p. 95.

currency was introduced.[1] The instructions to establish the Bombay Mint under local arrangements are contained in a letter to the "Generall and Council" from their "loveing Friends" the Governor and Directors of the Company in London, who observed that " it will be a pittiful Regency where such a principall part of Soveraigne Power is not exercised." [2]

Up to this time the English merchants had carried on their trade in India without engaging in war. Any fighting had been at sea, with the Portuguese and with the Dutch; and their military efforts had been confined to fortifying their settlements, a precaution which the home authorities had strongly disliked on the score of expense. But the war both by land and sea which was being waged between the Marathas and the Mogul forces all round Bombay made it clear in the words used by Aungier to the Directors in England a few months before his death in 1677, that " the trade could only be carried on sword in hand."

Four years later Sir Josia Child became the ruling spirit in the directorate at home, and the decision was taken to follow the Dutch example and build up on the Indian coast a military power which could defend itself from any aggressor. Bombay and Madras were to be strongly fortified, and adequate naval and military forces were to be raised to support the policy. To pay for these provisions for security rents, customs dues and municipal taxation were to be increased. The aims of the Company were defined [3] as being " to establish such a politie of civill and military power, and create and secure such a large, well-grounded sure English dominion in India for all time to come."

Sir Josia's policy was vigorously supported in India by his namesake, John Child, who became President and Governor in 1682. Aungier had recognized that, in the troubled state of the country, commercial enterprise needed military power to back it. But Sir Josia in London and John Child in India resolved to take

[1] *Camb. Hist. India*, Vol. V. pp. 100–101.
[2] Extract from letter dated 6th January 1687–88 (India Office MSS. Records).
[3] General letter to Fort St. George dated 12 December 1687, *Despatches from England* (Government Press, Madras, 1929), p. 100.

a strong line with the Mogul government over the levying of dues on the Company's trade, a cause of persistent friction in Bengal, without the necessary means to support their policy.

The East India Company had at first only enrolled European guards, who were quite undisciplined, and poorly armed Indian watchmen to safeguard their factories and add to the dignity of the local officials; and when the factories were fortified, gunners were supplied from the Company's ships to man the batteries. But after the transfer of Bombay by Charles II, military service under the Company was offered to the garrison of king's troops, who almost all volunteered. This nucleus of the future Bombay army consisted of 2 artillerymen with 21 guns, 5 officers, 139 other ranks and 54 " Topasses," who were soldiers of mixed descent from Goa. In 1683 two companies of Rajputs, a total of 200 men armed with their own weapons and under their own officers, were enlisted at Bombay. This was the beginning of the Indian army, and these were the land forces at the disposal of the Governor. In Bengal there were 30 European soldiers under an ensign.[1]

The first result of the new policy was, however, domestic. The garrison of Bombay, under its commander, Captain Keigwin, came out in revolt in 1683 against the methods used to raise revenue and cut down expenditure; and Keigwin governed Bombay in the king's name for a year before he surrendered on terms. Three years later Bombay took the place of Surat as the headquarters of the western presidency.

Keigwin's Rebellion.

President Child was appointed Captain-General, Admiral, Commander-in-Chief and Director of all mercantile affairs in 1687, and in these several capacities he rapidly embroiled himself with Aurangzeb. The seizure of some Mogul ships brought about a declaration of war. The English factors at Surat were imprisoned; Sir John Child captured a number of valuable Mogul merchant ships; Bombay was besieged by the Emperor's forces; and in 1690 the war ended in the Company paying a heavy indemnity. Child died during the peace negotiations.

[1] See *The Army in India and its Evolution* (Government Printing Press, Calcutta, 1924), pp. 2–6.

The difficulties with the Mogul government obliged the factories in Bengal to shut down, and, during the hostilities which followed, the post on the Hooghly selected by the Company's agent, Job Charnock, was in its turn abandoned. Charnock returned after peace was made and built a fortified factory in 1698 on the sites of the villages of Sutanati, Calcutta and Govindpur which he was allowed to rent. The factory was named after William of Orange, and became, in 1700, the head-quarters of Sir Charles Eyre, the first President and Governor of Fort William in Bengal.

Foundation of Calcutta.

The close of the century was a time of considerable anxiety for the East India Company. English pirates had become a scourge in the Arabian Sea, and, by capturing Indian vessels, caused complications with the Mogul government. While the appearance of the " English Company Trading to the East Indies " in 1698 with a duplicate trade monopoly from William III, and three discharged servants of the old Company as its presidents, raised a storm of bitter disputes and threatened the original enterprise with extinction.

The " Old and New " Companies.

But the East India Company was equal to the occasion. The " New Company " with its special ambassador, Sir William Norris, its factors and its fleet soon found it had to raise a further loan, and the " Old Company " promptly secured a strong position by subscribing £315,000 in the name of its treasurer. After further manœuvres the " New Company " saw the wisdom of amalgamation, and a provisional agreement was reached in 1702, which at least ended the undignified quarrels in India. In 1709 Lord Godolphin's award brought complete union in the form of a chartered joint-stock company under an Act of Parliament.

With its foundations set firmly in England and its trading centres established under their presidents at Madras, Bombay and Calcutta, the history of the East India Company has been carried up to the eighteenth century. But before returning to events in Mogul India there is one feature to which reference must be made—the beginnings of British justice in the country.

The Judiciary.

228

" Equal and impartial justice is one of the foundations on which British rule in India rests; it brought new ideals and prospects of peace, contentment and good government in a country where the administration of justice had hitherto been impeded by gross tyranny and corruption; and it affects the life and well-being of every villager and townsman in India." [1]

The charter of 1661 had empowered the Governor and Council of each factory to " judge all persons . . . under them, in all causes, whether civil or criminal, according to the laws of this kingdom and to execute judgment accordingly." From this limited jurisdiction the expansion of British justice developed. In 1672 a Court of Judicature was set up in Bombay where English law was first administered to Indians. By the religious freedom it allowed and by the reservation of capital punishment for murder only, the Company's law of this Court compared favourably with the severity of the law then existing in England. The English penal code was, however, forced upon Calcutta by the Supreme Court set up in 1774. One of the most interesting features of Aungier's judicial reforms was the introduction of trial by jury in both civil and criminal cases. When any party to a dispute was not English, six of the twelve jurors had to be non-English.

Zamindari (landholders') Courts had been presided over by English magistrates in Madras, in the position of Town Governor, since about 1654 to try Indian petty cases, inflicting punishments of whipping, fines, pillory and imprisonment; and almost similar Courts were held in Calcutta. Their jurisdiction was not derived from royal charter or commission as in the case of Bombay. Unlike Bombay, Madras and Calcutta had at that time no sovereign rights. These were then vested in Indian potentates, and judicial powers over the Indian inhabitants who were their subjects were derived from the suzerains. [2]

It must be noted, in the procedure of these early Courts, that

---

[1] Sir Charles Fawcett, formerly Judge of the Bombay High Court, in *The First Century of British Justice in India* (Oxford), 1934, from which this account of the Courts is taken.

[2] Fawcett, *op. cit.*, p. 208.

Indians were practically excluded from any share in the work of the Bench. Judicial powers were exercised by European Judges, or Justices who were servants of the Company, or at least dependent on its pleasure for their stay in India. The only exceptions were the appointment of Bombay merchants to the local Court of Judicature in 1718-28, to represent the four chief communities, and similar arrangements were made earlier in Madras.[1]

The charter of 1726[2] marks another forward step in the administration of justice according to the principles and practices of the English Courts of Law, which were to lead to the establishment of the improved Courts of the nineteenth century. Civil Courts, known as Mayor's Courts, and Criminal Courts of Sessions were substituted for the Company's Courts then existing, and these new Courts derived their authority from the king. The President and Council heard appeals from decisions in the Mayor's Court, subject to a right of appeal to the king in Council when the value of the disputed property exceeded Rs. 3000. The first appeal from India to the Privy Council was made from Madras in 1731.[3]

The charter of 1753 expressly excepted from the jurisdiction of the Mayor's Court all cases between Indians alone, unless both parties preferred that the action should be so settled. Purely Indian litigation, however, continued to form the bulk of the work of this Court.

By these two charters the only share in the administration of justice open to Indians was as jurors in the Sessions Court, but as this involved taking the same oath as jurors in England, all except Indian Christians were debarred. Sir Charles Fawcett observes: " There was of course a reason for this exclusion. In English settlements that were merely mercantile and liable to attack from hostile neighbours, such a policy was almost inevitable. It was not till the securer days of the nineteenth century that an effective start was made in associating Indians as judicial officers in the administra-

[1] Fawcett, op. cit. p. 183.
[2] See Government of India, Sir Courtenay Ilbert (2nd Edn.), pp. 32, 33, for details and legal implications of the Charters of 1726 and 1753.
[3] Fawcett, op. cit., p. 218, footnote.

tion of justice, with a successful development in the highest, as well as the lower, Courts that has made the British Courts in India one of the strongest ties between that country and Great Britain."

CHRONOLOGY

1527. French ship at Diu.
1591. Lancaster sailed from England to the Nicobars.
1595. Houtman's first voyage.
1600. Charter of the London East India Company.
1602. Formation of the Dutch United Company.
1605. Death of Akbar; Accession of Jahangir.
1605. Dutch factories set up at Masulipatam and Nizampatam.
1613. English factory at Surat permanently established.
1615–1619. Roe at the Mogul Court.
1619. Anglo-Dutch Treaty.
1620. Danish factory at Tranquebar.
1623. The Amboyna incident.
1629. Death of Jahangir; Accession of Shah Jahan.
1634. English trade concession in Bengal.
1639. Fort St. George founded.
c. 1651. English factory founded at Hooghly.
1653. Dutch factories established in Bengal.
1658. Enthronement of Aurangzeb.
1661. Charles II's Charter to East India Company.
1663. Dutch conquest of Portuguese settlements on Malabar coast.
1668. Bombay transferred to the East India Company.
1668. French fleet at Surat.
1673. Pondicherry founded by the French.
1688–1690. English war with Mogul Empire.
1690. Calcutta founded by Charnock.
1693. Dutch took Pondicherry (restored by treaty of Ryswick, 1697).
1700. Sir Charles Eyre first Governor of Fort William.
1702. Agreement between the rival English East India Companies.
1707. Death of Aurangzeb.

BIBLIOGRAPHY

Cambridge History of India, Vol. V., 1929. (Vol. IV. of the *Cambridge History of the British Empire*.)
Mughal Rule in India, Edwardes and Garrett, 1930.
Embassy of Sir Thomas Roe to India, ed. by Sir W. Forster, 1926.

European Travellers in India, E. F. Oaten, 1909.

India at the Death of Akbar, W. H. Moreland, 1920.

From Akbar to Aurangzeb, W. H. Moreland, 1923.

The Army in India and its Evolution (Government Printing Press, Calcutta), 1924.

The Presidential Armies in India, by Rivett-Carnac.

Glimpses of Old Bombay and *Bombay and Western India*, by Douglas.

State documents on military subjects are collected in:

Selections from the . . . State Papers . . . in the Bombay Secretariat, ed. by G. W. Forrest (Maratha Series and Home Series, 3 vols.).

Bengal . . . and Bombay Papers . . . from the East India Company relative to the Mahratta War, 1803, a very scarce volume printed by order of the House of Commons, 1804.

CHAPTER X

Mogul India after Akbar

PRINCE SALIM, the only surviving son of the Emperor Akbar, was
in his thirty-sixth year when he came to the throne
Jahangir. as Nur-ud-din Muhammad Jahangir Padshah Ghazi
on the 17th October 1605, and crowned himself on the 24th, after
a week of mourning.

In the course of half a century a great empire had taken the
place of a number of independent states, and Akbar's descendants
eventually conquered India as far south as the Cauvery river. But
the test of their power was their ability to maintain their authority
over a vast country through which communications were bad and
whose outlying provinces had the temptation to throw off their
allegiance. There was not, however, except among the Rajput
chiefs, a strong hereditary aristocracy, as there had been in Europe,
to challenge the power of an absolute monarch. The system of
escheat to the Emperor made that impossible, and each new and
impoverished generation had to establish its position afresh. On the
other hand, the difference in fighting value between the government
forces and an armed populace in revolt was not then overwhelming.

Akbar had won the goodwill of the people of India, with their
contrasting principles of Hindu caste and Moslem democracy, by
religious toleration. But that policy was reversed with increasing
emphasis by his successors, and when to the burden of the excessive
taxation of Shah Jahan there were added the fanatical persecutions
of Aurangzeb, Mogul supremacy came to an end.

Jahangir's first act after his accession was to promulgate a series
of reforms, of which the most important was the abolition of transit
and customs duties. These edicts were at least a manifestation of

good intentions, however much they were nullified by government officials.

The new Emperor, when his father was dying, had frustrated *Khusru's Revolt.* the intrigues to put his own son Khusru on the throne by engaging to uphold Islam and not to punish those who had plotted against him, and he kept both these promises. But within six months Khusru, evading his arrest in Agra fort, escaped to the Punjab and raised a rebellion. With Hussain Beg and Abdul Aziz as his chief adherents, about 650 retainers and an army of peasants and free-lances, Khusru marched upon Lahore, obtaining from the Sikh Guru Arjun a sum of money and his blessing, " not because he was a prince, but as he was needy and unfriended."

Dilawar Khan, governor of the province, rapidly put the city into a state of defence and held it with a small garrison until Khusru's forces were dispersed by the imperial troops. The leaders of the ill-starred rising were captured and brought before Jahangir. Khusru was partially blinded and sentenced to imprisonment for life. The fate of Hussain Beg and Abdul Aziz, and the wretched prisoners who were taken has been recorded by the Emperor himself.

" I ordered these two villains to be enclosed in the skins of a cow and an ass and to be placed on asses . . . and to be paraded round the city. As the skin of a cow dries quicker than the skin of an ass Hussain Beg only lived to the fourth watch (for twelve hours) and then died. Abdul Aziz, who was in the ass's skin and had moisture conveyed to him, survived for twenty-four hours and was then released. To strengthen and confirm our rule I directed that a dense row of stakes should be set up from the garden to the city and that the rebels . . . should be impaled thereon and thus receive their deserts in this most excruciating punishment." Jahangir then rode in state through the lines of his victims followed by Khusru, who was invited to accept the homage of his subjects.

An even more distinguished victim of the rebellion was Arjun, the Fifth Guru, and the compiler of the *Adi Granth*, the earlier of the Sikh sacred scriptures. Jahangir fined him heavily for helping the rebels and, on his refusal to pay, tortured him to death.

In 1611 Jahangir married Mehirunnisa, the widow of a Bengal fief-holder who had been killed four years earlier *Nur Jahan.* while resisting arrest on suspicion of treason. Jahangir and Nur Jahan—Light of the World—admirably suited each other, and the weak and self-indulgent Emperor was content to allow his strong-minded consort to gain complete influence over him.

Nur Jahan was thirty-four at the time of her second marriage, but she kept her remarkable beauty for many years; and to her personal charm were added a great charity, cultured intelligence and shrewd common sense. As the leader of society, her taste influenced the fashions for a century after her death. Her vitality found an outlet in riding and hunting with her husband, and her ambition brought her, in time, to the position of a reigning sovereign. With her name on the coinage and her signature added to Jahangir's on the imperial decrees, Nur Jahan emerged from the *purdah* and issued her orders to the nobles as she sat on the balcony of her palace. Jahangir, as his *Memoirs* record, was as proud of her prowess when tiger-shooting with her matchlock as he was of her wisdom in solving the difficulties of State affairs. The Emperor was a prey to the family failings of drink and drugs, but Nur Jahan was able eventually to moderate these habits which, outside the Mogul court circle, were not common, for Indian public opinion has always set its face against intemperance.

Early in the reign unrest had to be suppressed in Bengal. An unfortunate incursion into Tibet was made in 1612, *Wars and* and a year later came the successful campaign *Disturbances.* against the Portuguese. Hostilities with Udaipur (Mewar), which had been carried on intermittently for half a century, ended in 1614, when Rana Amar Singh capitulated to the Mogul army under Prince Khurram. Following Akbar's Rajput policy Jahangir, in making Udaipur a tributary state, granted most generous terms, and went so far as to erect statues of the Rana and his son below the audience window of the imperial palace at Agra.

In the Deccan the war with Ahmadnagar was prolonged throughout the reign by the genius of the Abyssinian eunuch Malik Ambar, minister and commander-in-chief, and while he lived the state kept its independence. He was a master of guerilla tactics, and although Prince Khurram took the capital in 1616 and was awarded the title of Shah Jahan, the war went on without decisive result; and Malik Ambar died in 1626, having, in the words of the *Iqbal-nama*, "maintained his exalted position and closed his career in honour."

But in 1616 the internal state of the country was more critical than the issue of any of Jahangir's foreign campaigns. The general unrest and the court intrigues over the rival heirs—Khusru the captive hero of the people and choice of the older nobility, and Khurram the favourite of the Queen's party—threatened the Emperor with assassination and the country with civil war. Sir Thomas Roe felt it necessary to warn the East India Company to keep their agents collected in a few places, not to extend their business up country and to avoid politics.[1] But the Queen's party extinguished the popular hopes by transferring Khusru from the guardianship of Ani Rai Singh Dalan to his enemies; and the unfortunate prince died in the custody of Khurram, now Shah Jahan, in 1621,[2] when Jahangir was lying seriously ill. The official announcement made at the beginning of 1622, that Khusru had died of colic, is contrary to the popular belief at the time that the prince was murdered by order of his brother. It is also against the weight of the evidence for and against cited in the *History of Jahangir*.[3]

A year earlier Jahangir had taken the Hindu stronghold of Kangra after a siege of fourteen months. On a subsequent visit he outraged the religious feelings of the inhabitants by ordering a bullock to be slaughtered and a mosque erected within the fort, which Professor Beni Prasad characterizes[4] as one of the few intolerant acts of his reign.

---

[1] *The Embassy of Sir Thomas Roe*, pp. 246–247, under date 16th October 1616.
[2] *History of Jahangir*, p. 336 and footnote. *Oxford History of India* has 1622, pp. 384, 385, but Professor Prasad gives reasons for his statement.
[3] *The Oxford History* and *Mughal Rule in India* both state that Khusru was murdered.
[4] *History of Jahangir*, p. 318.

PLATE XXXIX.

A MOGUL COURT. AMBASSADORS AND PORTUGUESE
MISSIONARIES IN ATTENDANCE

By permission of the Secretary of State for India in Council

PLATE XL.

HIMALAYAN BLUE-THROATED BARBET
Artist : Ustad Man Sur, Jahangir's Court Painter of Birds and Animals
By courtesy of Indian Museum, South Kensington

In 1622 Kandahar was taken by the Persians, and Shah Jahan
was given command of the army to be sent to
Rebellion of   recover the city. Prince Parviz, a drunken nonentity,
Shah Jahan.   was now his only rival to the throne, but Shah Jahan
felt that absence from the court, when his father might die at any
moment, was too great a risk to his own prospects. He refused to
obey the Emperor's orders, and by breaking into open rebellion
justified Nur Jahan's suspicions of his loyalty, and her conviction
that he had become a danger to the State.

Shah Jahan was joined by Abdurrahim, the Khan Khanan, an
old man of seventy who had been loaded with honours by Jahangir.
The rebel army marched on Agra and was met by the imperial
troops, nominally commanded by Prince Parviz and actually led
by Mahabat Khan. Shah Jahan was badly beaten at Bilochpur on
29th March 1623, and retreating through Malwa and the Deccan
reached Bengal, where he reorganized his forces and gained some
temporary success. But at Kampat, in 1624, Mahabat Khan again
defeated him and Shah Jahan escaped to the Deccan to take refuge
with his father's enemies.

The Khan Khanan had surrendered after Bilochpur and the
old minister was kindly treated by the Emperor. But it was more
than a year before Shah Jahan wrote to Jahangir imploring forgiveness. The answer came from Nur Jahan stating the conditions
on which his submission would be accepted; two strongholds
which he held must be surrendered and his sons Dara Shikoh and
Aurangzeb sent to the imperial court. The terms were accepted, but
Shah Jahan remained in the south until his father's death.

In under four years the situation of 1622 had entirely changed.
Shah Jahan was no longer a menace, but Mahabat
Mahabat Khan's   Khan, the victorious general and the most power-
Plot.   ful man in the Empire, was now a source of
danger as he had the drink-sodden Parviz, a prospective heir to
the throne, under his influence. The Queen realized the threat
to her power and, with the help of her brother Asaf Khan, took
steps to meet it. She succeeded in separating Parviz from Mahabat
Khan, and then found a pretext to order the general's recall to court.

Mahabat Khan, faced with ruin on a charge of wholesale embezzlement, resolved by a bold stroke to get control of the Emperor and end once for all the influence of Nur Jahan. With about five thousand Rajput horse he marched up country and surprised the imperial camp, then on the move from Kashmir to Kabul. Jahangir was made a prisoner and taken in custody to Kabul, but Nur Jahan evaded capture and succeeded in arranging the Emperor's escape to Rohtas, where imperial troops had been collected. Mahabat's scheme had failed and, making a virtue of necessity, he submitted. Ordered to proceed to Sind, in pursuit of Shah Jahan, whom rumour had credited with renewed disloyalty, Mahabat Khan promptly made his peace with the prince, whose position was greatly strengthened by the death of Parviz in October 1626.

While returning from his annual visit to Kashmir in 1627, Jahangir, *Death of Jahangir.* worn out with his excesses and suffering severely from asthma, was taken fatally ill and died on the 28th October at Chingiz Hatli in the foothills. He was buried at Shahdara, close to Lahore.

Jahangir possessed neither the complex character nor the outstanding intellect of his father, but he was far from *His Character.* incompetent. He lacked Akbar's insatiable spirit of inquiry, and religion did not vitally interest him. His devotion to Islam was outwardly orthodox, but it was largely a matter of secular policy. Like Akbar he enjoyed listening to debates between the Jesuit fathers and the *mullahs*, and although he surrounded himself with a gallery of pictures of the saints of the Catholic Church, this was in part due to his love of art, while his patronage of the Jesuit mission suited his foreign policy. Hinduism made no appeal to him and he ignored the teachings of the reformed sects, Moslem and Hindu, beyond persecuting popular preachers and fanatics when he believed them to be a danger to the State. He never instituted systematic religious persecution, and even the cases of Shaikh Ahmad of Sirhind who claimed to be the Mahdi, and the Svetambara Jains of Gujerat with their prophecy of the impending fall of the Empire, had at least some political pretext.

Kindly in his family life, Jahangir's temperament as a ruler was fairly described by the Reverend Edward Terry, chaplain to Sir Thomas Roe, as " composed of extremes; for sometimes he was barbarously cruel and at other times he would seem to be exceedingly fair and gentle."

His Culture. Jahangir took a keen and critical interest in the school of art founded by his father, and especially encouraged miniature painting. The influence of Hindu tradition became still more pronounced, and during his reign Mogul painting was at its best.

As may be seen from his *Memoirs*, Jahangir shared Babur's enthusiasm for gardening, and delighted in planning wonderful pleasances with their massed beds of tulips and every kind of rose, vistas of marble pavilions, waterfalls and trees, a characteristic of the dynasty which E. B. Havell has described as the greatest contribution of the Moguls to Indian art.

Although Jahangir's *Memoirs*, which cover eighteen years of his reign, have not the fascination of Babur's autobiography, they are a remarkably candid revelation of his character. Henry Beveridge has summed up the royal author as one who would have been a better and a happier man had he been head of a natural-history museum.[1]

Foreign Policy. The Emperor's inclination was to keep on friendly terms with Persia, but Kandahar was a perpetual source of contention, and after diplomatic negotiations were broken off it was lost to the Empire by the Persian invasion of 1622. Jahangir brought Udaipur, the last of the independent Rajput States, under his suzerainty, but his attempts to establish Mogul supremacy throughout the Deccan were unsuccessful.

The most important features of Jahangir's foreign policy were his relations with the European powers. At the beginning of his reign Portuguese supremacy in eastern waters was already on the wane, but their influence at the court was strong enough to prevent the earliest English merchants from obtaining trade concessions within the Empire. The situation at Agra changed in 1613, when the Portuguese, with insensate folly, plundered four imperial ships in which the Dowager Empress had a large interest. Jahangir expelled nearly

[1] *Memoirs of Jahangir*, Preface to Vol. II.

all the Portuguese from the Empire, interdicted Christianity and besieged Daman, while the Governor of Surat made an alliance with the English, who engaged and defeated the Portuguese Viceroy's fleet. The Portuguese then came to terms, and the treaty remained unbroken for the rest of Jahangir's reign.

The mischief, however, was done. English prestige rose as Portuguese influence declined, and the prospects of English traders were still further improved by the arrival of Sir Thomas Roe at the imperial court. Jahangir had no direct dealings with the Dutch United Company.

The government of the Mogul Empire has been described [1] as a union of despotism with bureaucracy. Unlike Akbar,

Administration.

Jahangir would never descend to details, and the local officials had in practice absolute powers over those with whom they came directly in contact, a successful appeal against oppression being extremely rare. The rule of Jahangir under the influence of Nur Jahan and her family council fell short of the government of Akbar, but for many years to come a sufficient number of foreign officials of the right stamp were available to save the administration from hopeless inefficiency. Jahangir's reign, however, marks the beginning of the decline in the general character of the higher (and alien) officials in the service of the ruler who, notwithstanding his father's national aspirations and policy, was described by Bernier as " The Great Mogul, a foreigner in Hindustan."

There was in Mogul India no code of law other than the canon law of Islam, which was recognized in theory; but outside his interpretation of religious obligations the Emperor was free to act as he pleased. Jahangir had a genuine desire to do justice without favouring the rich, but he was capricious and violent in temper, and the deliberation which had been a feature of the infliction of punishment by Akbar was replaced by speedy trials and quick executions. Until his health broke down, however, Jahangir undoubtedly tried to protect his subjects from official oppression, for the local authorities were notoriously corrupt, and popular opinion of the *kazis* (judges)

[1] *From Akbar to Aurangzeb*, p. 234.

has been crystallized in the saying: " When the *kazi's* bitch died, the whole town was at the funeral; when the *kazi* himself died, not a soul followed his coffin." [1]

Jahangir reverted to the *jagir* system of payment of officials, which Akbar had disliked as it gave the holders too much power and independence. But in general the principles of administration which Akbar had followed were observed by his son.

In a conversation with Sir Thomas Roe,[2] Mir Jamal-ud-din Hussain " Viceroy of Patan " in Bengal gave some illuminating details as to the pay and allowances of a high official in the Mogul government. Jamal-ud-din held the rank of Five Thousand horse, but he was allowed to maintain 1500 only (at an annual cost of 200 rupees a head) while drawing the pay of the total number, a net yearly gain of 700,000 rupees. He paid into the Treasury 1,100,000 rupees [3] annually for his province, it being understood that he could retain any surplus he was able to raise over and above the " rent." The Viceroy added that some governors had twice his income and more than twenty drew an equal amount. It may be mentioned that the pay which Sir Thomas received as ambassador at the Mogul court was £600 a year, equivalent, at the rate of exchange of the day, to just under 5540 rupees.

Francisco Pelsaert, chief of the Dutch factory at Agra, a highly *Social Conditions.* competent observer who stayed seven years in the country, shows us the other side of the picture. In his report [4] written in 1626 he contrasts the luxurious life of the nobles with the " stark want and utter subjection of the common people."

The French merchant Tavernier who made five visits to India and saw a great deal of the country between 1641 and 1667, and the

---

[1] Quoted in *Mughal Rule in India*, p. 191.

[2] *Sir T. Roe's Embassy*, pp. 209–211. The ambassador records the value of the rupee as 2s. 2d.

[3] In referring to sums in Indian currency the English method of notation is used in this book. But the general and official method would be to write " Rs. 11 lakhs " and Rs. 7,00,000 (*i.e.* 7 lakhs of rupees). A lakh is 100,000 and a crore 10,000,000.

[4] *Jahangir's India* (The Remonstrantie of F. Pelsaert), tr. by W. H. Moreland.

doctor François Bernier who was for twelve years at Aurangzeb's court, give accounts of the condition of the working classes. Tavernier [1] says of the peasants: " They are reduced to great poverty because if the governors become aware that they possess any property they seize it by right or by force. You may see in India whole provinces like deserts from whence the peasants have fled on account of the oppression of the governors." While Bernier wrote of the artisan in the city: " He can never become rich, and he feels it no trifling matter if he have the means of satisfying the cravings of hunger and covering his body with the coarsest garment. If money be gained it does not in any measure go into his pocket, but only serves to increase the wealth of the merchant."

Some of the Indian traders made large fortunes, and Virji Vora the merchant-prince of Surat, who controlled a number of syndicates for more than half the seventeenth century, was reputed to be the richest merchant in the world.[2]

Shah Jahan did not ascend the throne without opposition. His younger and only surviving brother Shahryar had married Nur Jahan's daughter by her first husband, and the Empress supported his claim. But Shah Jahan's father-in-law, Asaf Khan, brother of Nur Jahan, made short work of a claimant who had the misfortune to be slow-witted, irresolute and unpopular, and Shahryar was blinded and in prison before Shah Jahan came up from the Deccan. Asaf Khan took the additional precaution of creating a stop-gap Emperor, Dawar Baksh, son of the dead Prince Khusru.

Accession of Shah Jahan.

Before he started for the north Shah Jahan sent an express message to Asaf Khan in which he said " it would be well if Dawar Baksh the son, and Shahryar the useless brother of Khusru and the sons of Prince Daniyal were all sent out of the world." The almost

---

[1] Oaten deals briefly with the accounts of these two Frenchmen in *European Travellers in India*, Chs. XI. and XII. Full details are to be found in *Travels in India*, J. P. Tavernier, ed. W. Crooke, and in *Travels in the Mogul Empire*, ed. V. A. Smith.

[2] From *Akbar to Aurangzeb*, Ch. V.

wholesale family murders which accompanied the accession of the later Mogul emperors, with disastrous effect upon the dynasty, had begun. Dawar Baksh was the only one of the proscribed collaterals who escaped death; released from prison he went to Persia, where he spent the rest of his life as a pensioner of the Shah. Nur Jahan survived her husband eighteen years, living in complete retirement on the allowance of 200,000 rupees made to her by Shah Jahan.

The new Emperor, whose crown had been made safe by a holocaust of his nearest male relatives, was proclaimed at Agra early in February 1628.

Mumtaz Mahal. The Timurids were as a rule excellent husbands, and the redeeming feature of Shah Jahan's character was his devotion to his wife Mumtaz Mahal. Popularly known as Taj Bibi, the Lady Taj, Arjumand Bano Begam had married Prince Khurram, as he then was, in 1612, and throughout a happy married life her influence was always for good. Mumtaz Mahal died in child-birth in 1631 at the age of thirty-nine, and her sorrowing husband built in her memory at Agra a monument which has never been surpassed in beauty. Shah Jahan lived for another thirty-five years, but he did not marry again.

The Emperor's reign was to end in tragedy even more terrible than the circumstances of his accession. But under his rule of almost thirty years, frontier wars of no great importance and the revival of religious persecution were the only events which broke the peace of the country; and even repeated visitations of severe famine were not able to destroy the great outward prosperity of what is generally regarded as the golden period of Mogul dominion.[1]

Imperial Wealth. The wealth of the Mogul emperors at the height of their power was colossal. Akbar left behind him a fortune in coined money equivalent to at least two hundred million pounds today and a huge collection of gems, but this was exceeded by the treasure of his grandson. Shah Jahan was the very embodiment of oriental splendour, and his famous peacock throne of solid gold blazed with precious stones.

[1] *Mughal Rule in India*, p. 99.

Shah Jahan spent immense sums on architecture. The Taj Mahal alone cost 917 lakhs of rupees,[1] and 20,000 workmen
Architecture.
were employed on the building, which took twenty-three years to complete. His extravagant expenditure on tombs, mosques and palaces was a crushing burden upon the country and paved the way to national bankruptcy. The standard of assessment was raised by one-half, and production ceased " to be worth while because life, to the producer, was ceasing to be worth living." [2]

But Shah Jahan gave India its most lovely examples of the Indo-Persian style of architecture in the tomb of Jahangir at Shahdara, the Jama Masjid at Delhi, and the Pearl Mosque and the Taj Mahal at Agra. Rumour has for many years attributed the Taj, in part at least, to French or Italian experts. But Sir Jadunath Sarkar[3] gives documented reasons for the statement that it was built under the supervision of Mukarramat Khan and Mir Abdul Karim, working on a wooden model. Maulvi Moin-ud-din Ahmad ascribes the conception of the design to Isa Afandi, a Turko-Indian.[4]

The rebellions in Bundelkhand and in the south during the first
Rebellions of Raja Jujhar Singh and Khan Jahan Lodi.
two years of the reign were suppressed with little difficulty. The rising of the Bundela Rajputs in 1628 under Raja Jujhar Singh, the son of Jahangir's favourite, Bir Singh, was put down by Mahabat Khan, and the fugitive raja was killed by Gonds some years later.

The second rebellion, headed by Khan Jahan Lodi carrying out the traditional hostility of the Afghan chiefs to the Mogul dynasty, although backed by the ruler of Ahmadnagar, was soon dealt with by the imperial general Azam Khan; and Khan Jahan and his sons died in battle. This revolt, however, became ultimately the cause of greater interference in the Deccan than had ever yet been exercised by the Mogul sovereigns of Delhi.[5]

---

[1] *From Akbar to Aurangzeb*, p. 196. [2] *Mughal Rule in India*, p. 363.
[3] *Studies in Mughal India.* [4] *Mughal Rule in India*, p. 310.
[5] *Mughal Rule in India*, p. 71.

PLATE XLI.

(a) CRYSTAL BOWL

Early seventeenth century ; probably Agra work

By courtesy of Indian Museum, South Kensington

(b) JAHANGIR'S GREEN JADE DRINKING CUP

Mogul Delhi work, 1613

By courtesy of Indian Museum, South Kensington

PLATE XLII.

(a) PORTRAIT OF SHAH JAHAN
By Bichitr
By courtesy of Indian Museum, South Kensington

(b) PRINCE SALIM
Artist : Bichitr (Mogul School of Shah Jahan)
By courtesy of Indian Museum, South Kensington

(c) NUR JAHAN FEASTING WITH HER LADIES
By courtesy of Indian Museum, South Kensington

The failure of the monsoon brought about an appalling famine in
Famine. Gujerat and the Deccan between 1630 and 1632,
followed first by a plague of destructive vermin and
then by widespread pestilence. The Dutch merchant van Twist,
who afterwards became governor of Malacca, wrote an account of
what he saw, a terse description of fact more heartrending than the
emotional chronicle of Abdul Hamid Lahori.[1] Van Twist has
recorded: " No grass grew. Cattle died. As the famine increased
men abandoned towns and villages . . . deserted their wives and
children. Women sold themselves and their children as slaves.
Children deserted by their parents sold themselves. Some families
took poison and so died together . . . Others threw themselves into
the rivers so that they flowed full of corpses. Husbands (ate) their
wives, wives their husbands, children their parents. . . . Human flesh
was sold in open market. Some of the Dutchmen coming from
Amadabad found some people sitting at a little fire where hands and
feet were cooking; a terrible thing to see. The whole country was
covered with corpses lying unburied, which caused such a stench that
the whole air was filled with it. . . . This terrible divine punishment
fell chiefly on the poor who had nothing in store." [2]

The State measures of relief consisted in the opening of public
kitchens, the remission of a proportion of the taxes and grants of
money. But these measures could not cope with the calamity, there
was considerable delay before they were begun, and Peter Mundy[3]
observed that " the rich and strong (were) taking perforce all to
themselves." There was abundance of grain in the north but the
transport difficulties due in part to the Deccan war were insuperable;
and although English merchants ordered large stocks of grain from
Persia shipping facilities were quite inadequate for effective supply.
It was not until the end of 1631 that land and sea transport was able

[1] Abdul Hamid's account is quoted in *History of India as told by its own
Historians*, Elliott and Dowson, Vol. VII. p. 24, and in *Mughal Rule in India*,
p. 73.

[2] Quoted from van Twist's pamphlet by Moreland (*From Akbar to Aurangzeb*,
pp. 212, 213).

[3] *From Akbar to Aurangzeb*, p. 214. See also *Travels of Peter Mundy*, 1608–
1667. Ed. Sir R. C. Temple (Hakluyt Society), 4 vols. 1905–1924.

to meet the needs of the reduced population, though at prices still far above the normal.

Trade was dead in a depopulated land, and in December 1634 the factors at Surat wrote to London that the losses were incalculable. It was not until two years later that it became possible to report that the country had recovered from famine. There were seven other famines in different parts of the country, of varying severity, between 1632 and 1658.[1]

A comparison cannot fairly be drawn between the measures taken by the Mogul Government and the existing organization for famine relief. In 1630 there were no first-class roads; in 1930 nearly 42,000 miles of railway spread over the country. The effect of local shortage of food today is consequently soon spread over a wide area by importation; and modern civilization has been able to evolve a protective system which has practically put an end to famine on a large scale.

In 1632 Shah Jahan went to war with the Portuguese. Their increasing trade in Bengal was reducing the provincial revenues, but the Emperor's hostility was chiefly aroused by the Portuguese slave-trade coupled with the religious propaganda of the merchants. The Portuguese fortified settlement of Hooghly was invested by an army said to have numbered 150,000 men, and the little garrison of 300 Portuguese and 700 Indian Christians held out gallantly for three months. "The place was carried by assault at the end of September, very few of the Portuguese escaping. Four hundred prisoners were paraded before Shah Jahan in July 1633 and were given their choice between turning Muhammedans and perpetual imprisonment. A few adopted the former course and were rewarded." [2] The Mogul persecution of Christianity thus begun continued for about two years.

War with the Portuguese.

While the Christian prisoners of Hooghly were passing, as the author of the *Badshah-nama* viewed it, "from prison to hell," Shah Jahan began a violent persecution of the Hindus of Benares, and destroyed a large number of temples.

Hindu Persecution.

[1] See *From Akbar to Aurangzeb*, pp. 206–210.
[2] *Dutch Dagh Register*, 1631–1634, p. 145.

From the time of Akbar until Aurangzeb destroyed the last two
Sultanates of Golconda and Bijapur the Mogul
Operations in Emperors pursued a forward policy in the Deccan.
the Deccan. Shah Jahan's earliest operations were stopped by the
famine and by the death of Mumtaz Mahal. But in 1635 operations
were resumed with vigour. The Maratha chief Shahji had re-
established the power of what had once been the kingdom of
Ahmadnagar, and set up a youthful member of the Nizam Shahi
dynasty as nominal ruler. Shahji was the father of Sivaji, the popular
leader, " the wisdom of whose plans " in the words of James Grant
Duff " raised the despised Hindus to sovereignty . . . when the hand
that had framed them was low in the dust."

The Emperor sent an ultimatum to the rulers of Golconda and
Bijapur demanding a recognition of his suzerainty, the payment of
tribute and abstention from an alliance with Shahji and the State of
Ahmadnagar. Golconda accepted the terms; but the Adil Shah was
defiant and two imperial armies swept through Bijapur massacring
and enslaving the inhabitants. In May 1636 Muhammad Adil Shah
and Shahji made peace, and the settlement lasted for about twenty
years. Aurangzeb was appointed Viceroy of the Deccan provinces,
Khandesh, Berar, Telingana and Daulatabad. Daulatabad included
those parts of Ahmadnagar which were not ceded to Bijapur, now a
feudatory State of the Empire.

Shah Jahan by his own rebellion against his father had ruined
Jahangir's prospects of regaining Kandahar. He
The North- now resolved to win back the chief commercial
Western station on the trade route between India and
Campaigns. Persia. By judicious bribery the imperial governor of Kabul
induced the Persian, Ali Mardan Khan, to surrender Kandahar
in 1638.

Between the years 1645 and 1649 Shah Jahan waged unsuccessful
war to recover the lost Timurid territories of Balkh and Badakshan.
But in 1648 a large Persian army entered Afghanistan, and Kandahar
was taken in February 1649. Shah Jahan made several attempts to
recapture it. In May of the same year and again in 1652 Aurangzeb
was sent up, on the second occasion with new siege-guns, but he

failed to take the place; and Dara Shikoh was equally unsuccessful in 1653. Neither Shah Jahan nor his successors made any further attempt to regain it.

The loss of Kandahar was regrettable though not disastrous and the unsuccessful sieges had cost the government more than half the gross revenue of the Empire for one year,[1] but the loss of military prestige was considerable. The army of Akbar in spite of its usual encumbrances of an imperial court was efficient. But by the reign of Shah Jahan deterioration had already set in,[2] and the policy of increasing the weight of the heavy artillery did nothing to counteract it.

Aurangzeb had found the administration of the Deccan a thankless task. The country could not pay its way, which

Aurangzeb as Administrator.

landed him in financial difficulties, and he had to contend with the hostility of his eldest brother Dara Shikoh, who had complete influence over the Emperor. In 1644 he resigned his viceroyalty in protest against the persistent belittling of his authority and his consequent loss of prestige.[3]

A year later he was appointed to Gujerat. The country was infested with bandits and "the prevailing lawlessness added to the misery of the peasants and the poverty of the land by discouraging industry."[4] But the strong and energetic rule of Aurangzeb proved effective in establishing order and unusual security.

When the expeditionary force was sent up to Central Asia, Aurangzeb was given command, and on his return from active service in 1652 he was reappointed Viceroy of the Deccan. With the help of an exceptionally able and conscientious revenue officer, Murshid Quli Khan of Khurasan, who had been Paymaster to the Forces in Balkh, he reorganized the finances and introduced Todar Mal's system of land survey and assessment. The administration was overhauled, incompetent officials were dismissed or reduced, and agriculture was encouraged by irrigation works and loans. But at the same time Aurangzeb was betraying by his religious bigotry the

---

[1] *History of Aurangzib*, Vol. I. pp. 167, 168 and footnotes.
[2] *Mughal Rule in India*, pp. 174–180.
[3] *History of Aurangzib*, Vol. I. pp. 76, 77.   [4] *Ibid.*, Vol. I. p. 80.

limitations of his character, which finally blighted his fame and wrecked his Empire.[1]

The viceroy now turned his attention to foreign affairs, and resolved to attack the States of Bijapur and Golconda. The Shia Sultans of the Deccan were the objects of bitter hostility to the Mogul rulers, and Aurangzeb had no scruples as to the means he might employ to destroy them. He found a useful ally in Muhammad Said, known in history as Mir Jumla.[2]

The son of a Shia oil merchant of Isfahan, Mir Jumla had come to the Deccan in 1630 as a young man, and made a fortune in diamonds. Abdulla Qutb Shah (Kutbu-l-mulk), struck by his remarkable ability, made him chief minister of Golconda, and Mir Jumla proceeded to make himself virtual ruler of the State. Sent to subdue the hitherto unconquerable highlands of the Carnatic he handled the forces he had trained himself and stiffened with European artillerymen so effectively that he annexed a territory 300 miles long and 50 in breadth. Here he maintained his army on the proceeds of the local diamond mines and by digging up the treasure buried beneath the old Hindu temples. Qutb Shah found that he had raised up against himself a formidable and virtually independent ruler whom he had not the power to crush. To strengthen his position Mir Jumla began to intrigue against his master and so got in touch with Aurangzeb.

The would-be confederates were full of mutual suspicion but eventually Shah Jahan made Mir Jumla a Commander of Five Thousand in the Empire; and Aurangzeb declared war on Golconda. Hyderabad, one of the richest cities in India, was entered at the end of January 1656 and sacked. Aurangzeb then laid siege to the stronghold of Golconda where Qutb Shah had taken refuge. At this point Shah Jahan intervened and peace was made on the terms of an indemnity and the ceding of a district. After this campaign Shah Jahan made Mir Jumla chief minister of the Empire.

The kingdom of Bijapur, profiting by the peace of 1636, had reached the height of its power under Muhammad Adil Shah and

[1] *History of Aurangzib*, Vol. I. p. 173.
[2] *Ibid.*, pp. 216–242 give a documented account of the rise of this incredibly brilliant and unscrupulous adventurer.

extended from the Arabian Sea to the Bay of Bengal. But on the death of Muhammad in 1656, after a reign of thirty years, serious disturbances took place, and Aurangzeb made these the pretext for invading and plundering the country in 1657, with the assistance of Mir Jumla. Once again Shah Jahan intervened to prevent annexation by Aurangzeb. Ali Adil Shah II surrendered Bidar, Kalyan and Parenda and paid a heavy indemnity.

In the light of coming events one other incident of the Bijapur campaign deserves notice. The young Maratha chief Sivaji, profiting by the outbreak of war, raided the Mogul territory with his light horsemen and plundered the country almost to the gates of Ahmadnagar. But as soon as Aurangzeb organized movable columns and threatened Sivaji's capital of Poona, the Maratha chief made his submission.

Early in September 1657 Shah Jahan became so ill that he despaired of recovery and named Dara Shikoh his *War of the Mogul Succession.* successor. Dara Shikoh, then forty-two years of age, was the eldest of the four sons of Mumtaz Mahal, Shuja being forty-one, Aurangzeb thirty-nine and Murad Baksh six years younger. The brothers were all viceroys with large standing armies under their command, and they had no love for each other; indeed the bitter feeling between Dara Shikoh and Aurangzeb was a byword in the Empire. No one doubted that the succession to the throne would be won by civil war, possibly before the Emperor's death.

Dara Shikoh, Shah Jahan's trusted adviser for years, with a position only short of sovereignty in the unprecedented rank of Commander of Forty Thousand (raised to Sixty Thousand during the Emperor's illness), held every advantage Shah Jahan could bestow —save one. His experience in the field had been limited to five months before Kandahar and he had never been allowed to leave his father's side to learn the responsibilities of government and how to deal with men. He had conspicuous physical courage, but he was capricious, weak in character, and clouded with his own conceit, while a leaning towards Sufism, and a strong interest in Hinduism, made him suspect in the eyes of orthodox Sunni Moslems. In his

PLATE XLIII.

Central Press Photos Ltd.

THE TAJ MAHAL.

PLATE XLIV

PAGE FROM DARA SHIKOH'S ALBUM,
WITH THE INSCRIPTION TO HIS WIFE
By permission of the Secretary of State for India in Council

private life he was a good father, and devoted " to his nearest and dearest friend," his wife Nadirah Banu, a grand-daughter of Akbar.[1]

Shuja had proved himself a capable and courageous ruler in Bengal, but his energies were sapped by self-indulgence and he was under the disadvantage of being a Shia. Murad Baksh, brave, dissolute and brainless, was Viceroy of Gujerat and the west.[2]

During his illness the Emperor could not show himself as usual to the public, and Dara Shikoh allowed no one near his bedside. Rumours spread throughout the country that Shah Jahan was dead; and his sons prepared to fight for the throne. Shuja and Murad both declared themselves Emperor. Aurangzeb made no open move, but he began an intrigue with Murad to whom he offered a share of the Empire. Shuja advanced on Agra with an army but was defeated at Bahadurpur near Benares, in February 1658, by the imperial troops and driven back into Bengal.

The Emperor had recovered three months previously, but Aurangzeb now began to show his hand. Early in April he crossed the Narbada, effected a junction with Murad's army in Malwa, and overwhelmed the forces sent against him by Dara Shikoh at Dharmat on the 15th April. The Rajput clansmen fought with magnificent courage, but the divided command of the imperial army, under Raja Jaswant Singh of Marwar and Kasim Khan, stood no chance against the cool generalship of Aurangzeb.

Dara Shikoh now took the field to stem the tide of defeat. His father urged him to wait until Raja Jai Singh and Prince Sulaiman Shikoh returned from the campaign against Shuja, but Dara Shikoh would take no advice and marched to meet his brothers at Samugarh. The battle was fought on 29th May 1658, and in a desperate encounter Dara Shikoh was utterly defeated and his army scattered.

Aurangzeb marched on Agra and, throwing off his previous pretence of loyalty to the Emperor himself, laid siege to the fort.

[1] *History of Aurangzib*, Vol. I. pp. 294–302, Vol. II. p. 207. The reference to Nadirah is from the Persian inscription written in Dara Shikoh's handwriting in an album of paintings now in the India Office Library.

[2] *Mughal Rule in India*, p. 86.

Shah Jahan's appeal, in which he urged upon his son " that eternal prosperity comes only from remembering God and showing kindness to men," met with the curt reply " It is your own doing "; and on 8th June the fort surrendered with its immense hoard of treasure. Exasperated by the knowledge that the old Emperor's affection remained centred on Dara Shikoh, Aurangzeb made his father a close prisoner, and two days later publicly exercised imperial authority and accepted homage.

He was Emperor in all but name. Dara Shikoh's power was broken, and it only remained to end him altogether. Shuja had still to recover from his defeat, and had been sent an affectionate letter by " his true brother " giving him Bihar. Murad was in leading strings. But the junior member of the only fraternal alliance was beginning to distrust the promises made to him, and resented the absolute power which Aurangzeb was gathering into his own hands. Aurangzeb decided to deal with Murad and his growing pretensions before his brother's rapidly increasing forces became a danger.

The two brothers left Agra for Delhi at the head of their armies. While on the march Aurangzeb persuaded Murad to enter his camp and after entertaining him at dinner bound his guest and took him captive to Delhi, while Murad's army of 20,000 men entered his gaoler's service. Murad's subsequent fate is soon told. Although a prisoner his popularity made Aurangzeb uneasy, and he had his brother tried and executed in 1661 on a charge of murder.

At Delhi, Aurangzeb rested his army, reorganized the government of the provinces and, on the 21st July 1658, crowned himself Emperor under the title of Alamgir [1] Padshah Ghazi.

Dara Shikoh had not yet given up all hope, but with the resources and troops at his disposal he was unable to withstand the ruthless energy of Aurangzeb's pursuit. He was driven from Lahore to Multan, from Multan to Gujerat, and from Gujerat to Ajmer where, at Deori from the 12th to the 14th April 1659, he made his last stand. At last he came as a fugitive to the Bolan Pass, where his devoted wife died of dysentery. To fulfil her last request he sent Nadirah's body back to be buried in India with his remaining troopers as escort.

[1] Conqueror of the Universe.

Dara Shikoh went on with a few servants to seek refuge with the Afghan Malik Jiwan Khan of Dadar, whose life he had saved years before when Shah Jahan had sentenced the Khan to be trampled to death by an elephant. Jiwan Khan handed his benefactor over to his pursuers.

Dara Shikoh was brought before Aurangzeb at Delhi at the end of August 1659. There was a degrading parade through the streets amidst crowds roused to fury by the appearance of Jiwan Khan, and riots against the betrayer took place on the following day. That night Dara Shikoh was beheaded in his prison, after a violent struggle, on the grounds of heresy.

Sulaiman Shikoh, Dara Shikoh's eldest son, was captured when trying to escape over the passes into Ladak at the end of 1660. Aurangzeb received his nephew kindly, earnestly assured him that he would be treated with tenderness, and sent him to die by slow poison in Gwalior prison.

Aurangzeb, after dealing with Murad and having followed Dara Shikoh to the Indus in December 1658, was obliged to return from the Punjab. Shuja had taken his brother's promises for what they were worth and, profiting by his rival's absence, had seized Benares and advanced as far as Allahabad. Aurangzeb, coming up by forced marches, met him at Ewajah on the 3rd January 1659 and routed him. The pursuit of the defeated army was left to Mir Jumla, who had been deprived of his position as imperial minister on the outbreak of civil war, and now reappeared to become one of Aurangzeb's best generals. Shuja was chased across Bengal to the Deccan and then eastward to Arakan on the Burmese side of the Bay of Bengal. He crossed the Arakan border in May 1660 and was never heard of again.

Shah Jahan was kept in close confinement in Agra Fort, attended by his two surviving wives and his devoted daughter Jahanara, until his death in January 1666, at the age of seventy-four.[1]

---

[1] This account of the civil war is based on Sarkar's *History of Aurangzib*, Vols. I. to III.

CHRONOLOGY

1605. Accession of Jahangir.
1606. Rebellion of Prince Khusru.
1611. Jahangir married Nur Jahan.
1613. War with the Portuguese.
1614. Udaipur acknowledged Mogul suzerainty.
1615–1619. Sir Thomas Roe in India.
1616. Prince Khurram awarded title of Shah Jahan on capture of Ahmadnagar fortress.
1622. Kandahar taken by the Persians.
1623. Shah Jahan in rebellion defeated at Bilochpur.
1624. The rebellion ended by defeat at Kampat.
1626. Mahabat Khan's plot.
1627. October : death of Jahangir.
1628. February: accession of Shah Jahan.
Rising of the Bundela Rajputs.
1629. Rebellion of Khan Jahan Lodi.
1630–1632. Famine in Gujerat and the Deccan.
1632–1653. Building of the Taj Mahal.
1632. Hindu persecution.
1635–1636. Invasion of Bijapur.
1636–1644. First Deccan Viceroyalty of Aurangzeb.
1638. Kandahar surrendered to Shah Jahan.
1645–1649. Badakshan campaigns.
1649. Final loss of Kandahar.
1652. Second Deccan Viceroyalty of Aurangzeb.
1657. September: illness of Shah Jahan.
1658. February : beginning of the War of Succession.
June : Shah Jahan made prisoner by Aurangzeb.
July: Aurangzeb ascended the throne.

BIBLIOGRAPHY

Memoirs of Jahangir, tr. Rogers and Beveridge (Royal Asiatic Society), 2 vols., 1909–1914.
History of Jahangir, Professor Beni Prasad, Allahabad University (Studies in History, Oxford University Press, Madras), 1922.
Jahangir's India, F. Pelsaert, tr. W. H. Moreland and Dr. Geyl, 1925.
History of Aurangzib, Sir Jadunath Sarkar, 5 vols. (Calcutta), 1912–1924, Vols. I. to III.

Studies in Mughal India, Sir Jadunath Sarkar (Calcutta and Cambridge), 1919.
Mughal Rule in India, Edwardes and Garrett, 1930.
European Travellers in India, E. F. Oaten, 1909.
Embassy of Sir Thomas Roe to India, ed. Sir W. Foster, 1926.
From Akbar to Aurangzeb, W. H. Moreland, 1923.

CHAPTER XI

Aurangzeb

THE coronation of Aurangzeb in 1658 had been hurried and informal, and a year later he was enthroned with great ceremony.

Taxation. Failure of the monsoon and the breakdown in the administration caused by the civil war had brought widespread distress and famine upon the country, and the Emperor on his formal accession proclaimed a number of concessions to his subjects. Eighty imposts were officially abolished throughout Hindustan, ranging from transit dues and taxes on Hindu fairs down to the taxation of goats. But, in the words of Khafi Khan,[1] "although his gracious and beneficent Majesty remitted these taxes and issued strict orders prohibiting their collection, the avaricious propensities of men prevailed," and except in the towns, where strict supervision was possible, the concessions were a dead letter.

The higher officials, as Bernier observed, were heavily in debt on account of the extravagance of their households of wives and servants and their stables of horses and camels; they were expected, moreover, to give the Emperor costly presents at various annual festivals. To meet these expenses they raised money in unauthorised ways, and the imperial government only interfered in the local administration when the scandal became notorious, or the people were driven into rebellion.[2]

But the oppression of the poor, to which Indian historians and foreign visitors allude, cannot be directly charged to the central government. "The principles of the land-revenue system were

[1] *Mughal Rule in India*, p. 212.
[2] *From Akbar to Aurangzeb*, pp. 271, 272.

256

thoroughly sound and were conveyed to the officials in a series of instructions which were all that could be desired." One has only to read the rules for the guidance of the collectors of revenue included in the *Ain-i-Akbari* to realize that fact [1]; and Aurangzeb's revenue regulations of 1668–69 [2] emphasize a policy " to give ease to the *ryots* (cultivators), so that the signs of agriculture may increase . . . while benefiting the government," to quote from the imperial decree.

The reign of Aurangzeb, a time of almost ceaseless warfare, lasted forty-seven years, and falls into two parts. The earlier half is centred in Northern India, the second period in the south, when the Emperor was engaged in the twenty-six years of fighting which sapped the resources of the Mogul Empire. As Sir Jadunath Sarkar has said: " In the closing years of Aurangzeb's life, Hindustan merely meant a place where the much-needed money for the Deccan wars was to be raised and from which disturbances were reported with annoying frequency." [3]

After the civil war was over, and before the imperial armies moved to fight on the eastern and north-western frontiers, Aurangzeb received a procession of ambassadors from the Moslem world. Persia and Mecca were the greatest of these powers to send their envoys, and the Dutch sent their representative from Batavia.

Foreign Embassies.

" The fame of his victories had spread far and wide and he was congratulated on his accession. His policy at the beginning was to dazzle the eyes of foreign princes by . . . lavish presents to them and their envoys and thus induce the outer Moslem world to forget his treatment of his father and brothers, or at least to show courtesy to the successful man of action and master of India's untold wealth, especially when he was so free with his money." [4] Later in his reign he stopped this liberality but he always maintained friendly intercourse with the Moslem states.

[1] *Mughal Rule in India*, pp. 204, 205.
[2] *Studies in Mughal India*, pp. 169–197.
[3] *History of Aurangzib*, Vol. III. p. 3.
[4] *Ibid.*, Vol. III. pp. 115, 116.

Invasion of Assam. The history of Assam as a kingdom starts with the invasion of the Ahoms, an offshoot of the Shan race, early in the thirteenth century; and they gradually conquered the whole of the Brahmaputra Valley. By the end of the sixteenth century, through intermarriage with the people of Cooch Behar, the Ahoms had generally adopted Hinduism.

Moslem invasion of Assam from the thirteenth century onwards had invariably failed. The great valley, with the Brahmaputra as its only gateway, was as isolated as Kashmir. But, unlike Kashmir, Assam was protected by masses of almost impenetrable forest. The climate was desperately unhealthy and a record rainfall flooded the country regularly every year, disabilities which, of course, still exist.[1]

In the disorders of the war of succession the rulers of Cooch Behar and Assam crossed the Bengal frontier and seized part of Kamrup. But when Aurangzeb's position became secure, Mir Jumla was sent up from Dacca with a strong force, well supplied with boats. Cooch Behar was occupied without opposition at the end of 1661 and the country annexed. At the beginning of 1662 Mir Jumla invaded Assam and during the next three months swept all before him, capturing stockaded positions, sinking the Assamese river flotilla, and taking a large amount of arms and ammunition at the capture of the capital Garhaon.

After March, Mir Jumla had to contend with a more formidable enemy than the Assamese. His lines of communication were broken by floods and he had the greatest difficulty in maintaining himself in the country. But Mir Jumla was a commander who not only held the confidence and affection of his men by sharing all their hardships, but "no other general of his age conducted war with so much humanity." [2] He permitted no ill-treatment whatsoever of the inhabitants, who consequently freely brought in supplies for the army.

[1] The description of the country given by Shihab-ud-din, who accompanied Mir Jumla's expedition and wrote the *Fatiyeh-i-Ibrayah*, is quoted at length by Sir Edward Gait in his authoritative *History of Assam*, pp. 141-151 (2nd Edn., Calcutta, 1926).

[2] *History of Aurangzib*, Vol. III. p. 206.

Although fatally ill with fever and pleurisy, Mir Jumla resumed the offensive at the beginning of the cold weather, and on the 5th January 1663 peace was concluded with the Ahom King Sutyinpha. By the terms of the treaty a large indemnity and an annual tribute of elephants were exacted and territory on both banks of the Brahmaputra was ceded. Mir Jumla died on the 30th March on his way back to Dacca, and the country was lost to the Mogul Empire, mainly through the oppression of local officials, by 1681.

Mir Jumla was followed as Governor of Bengal by Aurangzeb's maternal uncle Shayista Khan. Sent in 1660 to deal with Sivaji, Shayista had entirely failed to cope with the rapid and unexpected movements of a past-master in the art of raiding, and was relieved of his command in the Deccan. When he reached Dacca he found that the Bay of Bengal and the waterways of the province as far inland as Hooghly and the provincial capital were dominated by the pirates of Chittagong, who habitually pillaged when and where they pleased.

Suppression of Piracy.

The kings of Arakan had long taken advantage of the weakness of the Mogul Empire at sea, and built up a fleet manned by their Magh subjects and by Portuguese adventurers and half-castes. As early as 1625 the "swift galleasses of the Arrakanese" had sacked Dacca, obliged the Mogul viceroy to move his headquarters, and they had levied blackmail on Eastern Bengal for years. The Maghs kept the Muhammadans and Hindus they captured as farm and household slaves, making concubines of the women; the Portuguese sold their prisoners to Dutch, English and French merchants at the Deccan ports.[1]

The loss caused to the provincial revenue by the ravages of the pirates was considerable, the blow to Mogul prestige was intolerable, and Shayista Khan was given a free hand by the Emperor to stamp out the piracy. The expedition to Assam had taken a heavy toll of the Mogul fleet, such as it was, and Mir Jumla had died before he could reorganize it. Shayista Khan had to create a new navy, and one which could oppose the numerous well-armed pirate vessels. He collected every available shipwright and built nearly 300 ships

[1] *History of Aurangzib*, Vol. III. p. 225.

in little over a year in the dockyards of Dacca and the smaller ports, while he made fortified bases for the fleet.

Towards the end of December 1665 Shayista Khan began his combined operations with his fleet and army, and by the 26th January 1666 Chittagong was taken and the pirate fleet destroyed or captured. "We can easily imagine," the Governor wrote in his report to the Emperor, "how fast cultivation will increase in Bengal, now that Magh violence has been put down." [1]

A year later Mogul troops were fighting on the Afghan border, fifteen hundred miles from Chittagong.

First Afghan War. The Pathans had settled in the valleys of the north-western highlands at the beginning of the sixteenth century; and by consistently regarding the plains and prosperous towns below them as their lawful prey, have made the history of that frontier a tale of almost continuous fighting from that day to this. Akbar's efforts to subdue the tribes ended in the disaster of 1586 and the payment of subsidies to the *maliks* (chiefs). Jahangir and Shah Jahan left the frontier province to take care of itself, but Aurangzeb decided that imperial prestige could no longer allow habitual raiding.

Early in 1667 a *lashkar*, or tribal force, of 5000 Yusufzais came down into the Hazara district and strong raiding parties appeared on the Kabul River. The Yusufzais were badly beaten at the beginning of April by the Governor of Attock, and when reinforcements arrived from Lahore and Kabul the Yusufzai country was entered and the tribesmen were taught a salutary lesson.

The Afridis were the next tribe to give trouble. In 1672 Acmal Khan, who had gained control over the clans, seized *Second Afghan War.* the country between Peshawar and Kabul and annihilated a Mogul army in the Khyber Pass. Muhammad Amin Khan, Governor of Kabul, and a few of his officers escaped to Peshawar with their lives, but everything else was lost.

The Mogul casualties were 10,000 killed, and 20,000 men and

[1] *History of Aurangzib*, Vol. III. p. 240.

women were captured and sent into slavery in Central Asia, while the booty was considerable. As inevitably happens upon the frontier after a disaster, the whole border rose, from Kandahar to Attock.

Aurangzeb ordered Mahabat Khan, who had long experience as a frontier officer, but was now nearly seventy, up from the Deccan, and as he showed small inclination to risk an engagement, large reinforcements were sent up under Shujaat Khan in November 1673. Mahabat and Shujaat were told to co-operate with Maharaja Jaswant Singh who was holding Jamrud.

History never repeats itself more closely than on the north-west frontier. The Pathan leaders had served in the imperial army and knew its organization and tactics, and they were fighting in their own country. Except for artillery—and the Mogul guns were almost immobile—there was little difference in armament. The Indian troops were unused to mountain warfare and found the intense winter cold exceedingly trying. But added to this was jealousy in the high command.

The concentration of so large a force induced a number of the clans to send deputations into Peshawar to sue for peace. But Shujaat Khan, without waiting for the remainder to submit and ignoring Jaswant's advice, advanced into the hills upon Kabul. His camp on the Karapa kotal (saddle) was heavily attacked on a stormy night in February 1674. Shujaat Khan was killed, and next morning the Pathans came down from the heights to complete their victory. What was left of Shujaat's column was extricated only by the skilful handling and magnificent behaviour of a small body of Rajput infantry with guns which had been sent in support by Jaswant Singh.

Aurangzeb came up to the frontier after this second disaster, and with the combination of overwhelming force and the distribution of money, *jagirs* and posts in the imperial army to the *maliks*, won the submission of many of the clans.

In the meanwhile Aghar Khan, an able and experienced Turki general, had been brought up from the Deccan. He reduced the Mohmands to order, making for himself a name on the frontier which was echoed in John Nicholson nearly two hundred years later, and at the end of a vigorous campaign defeated a strong force of Afghans at Gandamak.

In June 1675 the Moguls met with a heavy reverse in Bajaur, but Aghar Khan restored the situation. It was not, however, until Amir Khan was made governor of Afghanistan in 1678 that peace reigned, as much as it ever could reign on the frontier, and lasted during the whole of his twenty years' administration. The Mogul policy was to play one clan off against another, and to keep the Khyber route open by the payment of regular subsidies, an arrangement which still survives under what is known as the *khassadar* system.

Affairs in Afghanistan had been serious enough, but the religious *Religious Policy.* policy in which the Emperor persisted, and upon which he had already embarked, was to have a decisive effect upon the fortunes of the Mogul Empire.

Aurangzeb had entered the war of succession as the defender of orthodox Islam and ordered the execution of his unsuccessful rival and elder brother Dara Shikoh on the grounds of heresy. His attitude was perfectly sincere. He was a religious fanatic, living a simple and abstemious life with only three wives,[1] while he scrupulously followed every precept of the Koran. In the eleventh year of his reign he even forbade the playing of music at court, and pensioned off the musicians. His jealous orthodoxy as a Sunni estranged the Shia Moslem population; and by his sectarian intolerance he stopped the flow of Shia immigrants from Persia and Khurasan, depriving the government service of its ablest recruits. This source of supply had already been considerably diminished by Akbar's policy of " India for the Indians." Foreign stock is apt to deteriorate rapidly on Indian soil, as the Portuguese found to their cost, and the alien Mogul state vitally required the constant immigration of strong new blood from outside. Nor did Aurangzeb take steps to obtain an adequate supply of military recruits from beyond the north-western border. The Mogul army of Indian Muhammadans with its stiffening of Rajputs had lost much of its earlier efficiency when it came to meet the Maratha horse and their famous light infantry.

But it was the complete reversal of Akbar's policy of toleration

[1] The Koran allows four wives.

towards Hinduism which led more than anything else to the downfall of the Empire. Aurangzeb firmly believed that he was com-
pounding with sin if he tolerated any sect outside the fold of orthodox
Islam, and that his duty to enforce the faith upon all his subjects
lay clear before him. In a charter to a Benares priest in the first
year of his reign he significantly quoted the canon law that while
" long-standing temples should not be demolished, no new temple
(should be) allowed to be built." [1]

Had he stopped at this his Hindu subjects would probably have
quietly accepted the restriction. But in 1669 he issued a general
order " to demolish all the schools and temples of the infidels, and
to put down their religious teaching and practices," [2] and the great
temple at Somnath and the Vishvanath temple at Benares were
pulled down during the year. In January 1670 the great shrine at
Mathura, Kesav Rai's temple, built in the reign of Jahangir, whose
gilded pinnacle could be seen from Agra, was levelled to the ground.
A large mosque was then built on the site, and the Emperor ordered
that the name of the city should be changed to Islamabad. The
jewelled idols were taken to Agra and placed under the steps leading
to the Nawab Begam Sahib's mosque " to be pressed under foot by
the true believers." [3]

In order that the destruction of the Hindu temples should be
thorough, muhtasibs (censors of morals) were appointed under an
inspector-general, and their duties also included the enforcement
of the Islamic code, which forbade gambling and the use of wine
and drugs.

At the same time economic pressure was added to direct religious
persecution. By an ordinance of 1665 the custom duty on all commodities brought in for sale was fixed at 2½ per cent. ad valorem
in the case of Moslems and 5 per cent. in the case of Hindus. Two
years later the duty was abolished for Moslem traders, and retained
at its old level for Hindus. [4]

[1] 28th February 1659. History of Aurangzib, Vol. III. pp. 319, 320.
[2] Ibid., Vol. III. p. 302.
[3] Masir-i-Alamgiri, quoted by Sarkar, History of Aurangzib, Vol. III. p. 321.
[4] History of Aurangzib, Vol. III. p. 313.

In 1671 Aurangzeb struck a blow at the large body of middle-class educated Hindus who had served from time immemorial as clerks in the revenue department by issuing a decree which, in the words of the official historian of the reign, " by one stroke of the pen . . . dismissed all the Hindu writers from his service." But it was found that the secretariats were unable to function without their Hindu head clerks and accountants, and eventually the Emperor allowed half the clerks in the revenue and accounts departments to be Hindus.[1]

Further and heavier restrictions were to follow, but discontent and hatred of Mogul rule was already making itself felt. The Jats of the Mathura district, infuriated by the destruction of their temple, rose in revolt, and the imperial troops, under Aurangzeb himself on one occasion, were unable entirely to suppress them.[2] These risings continued during the reigns of the Emperor's successors; while the epithet " Turk " passed into Jat speech as the name for an oppressor.[3]

The Satnami Rebellion. The Jat risings were definite revolts of the Hindu peasantry against religious persecution, but the rebellion of the Hindu sect of Satnamis in May 1672 was started by a quarrel between some of their members and a soldier in the Narnaul district. From this beginning the disturbance spread and assumed the form of a religious war. Small bodies of troops were defeated, the garrison of Narnaul was driven out, the town was plundered and the mosques destroyed. The insurgents then set up their own local government and collected revenue in the district.

Emboldened by success they advanced on Delhi in March 1673, to the alarm of the citizens, who credited the Satnamis with occult powers making them invulnerable to ordinary weapons. Aurangzeb sent a strong force to meet the insurgents and countered the magic which had shaken the morale of the troops by binding amulets to their standards. After a hard fight the Satnamis were almost annihilated. The successful general, Radandaz Khan, was given the

[1] *History of Aurangzib*, Vol. III. p. 315.
[2] *Ibid.*, Vol. III. pp. 330–336.
[3] *History of the Sikhs*, J. D. Cunningham, ed. H. L. O. Garrett (1918), p. 5.

title of Shujaat Khan and, less than two years later, was killed in action on the north-west frontier.

The son and the grandson of Akbar both had trouble with the Sikhs for secular causes. Jahangir had executed Arjun as a rebel and partisan of Prince Khusru[1]; and Shah Jahan had been obliged shortly after his accession to assert the imperial authority over his Sikh subjects at the cost of more than one defeat. But Aurangzeb came into conflict with the growing power of Sikhism on purely religious grounds.

Aurangzeb and the Sikhs.

The founder of the Sikh faith, Nanak, a Hindu of Talwandi (Nankana), who lived from 1469 to 1539,[2] preached a religion which entirely rejected Brahmanism, but accepted the doctrine of transmigration. The Japji, which is an epitome of the Sikh Scriptures, begins with the words: " There is but one God whose name is true, the Creator." [3] The religion forbids idolatry, caste exclusiveness, *sati*, the immurement of women, wine, tobacco, infanticide and pilgrimages to Hindu sacred places.[4]

The Sikhs, as Sir Patrick Fagan [5] has said, are " neither a race, nor a nationality, nor a caste, but primarily the followers of a religion." Arjun organized the Sikhs into a theocratic community, with the *Granth* as its religious code, the pool and temple at Amritsar as its centre, and a chief in the person of the guru.[6]

This was the religious association whose " temples Aurangzeb ordered to be destroyed, and the guru's agents for collecting the tithes (one-tenth of the total income) and presents of the faithful to be expelled from the cities." [7] When Aurangzeb's indiscriminate persecution began the guru was Tegh Bahadur, whose sympathies had led him in 1668 to serve in the Mogul ranks on an expedition to Assam. Tegh Bahadur was not one to submit to religious oppression and he openly defied Aurangzeb. When he was captured

---

[1] *History of the Sikhs*, p. 53.
[2] *Ibid.*, p. 41 and footnote. Some authorities give 1538.
[3] *The Sikh Religion*, M. A. Macauliffe (1909), Vol. I. p. 195.
[4] *Ibid.*, Preface, p. xxiii.
[5] *Political India*, p. 124.   [6] *History of the Sikhs*, pp. 51, 52.
[7] Khafi Khan, quoted in *History of Aurangzib*, Vol. III. p. 354, footnote.

and taken to Delhi the Emperor ordered him to accept Islam, and on his refusal the guru was beheaded after five days' torture at the end of 1675. Tegh Bahadur may not, if certain modern critics are right, have made the celebrated prophecy attributed to him when confronting Aurangzeb: " I see a power rising in the West which will sweep your empire into the dust." But the saying was handed down by the Sikhs and remembered by the Punjab regiments in 1857 before the walls of Delhi.

Tegh Bahadur left behind him a son Govind, then a boy of fifteen, of whom it had been prophesied before his birth that " he would convert jackals into tigers and sparrows into hawks." Govind, the tenth and last guru, inspired the Sikhs, who now added Singh (lion) to their names, with an undying hatred of Islam; and he created the Khalsa, a combination of religious fervour and warlike temper, which was destined to exert a profound influence upon Northern India.

In 1679 Aurangzeb reimposed the *jizya*, the tax on *zimmi*, or unbelievers, which had been abolished for a hundred and fifteen years, " in order to spread Islam and put down the practice of infidelity." The Emperor interpreted the expression in the Koran, that the tax should be paid " with the hand of humility," to enforce personal payment to the collector under insulting conditions. The renewal of the tax caused considerable outcry and brought a reasoned and outspoken letter of remonstrance from Sivaji.[1] In the Mogul portion of the Deccan the *jizya* could only be collected by force, but it succeeded to an appreciable extent in its object as " many Hindus who were unable to pay turned Muhammadan to obtain relief from the insults of the collectors." [2]

Reimposition of the Jizya.

There were, however, exemptions, comprising all government officials (who were best able to afford the tax), women, children below fourteen, and slaves. The poorest class scheduled, such as dyers and shoe-makers, only paid when their gross professional

[1] Given at the end of this Chapter.
[2] Quoted from Manucci, *Mughal Rule in India*, pp. 117, 118.

income left a sufficient margin to maintain their families. The three grades of the tax were 12, 24 and 48 *dirhams* ($3\frac{1}{3}$, $6\frac{2}{3}$ and $13\frac{1}{3}$ rupees) a year, which Sir Jadunath Sarkar estimates to have meant 6 per cent. to the poorest class and less than $2\frac{1}{2}$ per thousand to the richest.[1] Moreover, in the case of the poorest the tax annually took the full value of one year's food as the price of religious indulgence.[2]

Jodhpur, the Succession. In December 1678 Maharaja Jaswant Singh of Jodhpur (Marwar), who commanded in the Khaibar, died at Jamrud. Jodhpur lay on the main trade route between the Mogul capital and Ahmadabad, and Aurangzeb had always disliked its semi-independence. There was at the moment no direct heir to the throne, Jaswant's best troops were on the Afghan frontier, and the Emperor seized his opportunity to annex the country. Muhammadan officers were posted to the Jodhpur administration and arrangements were made for new revenue statements. At the same time Aurangzeb occupied the country in force, and resistance was impossible. After the Emperor's return to Delhi at the beginning of April to impose the *jizya* the temples of Jodhpur city were demolished.

But in the meanwhile, in February 1679, Ajit Singh, a posthumous son of the late Maharaja, was born in Lahore. The Rajput ministers then petitioned the Emperor to recognize Ajit Singh as their future ruler. Aurangzeb ordered the boy, who was taken to Delhi in June, to be brought up in his harem with the promise of rank as a Mogul noble and investiture as raja when he came of age. One account affirms that the throne was offered to Ajit Singh on condition that he turned Moslem.[3]

---

[1] *History of Aurangzib*, p. 307.

[2] Sarkar's calculation. It is based on the market rates given for the end of the sixteenth century in the *Ain-i-Akbari*, i. 63. W. H. Moreland (*From Akbar to Aurangzeb*, Ch. V.) reaches the conclusion that the price of food, periods of famine excepted, remained almost stationary throughout the seventeenth century with no rise in wages.

[3] This account is based on Ch. XXVI. of the *History of Aurangzib*, Vol. III. The probability of the religious condition is discussed on p. 374.

Aurangzeb's attitude towards the rightful heir roused the Rajputs to action, and Durgadas, the intrepid and gifted son of Jaswant's minister Askaran, resolved to rescue Ajit Singh and his mother from the fortress where they were guarded. In this he succeeded, but of the band who cut their way through the streets of Delhi and kept their Mogul pursuers at bay along the road to safety only Durgadas and seven of his Rathor Rajputs came back alive to Jodhpur.

The imperial edicts against Hinduism had infuriated the Rajputs, and it was now open war between Aurangzeb and Rajasthan, only Jaipur holding aloof. The Emperor took the field in overwhelming force with his three sons, Muazzam, Azam and Akbar in the higher commands, and the Rajputs, under Maharana Raj Singh of Udaipur, retired before the invaders into the Aravali hills between the two main lines of advance. Aurangzeb occupied Jodhpur, Udaipur and Chitor before the end of February 1680 without serious opposition, to find his lines of communication incessantly attacked and his outposts surprised by an enemy who had once been the backbone of the Mogul army. The imperial forces lost their morale and their mobility, the army in Mewar was threatened with starvation by the capture of supply trains; and Aurangzeb holding Akbar responsible relieved him of his command.

Akbar was a young man of twenty-three, full of energy and restless ambition, and he felt his relegation keenly. *Prince Akbar and his Father.* The Rajputs were quick to take the opportunity this offered and through Tahavvur Khan, the prince's second in command, Akbar was led to listen to their proposals. Durgadas pointed out (as Sivaji had written to the Emperor) that Aurangzeb's bigotry threatened the existence of the Mogul empire; and if his heritage was to be saved Akbar must seize the throne and return to the policy of his ancestors. He would have at his back the armed strength of the two greatest Rajput clans, the Sisodias and the Rathors. Akbar had not far to go to find a precedent for filial disloyalty, and four of his theologians formally declared that Aurangzeb had forfeited the throne by his violation of Islamic canon law.[1]

[1] *History of Aurangzib*, Vol. III. pp. 404–406.

On the 2nd January 1681 Akbar marched from Marwar, and on the 15th he was within three miles of imperial headquarters. The Mogul armies were at Chitor and the Raj Samudra lake, the bodyguard was away on special service, and the court officials and servants, clerical staff and invalided soldiers on light duty totalled about ten thousand men. Aurangzeb was in no position to fight a host of 70,000 with the flower of the Rajput army in its ranks. But the Emperor was a master of political manœuvre. That night he wrote a letter which Louis XI of France might well have envied, in which it appeared that he and his son were in collusion and that Akbar was playing his confederates false in a deeply laid plot; and he saw that this letter fell into the hands of the Rajputs. At the same time he decoyed Tahavvur Khan, the mainspring of Akbar's revolt, over to his camp and murdered him. The sudden disappearance of Tahavvur Khan lent additional force to the incriminating letter, and the entire Rajput army disappeared in the night leaving the prince with no more than his personal bodyguard of 350 mounted men.

Akbar rode after the Rajputs and succeeded in persuading them of his loyalty. But the opportunity had gone for ever. Durgadas escorted the prince to the court of Sivaji's son Sambaji, and a year or so later Akbar took ship to Persia where he spent the remainder of his life.

In June 1681 peace was made with Udaipur, by which the maharana ceded a few districts and the Emperor agreed not to impose the *jizya* on the Rajput kingdom. The war with Jodhpur dragged on until 1709 when Ajit Singh entered his capital in triumph and Aurangzeb's son and successor, Bahadur Shah I, acknowledged him as ruler of the state.

But Aurangzeb had lost the support of more than Udaipur and Jodhpur. The loyalty of almost all the Rajput clans was alienated. Lawlessness overflowed fitfully into Malwa and endangered the vitally important Mogul road to the Deccan; and in the incessant wars which filled the rest of the reign the Bundela clan and a few Hada and Kachhwah families supplied the only Rajput soldiers the Emperor could enlist to fight in his armies.[1]

[1] *History of Aurangzib*, Vol. III. Ch. XXXVII.

Aurangzeb, having come to terms with the Maharana of Udaipur in June 1681, turned his attention to the Deccan.

The Deccan.

Sivaji had created a state in the Konkan and it was protected by chains of strong hill forts with the support of the celebrated Maratha infantry. The power to which Sivaji's son Sambaji had succeeded in 1680 was too strong to be ignored. Moreover, the Emperor, a fervent Sunni, was hostile to the Shia rulers of Bijapur and Golconda, kingdoms which had not as yet been forced to acknowledge Mogul supremacy. The Emperor made up his mind to establish his ascendancy in the Deccan, and when he moved south Northern India became a group of provincial governments while the resources of the overgrown empire were being exhausted beyond the Vindhya hills.

But before dealing with the campaigns which occupied Aurangzeb for the rest of his reign it is necessary to describe the original foundation of the power which was destined to expand in the eighteenth century into the Maratha Confederacy.

Maharashtra, the land of the Marathas, was the hilly country east of the Western Ghats. With a good climate

The Marathas.

and a poor soil its people, the Kunbis (the great agricultural caste of the Deccan), have always been hardy and self-reliant, energetic and courageous. Social differences were not so sharply defined as in other parts of Hindu India, and this spirit of the early days of Maratha political dominance may be partly attributed to the great literary movement of Maharashtra, its Bhakti school of poetry.

The first of these poets was Eknath, who was persecuted by his brother Brahmans for his bold denunciation of the caste system. The most famous of his works is the Marathi rendering of the *Bhagavat* with its doctrine of personal service of God as the only road to salvation; a lasting memorial of his struggle on behalf of the language of the common people of Maharashtra. Eknath died in 1608, the year in which Tukaram, the greatest of the Bhakti devotional poets, was born. Tukaram was not only foremost in the crusade against the " empty ritual and barren ceremonial of Brahman priestcraft "; he has been described as the Kabir of the Marathas, and no other poet has contributed so many familiar quotations to the common speech of Maharashtra.

It was, however, the rise to power of the Sudra Sivaji, with the admixture of castes that filled his civil administration and flocked to his standard, which gave the mass of the people their most definite ideas of a common nationality and the limitations of an exclusive caste system. But in the words of S. M. Edwardes [1]: " When Sivaji's descendants degenerated into a line of royal phantoms and the Peshwas " (who were Konkani Brahmans) " usurped all power, the ancient spirit of caste-exclusiveness reasserted itself with re-doubled force."

The Marathas were a stout-hearted people who had been re-nowned as soldiers since the days when they fought under Pulikesin II against the Emperor Harsha. The Moslem conquests had turned them into first-rate mercenary troops who sold their swords to the new rulers of the Deccan, and some of them rose to positions of importance.

The most successful of these adventurers was the father of Sivaji. Born in 1594, Shahji Bhonsla had lived in troublous times. He married Jiji Bai the daughter of one of the great Ahmadnagar nobles, and he first saw service under Malik Ambar. Later he fought for his own hand, joined the Moguls and deserted their service, sided against the Bijapuris, and then finally threw in his lot with them. Shahji was powerful enough, by the year 1633, when the kingdom of Ahmadnagar was destroyed by Shah Jahan, to set up a puppet Nizam Shah and govern in his name the wide extent of the old Nizam Shahi dominions which he was able to conquer. Shahji's enterprising rule ended with his complete defeat in 1636 by the Moguls and, returning to the service of Bijapur, he was confirmed in his *jagirs* of Chamargunda and Poona.

Sivaji was born in 1627, and on the foundation of his father's position he began, at the age of nineteen, to build *Sivaji.* up a lordship for himself with the band of lawless Mavali hillmen whom he gathered together. Fort after fort fell

[1] In his editorial introduction to Grant Duff's *History of the Mahrattas* (ed. 1921), where a summary of Marathi literature is given.

into his hands until he possessed a large and strongly protected domain in the neighbourhood of Poona. While he was extending his authority in the highlands Sivaji was careful to keep friendly with the State of Bijapur in which his father was serving.

But in 1649 the rich strip of country between the Western Ghats and the sea became too strong a temptation, and he came down and seized the seaport towns in the Kalyan and Kolaba districts. The Bijapur government promptly used Shahji as a hostage, and Sivaji was forced to remain quiet for the next five years. " This was the beginning," in the words of Khafi Khan, " of that system of violence which he and his descendants spread over . . . the Konkan. . . . Whenever he heard of a prosperous town or of a district inhabited by thriving cultivators, he plundered it and took possession of it."

But while cruelty, treachery and murder are, in Grant Duff's estimate of Sivaji's character,[1] justly alleged against him, the great Maratha leader proved by his actions his genuine and impartial respect for the holy men of all sects, Moslem as much as Hindu; and his chivalry to women and strict enforcement of morality in his camp were a wonder in that age and extorted the admiration of hostile critics like Khafi Khan.[2] The influence of his mother, a devout Hindu lady, was, to quote Mr. Justice Ranade, " a factor of prime importance in the making of Sivaji's career and the chief source of his strength." As long as she lived he is said to have consulted her in all the great crises of his life.[3]

In 1655 Sivaji, who had been steadily consolidating his conquests, took advantage of the hostilities between Aurangzeb (then Mogul Viceroy of the Deccan) and the State of Bijapur to seize almost the whole of the Konkan, and its important seaports now fell into his hands. But when peace was declared between the Moguls and Bijapur, the Deccan kingdom was able to turn its attention to Sivaji, and in 1659 an expedition was sent under Afzal Khan against the Maratha State.

[1] *History of the Mahrattas*, Vol. I. pp. 228, 229.
[2] *History of Aurangzib*, Vol. IV. pp. 233, 235.
[3] *Mughal Rule in India*, pp. 128, 129.

The Bijapur forces made slow progress through the hills, and Afzal Khan conceived the misguided plan of capturing by treachery an adversary infinitely more cunning than himself. Sivaji was invited to a parley and, having learnt the details of his opponent's scheme, accepted, and made his own plans accordingly. The understanding was that neither leader should carry weapons, though each was to bring two armed retainers and an envoy. But when Afzal Khan suddenly attacked him with a dagger which the Maratha's concealed armour made harmless, Sivaji produced his own hidden weapons, a set of steel claws in the form of a knuckle-duster and a workmanlike dagger, with which he mortally wounded his adversary. In the scuffle which followed Afzal Khan was finished off, and Sivaji, by a preconcerted signal, launched his whole army from their ambush upon the leaderless Bijapur forces. The Bijapur army was overwhelmed. The losses amounted to 3000 killed and a large number of prisoners, while 65 elephants, 4000 horses, 1200 camels and a large quantity of treasure fell into Sivaji's hands. The Marathas then carried the war into the enemy's country, and continued their successful invasion until April 1660, when Sivaji was recalled by a dangerous threat against his own dominions.

After his second coronation in 1659 Aurangzeb sent Shayista Khan to replace Prince Muazzam as Viceroy of the Deccan, with orders to suppress Sivaji. Shayista made an alliance with Bijapur, and in May 1660 the campaign began, the two armies operating respectively from the north and south.

The Mogul Invasion.

The Marathas retired into the hills, where they could meet their enemies on more favourable terms, but by the middle of August Sivaji had lost the forts of Panhala and Chakan. Hostilities then slackened into desultory warfare, as Shayista Khan was apparently reluctant to face the heavy losses incurred by assaulting the hill forts.[1] But in April 1663 Sivaji made a characteristically daring raid upon Shayista Khan's headquarters at Poona, where the general had been in otiose residence for nearly three years. Pretending to be Deccani troops, Sivaji with 400 men entered the Mogul camp

[1] *History of the Mahrattas*, Vol. I. pp. 151, 152.

after dark. At midnight they broke into the general's house, forced their way into Shayista's own room, indiscriminately cut down about fifty people of both sexes in the darkness, the general himself being wounded, and then safely withdrew in the confusion.[1]

The fame of this exploit added enormously to Sivaji's prestige, but it broke Shayista, who had promptly retired to a safer residence at Aurangabad. The Viceroy was shortly transferred to Bengal, then regarded as a penal province and described by Aurangzeb as " a hell well stocked with bread," where Shayista Khan ruled firmly and humanely for about thirty years.[2]

In January 1664 Sivaji followed up this enterprise by attacking and sacking the Mogul seaport of Surat, with the exception of the English and Dutch factories which successfully defied the raiders.

Aurangzeb was now thoroughly roused and poured troops into the Maratha country. The villages were ravaged, Rajgarh the capital was threatened, and in June 1665 Sivaji made peace by which he surrendered twenty of his forts.

In the following year the Maratha chief and his son Sambaji were persuaded to attend the court at Agra. But the Emperor deliberately slighted him in open darbar and made Sivaji virtually a prisoner in his own house, from which the two Marathas escaped concealed in a large fruit basket. If Aurangzeb had shown ordinary tact and recognized the importance of the Maratha chief, Sivaji would in all probability have helped the Emperor to conquer Bijapur and Golconda and as a vassal would have brought the whole of the Deccan, at least for a time, within the Empire.[3] But Aurangzeb was not the man to seek the friendship or the alliance of those whom he hated as infidels.

From 1666 until 1668 Sivaji organized his internal administration and two years later renewed his external activities
Sivaji Establishes a Kingdom. by again sacking Surat and by instituting his system of blackmail on districts within the Mogul empire. This was a levy of one-fourth of the yearly revenue due to the

---

[1] *History of Aurangzib*, Vol. IV. pp. 47–51.
[2] See *Studies in Mughal India*, pp. 118–167.
[3] *Mughal Rule in India*, pp. 137, 138.

government, and was known as *chauth*. The sack of Surat caused fresh hostilities with the empire; but the Mogul forces met with little or no success, and in June 1674 Sivaji was enthroned with full Vedic rites as sovereign ruler of Maharashtra.[1]

Between 1676 and 1680 Sivaji was actively at war. In a succession of brilliant campaigns the great fortresses of Jinji and Vellore were taken, and by annexing the Western Carnatic from Belgaum to the Tungabhadra he established his rule over a large portion of the old Hindu Empire of Vijayanagar.

Sivaji's eldest son, a youth of nineteen, violent and capricious in character and notoriously depraved in morals, was a source of great anxiety to his father; and in 1678 Sambaji went over to the enemy and joined Dilir Khan, the Afghan general commanding the Mogul army in the south, then mobilizing to invade Bijapur. Sambaji was appointed a Commander of Seven Thousand, but his value as an ally was negligible and in little over a year he returned to his father.

Sivaji died of fever and dysentery on the 5th April 1680 before he had completed his fifty-third year.

The form of government organized by Sivaji was the system laid down by Kautalya. As Grant Duff observes, *Sivaji's Administration.* nothing in regard to him is more remarkable than the fitness of his arrangements for the genius of his countrymen; and the root of all the Maratha systems of government which appeared later, however much amended, is found in the institutions of Sivaji. The central government consisted of a council of state with eight members who were in charge of the government departments; and all these ministers, except the superintendent of judicial affairs and the adviser on religion, judicial astrology and science, held military commands. The immemorial Hindu institution of a jury of neighbours, the *panchayat*, was preserved intact, and almost all civil disputes were settled by that body.

The three viceregal provinces into which the Maratha kingdom

---

[1] *Mughal Rule in India*, p. 140.

was divided were administered on similar lines. Agriculture was encouraged by loans, and in the districts under the central government (known as *swaraj*) revenue officials with regular salaries took the place of the bad old method of farming out land revenue to hereditary landlords. These revenue officers had no political powers over the inhabitants of the district. There were other districts (*Mughlai*) under the government of other rulers over whom the Marathas claimed suzerainty and from whom one-fourth of the revenue (*chauth*) and an additional payment of one-tenth of the authorized annual assessment were levied.

Originally the Maratha forces consisted almost entirely of mounted yeomen who spent half the year on their fields. But Sivaji introduced a standing army and founded his power upon his infantry, though his cavalry later on were to "spread the terror of the Maratha name where the existence of such a people was unknown."[1] He also strongly fortified the harbours of Kolaba, Suvarndrug and Geriah, and built up a navy. Under Darya and Mai Naik there began the Maratha piracy which became so great a menace to shipping in the eighteenth century.

In regard to the Maratha administration Sarkar has observed: "There was no attempt at . . . organized communal improvement, spread of education or unification of the people, either under Sivaji or under the Peshwas. The cohesion of the people in the Maratha State was not organic but artificial, accidental and therefore precarious. It was solely dependent on the ruler's extraordinary personality, and disappeared when the country ceased to produce supermen."[2]

Sambaji.

On Sivaji's death his younger son Raja Ram attempted to gain the throne. But at the end of four months Sambaji deposed his brother, crushed all opposition with vindictive cruelty and was crowned with full ceremony in February 1681.

[1] Grant Duff, *History of the Mahrattas*, Vol. I. p. 175.
[2] *Shivaji and his Times* (Calcutta), 1919, pp. 485, 486.

To complete the description of the political situation in the
Deccan at this period a reference must be made to
The Shia Kingdoms. the two Shia kingdoms.

" The history of Bijapur from 1672 to 1686 is
really the history of its *wazirs* (chief ministers). It was a period
marked by chronic civil war among the factious nobles, independence
of the provincial governors, paralysis of the central administration
in the capital itself, occasional but indecisive Mogul invasions, and
a secret alliance but pretended hostility with the Marathas." [1]

For nearly half a century Golconda was ruled in name by the
worthless and profligate Abdullah Qutb Shah (1626–72), and the
State was at the mercy of disorder and tyranny. The impoverishment
of the country, under the farming system of revenue collection by
district officers liable to flogging in case of default, has been described
at length by Moreland.[2] Bijapur, where the Hindus seem to have
been depressed as a deliberate policy, was in hardly a better condition, and revenue farming with its attendant evils was the regular
practice in the Hindu territories of the south.[3]

Only the astute diplomacy of his mother and his eldest son-in-
law saved Golconda during the reign of Abdullah from complete
annexation. After Abdullah's death Abdul Hassan fought his
way to the throne and the Brahman Madanna, under the title of
Surya Prakash Rao, became his prime minister. In the opinion
of the East India Company's officials at Madras in 1676: " Madanna
has sole control and nothing is thought of but peeling and squeezing
the people." With Bijapur in a state of chaos, faction fights and
changes of regency, Madanna exchanged the foreign policy of a
secret understanding with the Adil-Shahi government for an alliance
with Sivaji; and this alliance, with the subsidy to the Marathas
which cemented it, was renewed with his successor.[4]

The political situation in the Deccan in 1681 has been summed
up by Sarkar: " The Sultans of Bijapur and Golconda could never
for a moment forget that the sleepless aim of the Mogul Emperor

[1] *History of Aurangzib*, Vol. IV. p. 136.
[2] *From Akbar to Aurangzeb*, pp. 239–243. [3] *Ibid.*, pp. 244–245.
[4] *History of Aurangzib*, Vol. IV. pp. 330–335.

was their . . . extinction and the annexation of all their territories. They had at all times had Maratha auxiliaries . . . Shahji Bhonsla . . . Sivaji . . . and Sambaji their only shield in the hour of supreme danger. A union of hearts between Bijapur and Golconda and the Mogul Empire was a psychological impossibility." [1]

Aurangzeb Invades the Deccan. Aurangzeb's determination to make an end of the Shia and Maratha powers of the Deccan was strengthened by the danger to his throne which threatened from the presence of his rebel son Akbar at Sambaji's court. The Emperor accordingly moved south with his great army and splendid camp equipage to spend the last twenty-six years of his life in the field while the Deccan ulcer ate away his power.

Annexation of Bijapur. He reached Aurangabad on the 22nd March 1682, and Muazzam and Azam were sent against the Marathas and Bijapur at the end of 1683. The next two years are a tale of military failure, of the escape of Akbar to Persia, and of heavy losses due to the unhealthiness of the climate of the Konkan. One or two Maratha forts were taken, but this was more than offset by the sack of Broach and Burhanpur. Then in April 1685 the Emperor advanced in person and laid siege to Bijapur, which fell in October 1686. Sikandar Ali Khan was made prisoner and the kingdom annexed.

Annexation of Golconda. The Mogul forces then invaded Golconda, and Hyderabad the capital with its fortress of immense strength was invested at the end of January 1687. Assaults and mining operations all failed, but eventually bribery and treachery succeeded. The fortress of Golconda was captured in September after a siege of eight months, and with it fell the last of the Shia kingdoms of the Deccan.[2]

Death of Sambaji. Sambaji and his chief adviser Kalusha, a Brahman from Northern India, had watched the downfall of the Deccan kingdoms without striking a blow to save them. Sambaji was personally brave, and he had thoroughly beaten the

[1] *History of Aurangzib*, Vol. IV. pp. 5, 6.
[2] A full description may be found in the *History of Aurangzib*, Vol. IV. Ch. XLVII.

Portuguese in 1683, although he failed before Chaul and Goa. But both he and his minister preferred debauchery to campaigning, conduct which had alienated many of the Maratha chiefs.

In January 1689, Muqarrab Khan, who had deserted from Golconda during the siege and been rewarded with a high command by Aurangzeb, located Sambaji at Sangmeshwar and his spies reported that the usual Maratha military precautions had been relaxed. Muqarrab Khan started at once with a flying column through the hills and forests of the Western Ghats and with 300 troopers covered the ninety miles from Kolhapur in under three days. Sambaji and his minister were captured and taken to imperial headquarters. On their refusing to turn Muhammadan they were tortured to death in March 1689.[1]

Rajgarh the Maratha capital fell in October and the entire royal family with the exception of Raja Ram were captured. With his objectives gained Aurangzeb pushed south and carried his conquests as far as Tanjore and Trichinopoly. As Sarkar has said in his *Studies in Mughal India*[2] : " All seemed to have been gained by Aurangzeb now, but in reality all was lost. . . . The Empire had become too large to be ruled by one man or from one centre. . . . His enemies rose on all sides; he could defeat but not crush them for ever. Lawlessness reigned in many parts of Northern and Central India. The administration grew slack and corrupt." The war in the Deccan so depleted the imperial treasury that for the last ten years of the reign the pay of the troops was usually three years in arrears.[3]

Aurangzeb was soon to discover that the Marathas were far from being subdued. Raja Ram had escaped to Jinji, one of the strongest fortresses in the south, and for seven years repeated efforts by the best imperial generals failed to take it. Finally it fell by escalade in January 1698. Raja Ram, who had conducted the defence, made his escape to Satara where he collected a large force and continued his operations in the field.

The years of warfare with the Marathas from 1689 to 1707

---

[1] *History of Aurangzib*, Vol. IV. pp. 396–403.
[2] In the Chapter " Aurangzib," p. 50.
[3] *The Later Mughals*, W. Irvine, Vol. I. p. 9, footnote.

proved a disheartening struggle for the imperial armies. In the Western Ghats the forts offered obstinate resistance, and in the Deccan itself the Marathas plundered the country, cut off convoys and repeatedly defeated the Mogul columns. Gemelli Careri, an Italian doctor who visited imperial headquarters in 1695, gives an interesting account of the great camp at Galgala. The tide of demoralization which eventually reduced the Mogul armies to a laughing-stock had just begun to flow in full force, though to all appearance Aurangzeb was the lord paramount of Northern India, the Deccan and the south as far as Tanjore.

The camp was thirty miles in circumference, and held about a million people, the army consisting of 60,000 cavalry, 100,000 infantry, 3000 elephants and 50,000 camels. This huge population ate up all the provisions for miles around, and whenever the lines of communication with the north were cut by the Marathas, Galgala ran considerable danger of starvation. The Emperor's simple way of living was not followed by his officers. Luxury, effeminacy and corruption were rampant. Discipline, even among the French mercenaries, did not exist.[1]

In March 1700 Raja Ram died, and in April Satara surrendered on terms. But Raja Ram's widow Tara Bai carried on the campaign with equal energy and considerable success. The Mogul troops would capture a position one day only to lose it the next, while famine, pestilence and flood weakened the ranks of a demoralized army.

In October 1705 Aurangzeb became seriously ill and " slowly and with difficulty " reached Ahmadnagar in the following January pursued by the Maratha horse. The old man of ninety lingered on for a year, while his second son Azam was deep in intrigue to secure the throne and busy plotting against the life of his younger brother Kam Baksh, Aurangzeb's favourite son.

Early in February 1707 the Emperor realized that he was dying, and he sent Azam and Kam Baksh to their provinces of Bijapur and Malwa. Then with the fear of future torment in his heart he prepared for death. Like another puritan and iconoclast, Crom-

[1] *Travellers in India*, E. F. Oaten, pp. 232–236.

well, the one dictator of England, his spirit passed in the midst of a violent storm; and Aurangzeb died on the 20th February 1707.

During the closing years of the reign the tenth Sikh Guru Govind emerged from a retirement which had lasted twenty years to found the Khalsa among the Jats, and proclaimed his aspirations to vanquish the Mogul armies and destroy the empire of "unbelieving" oppressors. In 1695 he established forts in the foothills between the Sutlej and the Jumna, and between that date and 1701 he routed two Mogul commanders who were sent against him. Aurangzeb then ordered the Governors of Lahore and Sirhind to crush the leader who called himself the True King, and Govind Singh was surrounded at Anandpur. The guru succeeded in escaping, but his forces were broken by defeat and desertion, his sons were killed and Govind Singh became a fugitive until after the death of Aurangzeb, when he took service with Bahadur Shah.[1]

Govind Singh.

Aurangzeb had carefully prepared himself for the kingship, and he set himself a course of policy from which nothing could make him swerve. He spent his whole life doing what he held to be his duty to his religion, and he believed treachery, violence and intolerance to be fully justified in furthering his ideals. He had ruthlessly exterminated all his rivals of his own family to secure the throne; and for this he felt no remorse. His one reference in his death-bed letters [2] to the horrors accompanying his succession was to Kam Baksh : " Dara Shikoh made unsound arrangements and hence he failed to reach his point. He increased the salaries of his retainers . . . but at the time of need got less and less work out of them. Hence he was unhappy." In the pursuit of what he believed to be right, the suppression of infidelity, Aurangzeb hastened the ruin of a great Empire. This he realized, and he is reported to have said towards the end of his career: " After me will come the deluge." [3]

Aurangzeb's Character.

[1] *History of the Sikhs*, pp. 66–81.
[2] *History of Aurangzib*, Vol. V. pp. 259–262 ; *Mughal Rule in India*, pp. 155–157.
[3] *Mughal Rule in India*, p. 155.

His industry in conducting the affairs of State was stupendous. But his suspicious nature led him to interfere incessantly with his governors and other officials. Their initiative was consequently destroyed, to the serious detriment of the public service, and towards the end of his life his ministers had become little more than clerks to register his edicts.

But apart from his actions as a ruler there is much to admire in Aurangzeb. His coolness and courage were proverbial, and throughout his long reign he was never known to lose his temper. He possessed the royal attribute of never forgetting a face, and both as Prince and Emperor he displayed a tact, sagacity and humility which made the highest nobles of the court his friends.[1]

Doctor Gemelli Careri [2] gives an interesting description of the Emperor when nearly eighty: " Aurangzeb was of a low stature, with a large nose, slender and stooping with age. The whiteness of his round beard was more visible on his olive skin. He was clothed in plain white muslin and wore a turban adorned with a large emerald. I admired to see him endorse the petitions with his own hand, without spectacles, and by his cheerful smiling countenance seem to be pleased with his employment."

In the rigid austerity of his way of living the Emperor allowed himself no relaxations, and his Moslem subjects regarded him as a saint. The simplicity of his life is illustrated by the instructions he gave for his funeral. He was buried in a coffin which cost five rupees, the proceeds of the sale of caps which he had quilted himself, while the 300 rupees which he ordered to be distributed to the poor had been earned by making copies of the Koran.[3]

Aurangzeb possessed a distinctly sardonic humour. The story is told by Manucci [4] that the Emperor on his way to the mosque one Friday, after he had prohibited music, met a funeral attended by about a thousand people. When he asked who was dead he

[1] *History of Aurangzib*, Vol. V. pp. 473–476.
[2] *Ibid.*, pp. 476, 477, quoting *Churchill's Voyages*, IV. p. 222, and *Travellers in India*, p. 235.
[3] *Mughal Rule in India*, p. 154.
[4] *Storio do Mogor*, tr. by W. Irvine (Indian Text Series, London, 1907), Vol. II. p. 8.

was told: " The king by his orders has killed Music and we are bearing her to her grave." " Pray for the soul of Music," replied Aurangzeb, " and see that she is thoroughly well buried."

On another occasion the Emperor does not figure with equal success. A strict abstainer himself, the use of alcohol by his subjects infuriated him. As Manucci tells the story: " Aurangzeb said one day that in all Hindustan no more than two men could be found who did not drink, namely himself and Abd-ul-Wahlab the chief Kazi appointed by him. But with respect to Abd-ul-Wahlab he was in error, for I myself sent him every day a bottle of spirits which he drank in secret so that the king did not find it out." [1]

Aurangzeb was a widely read and accurate scholar; and to his initiative the country owes its greatest digest of Moslem law, the *Fatawah-i-Alamgiri*.[2]

Arts and Sciences.

There was but little building during the reign, and the style of Mogul architecture rapidly degenerated after Aurangzeb's accession; while the art of painting, though not discouraged by the Emperor, noticeably deteriorated.[3] " Not a single grand edifice, finely written manuscript, or exquisite picture commemorates Aurangzeb's reign." [4]

The causes which led to the fall of the Mogul Empire all existed in the reign of Aurangzeb. His successors were weak and, with the exception of Bahadur Shah, quite incompetent, who soon became puppets in the hands of their ministers, but the forces which had sprung up in the vast overgrown empire were too strong for any one ruler to control. The death of Aurangzeb opened the flood-gates of civil war, revolt and foreign invasion, the empire crumbled to pieces, and Mogul supremacy vanished for ever. Yet such was the prestige of the Timurid dynasty that " their name continued to be invoked by the powers that contended for supremacy . . . even when they fought against the Emperor's

---

[1] Quoted from the *Storio*, II. pp. 5, 6.
[2] *History of Aurangzib*, V. pp. 477, 478.
[3] *Mughal Rule in India*, Ch. VIII.
[4] *Studies in Mughal India*, p. 51.

own authority. . . . (These) rising powers . . . were not necessarily rebels by intention. They sought some centre of authority; when Delhi broke down they attempted to substitute themselves as representing the Padishah better than any other power." [1]

Nor was this attitude confined to Muhammadan princes, to whom even the later Mogul Emperors symbolized religious as well as political sentiments. The Marathas under the rule of their ministers, the Peshwas, though they habitually raided the shrunken territories of Delhi, frequently acted in the Emperor's name, and were proud of such titles as they received, or extorted, from him. The rival European companies took this sentiment into account. Dupleix with his Mogul title of Zafar Jang Bahadur made use of imperial prestige in his schemes to drive out the English; the essential preliminary to the substitution " of a French government for that of the Moguls gradually and by degrees." [2] The East India Company developed their sovereignty in Bengal under the imperial name, and in the early years of the nineteenth century were still purporting to act under the authority of the Mogul Emperor.

After the death of Aurangzeb there began a conflict of rival influences, Maratha, Muhammadan and later, for a brief period, the French. It was half a century before any sign appeared that out of chaos a power would emerge capable of establishing, slowly but surely, a government which could give peace and unity to India.

APPENDIX TO CHAPTER XI

SIVAJI'S LETTER TO AURANGZEB

Sivaji was, amongst other things, a clear-sighted statesman of the highest rank, but he was too illiterate to present the case for religious toleration in so polished a form. From the evidence it would seem that the letter sent by Sivaji was cast into shape by Munshi Nil Prabhu. This remarkably candid State paper is lightened by the reference to the Maratha leader's escape from Agra concealed in a country basket.

---

[1] A. Yusuf Ali, *The Making of India*, Edn. 1925, p. 168.
[2] De Bussy to Dupleix on French policy, 26th February 1754, quoted in *Camb. Hist. British Empire*, IV. p. 139.

PLATE XLV.

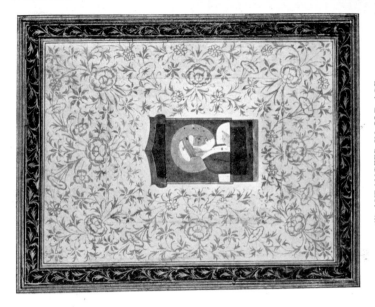

(b) AURANGZEB IN OLD AGE

By courtesy of Indian Museum, South Kensington

(a) THE OLD MULLAH

Artist : Farrukh Beg (School of Jahangir)

By courtesy of Indian Museum, South Kensington

PLATE XLVI.

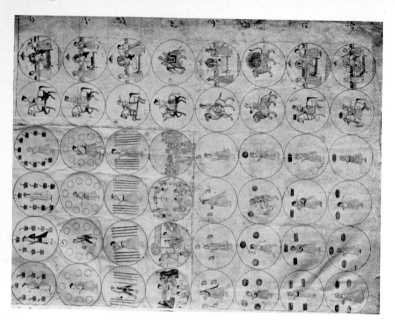

By permission of the Secretary of State for India in Council

(c) INDIAN CARDS

(a)

(b)

(a) TENT PANEL
Mogul Embroidery, early eighteenth century

(b) EMBROIDERY PANEL FROM
SHIELD PAD
Rajput work, c. 1700

By courtesy of Indian Museum, South
Kensington

The letter is given in the *History of Aurangzib*, Vol. III. pp. 325–329, and the original is now in the possession of the Maharaja of Kolapur. For evidence as to its genuineness see *ibid.*, p. 329, and *History of the Mahrattas*, by Grant Duff (Edn. 1921), Vol. I. footnote to p. 172.

Sivaji's historical summary is so admirable that, with the exception of two quotations, it is given below in full:

To the EMPEROR ALAMGIR—

" This firm and constant well-wisher Sivaji, after rendering thanks for the grace of God and the favours of the Emperor,—which are clearer than the Sun,—begs to inform your Majesty that, although this well-wisher was led by his adverse Fate to come away from your august presence without taking leave, yet he is ever ready to perform, to the fullest extent possible and proper, everything that duty as a servant and gratitude demand of him.

" My excellent services and devotion to the welfare of the State are fully known to the princes, *khans, amirs, rajahs* and *rais* of India, to the rulers of Persia, Central Asia, Turkey and Syria, to the inhabitants of the seven climes of the globe, and to wayfarers on land and sea; and very likely their light has flashed on your Majesty's capacious mind. So with a view to rendering good service and earning the imperial favour, I submit the following words in a spirit of devotion to the public welfare :

" It has recently come to my ears that, on the ground of the war with me having exhausted your wealth and emptied the imperial treasury, your Majesty has ordered that money under the name of *jaziya* should be collected from the Hindus and the imperial needs supplied with it. May it please your Majesty! That architect of the fabric of empire (Jalaluddin), Akbar Padishah, reigned with full power for 52 (lunar) years. He adopted the admirable policy of perfect harmony in relation to all the various sects, such as Christians, Jews, Muslims, Dadu's followers, sky-worshippers, materialists, atheists, Brahman and Jain priests. The aim of his liberal heart was to cherish and protect all the people. So, he became famous under the title of ' the World's spiritual Guide.'

" Next, the Emperor Nuruddin Jahangir for 22 years spread his gracious shade on the head of the world and its dwellers, gave his heart to his friends and his hand to his work, and gained his desires. The Emperor Shah Jahan for 32 years cast his blessed shade on the head of the world and gathered in the fruit of eternal life,—which is only another name for goodness and fair fame,—as the result of his happy time on earth.

" Through the auspicious effect of this sublime disposition, wherever he (Akbar) bent the glance of his august wish, Victory and Success advanced to welcome him on the way. In his reign many kingdoms and forts were conquered. The state and power of these emperors can be easily understood from the fact that Alamgir Padishah has failed and become bewildered in the attempt to merely follow their political system. They, too, had the power of levying the *jaziya*; but they did not give place to bigotry in their hearts, as they considered all men, high and low, created by God, to be (living) examples of the nature of diverse creeds and temperaments. Their kindness and benevolence endure on the pages of Time as their memorial, and so prayer and praise for these (three) pure souls will dwell for ever in the hearts and tongues of mankind, among both great and small. Prosperity is the fruit of one's intentions. Therefore, their wealth and good fortune continued to increase, as God's creatures reposed in the cradle of peace and safety (in their reigns) and their undertakings were achieved.

" But in *your* Majesty's reign, many of the forts and provinces have gone out of your possession, and the rest will soon do so, too, because there will be no slackness on my part in ruining and devastating them. Your peasants are downtrodden; the yield of every village has declined, in the place of one lakh (of Rupees) only one thousand, and in the place of a thousand only ten are collected, and that too with difficulty. When Poverty and Beggary have made their homes in the palaces of the Emperor and the Princes, the condition of the grandees and officers can be easily imagined. It is a reign in which the army is in a ferment, the merchants complain; the Moslems cry, the Hindus are grilled; most men lack bread at night, and in the day inflame their own cheeks by slapping them (in anguish). How can the royal spirit permit you to add the hardship of the *jaziya* to this grievous state of things? The infamy will quickly spread from west to east and become recorded in books of history that the Emperor of Hindustan, coveting the beggars' bowls, takes *jaziya* from Brahmans and Jain monks, paupers, mendicants, ruined wretches and the famine-stricken,—that his valour is shown by attacks on the wallets of beggars,—that he dashes down (to the ground) the name and honour of the Timurids!

" May it please your Majesty! If you believe in the true Divine Book and Word of God (*i.e.*, the Quran), you will find there (that God is styled) Rabb-ul-alamin, the Lord of all men, and not Rabb-ul-musalmin, the Lord of the Muhammadans only. Verily, Islam and Hinduism are antithetical terms. They are (diverse pigments) used by the true Divine Painter for blending the colours and filling in the outlines (of His picture of the entire human species). If it be a mosque, the call to prayer is chanted in remembrance of Him. If it be a temple, the bell is rung in yearning for Him only. To show bigotry for any man's creed and practices is (really) altering the words of the Holy

286

Book. To draw (new) lines on a picture is to find fault with the painter.

" In strict justice the *jaziya* is not at all lawful. From the point of view of administration it can be right only if a beautiful woman wearing gold ornaments can pass from one country to another without fear or molestation. (But) in these days even the cities are being plundered, what of the open country? Not to speak of its injustice, this imposition of the *jaziya* is an innovation in India and inexpedient.

" If you imagine piety to consist in oppressing the people and terrorizing the Hindus, you ought first to levy *jaziya* from Rana Raj Singh, who is the head of the Hindus. Then it will not be so very difficult to collect it from me, as I am at your service. But to oppress ants and flies is far from displaying valour and spirit.

" I wonder at the strange fidelity of your officers that they neglect to tell you of the true state of things, but cover a blazing fire with straw! May the sun of your royalty continue to shine above the horizon of greatness! "

CHRONOLOGY

1659. Formal enthronement of Aurangzeb.
1662–1663. Invasion of Assam by Mir Jumla.
1664. Foundation of French *Compagnie des Indes*.
    Sack of Surat by Sivaji.
1666. Death of Shah Jahan.
    Capture of Chittagong and extermination of Arakan pirates.
1667. Defeat of the Yusufzais.
1669. Aurangzeb began his Hindu persecutions.
    First of succession of Jat rebellions.
1672. Satnami rebellion.
1672–1678. Afridi rising.
1674. Enthronement of Sivaji.
1675. Execution of Tegh Bahadur the Sikh Guru.
1676–1680. Sivaji's conquests in Southern India.
1678. Death of Maharaja Jaswant Singh of Jodhpur.
1679. Reimposition of the *jizya*.
1680. Rajput war begins (to end with Jodhpur in 1709).
1680. Death of Sivaji.
1681. Revolt of Prince Akbar.
    Accession of Sambaji.
1681. Peace with Udaipur.
1682. Aurangzeb invades the Deccan in person.

1686. Annexation of Bijapur.
1687. Annexation of Golconda.
1689. Execution of Sambaji.
       Capture of Rajgarh and commencement of the indecisive campaigns against the Marathas.
1707. 20th February: death of Aurangzeb.

BIBLIOGRAPHY

History of Aurangzib, Sarkar, 5 vols. (Calcutta), 1912–1924.
Studies in Mughal India, Sarkar (Calcutta and Cambridge), 1919.
Mughal Rule in India, Edwardes and Garrett, 1930.
European Travellers in India, Oaten, 1909.
From Akbar to Aurangzeb, Moreland, 1923.
History of the Mahrattas, J. C. Grant Duff, revised Edwardes, 1921, Vol. I.

NOTE.—INDIAN MUSIC

The many systems of music in India may be classified as the " celestial " and the " terrestrial," the latter being broadly divided into the Hindustani and Carnatic schools. The Hindustani school of Northern and Western India and the Deccan is considered to be directly traceable to the systems set forth in Bharata's *Natya-Sastra* (*c.* fifth century A.D.) and the *Sangit Ratnakar* of Sarangdev, a Kashmiri of the thirteenth century (*Introduction to the Study of Indian Music*, E. Clements (London), 1913). Southern India generally was far less disturbed by invasion than the north, and remained more subject to Hindu rule, consequently its Carnatic school of music keeps the old Sanskrit forms. From early Sanskrit treatises and from paintings as at Ajanta, it appears that the instruments now used have hardly altered at all in two thousand years. The Amravati sculptures (visited by Yuan Chwang) depict an orchestra of eighteen women with drums, a shell trumpet, a chanter, two dulcimers and a harp. (*Music of Southern India*, C. R. Day, 1891, gives coloured plates of musical instruments.) Indian music is played with a drone or pedal accompaniment. Music has been closely knit up with the lives of every grade of society and vividly expressed in religion and the drama since Vedic times, and it succeeded in surviving the antagonism of Aurangzeb. A worse enemy has been the insidious effect of latter-day Western influence. Hindu dancing (which is treated in the *Bharat-sastra*) consists of slow, meticulously regulated gestures centred in the stamping of the feet on the ground, while great restraint in facial expression contrasts with bird-like motions of the head and exquisite fluttering movements of the hands and arms.